PROMOT[IONAL]
PACKAGING
AND DESIGN

CREATIVE CONCEPTS,
FOLDINGS AND TEMPLATES

DESIGN ET
PACKAGING
PROMOTIONNEL

CONCEPTS CRÉATIFS,
PLIAGES ET PATRONS

DISEÑO
Y PACKAGING
PROMOCIONAL

CONCEPTOS CREATIVOS,
PLIEGUES Y PLANTILLAS

PROMOTIONAL PACKAGING AND DESIGN

CREATIVE CONCEPTS, FOLDINGS AND TEMPLATES

DESIGN ET PACKAGING PROMOTIONNEL

CONCEPTS CRÉATIFS, PLIAGES ET PATRONS

DISEÑO Y PACKAGING PROMOCIONAL

CONCEPTOS CREATIVOS, PLIEGUES Y PLANTILLAS

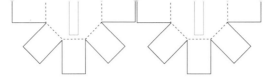
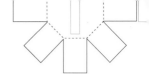

PROMOTIONAL PACKAGING AND DESIGN. CREATIVE CONCEPTS, FOLDINGS AND TEMPLATES
DESIGN ET PACKAGING PROMOTIONNEL : CONCEPTS CRÉATIFS, PLIAGES ET PATRONS
DISEÑO Y PACKAGING PROMOCIONAL: CONCEPTOS CREATIVOS, PLIEGUES Y PLANTILLAS

Editorial coordination: Anja Llorella Oriol

Editor: Cristian Campos

Texts: Cristian Campos

Illustrations: Thais Caballero

English translation: Cillero & de Motta

French translation: Cillero & de Motta

Art director: Emma Termes Parera

Layout: Esperanza Escudero Pino

Cover design: Esperanza Escudero Pino

PROMOPRESS is a brand of:
PROMOTORA DE PRENSA INTERNACIONAL SA
Ausiàs March, 124
08013 Barcelona, Spain
T: +34 932 451 464
F: +34 932 654 883
E-mail: info@promopress.es
www.promopress.info

First published in English, French and Spanish: 2010

ISBN 978-84-936508-1-0
Printed in Spain

Table of Contents ı Sommaire ı Índice

6 Introduction ı Introduction ı Introducción

8 Icons and captions ı Icônes et légendes ı Iconos y leyendas

10 Products and services ı Produits et services ı Productos y servicios

32 Interview with Evelio Mattos (Design Packaging) ı Interview avec Evelio Mattos (Design Packaging) ı Entrevista con Evelio Mattos (Design Packaging)

62 Interview with Imelda Ramovic + Mirel Hadzijusufovic (Bruketa&ZinicOM) ı Interview avec Imelda Ramovic + Mirel Hadzijusufovic (Bruketa&ZinicOM) ı Entrevista con Imelda Ramovic + Mirel Hadzijusufovic (Bruketa&ZinicOM)

82 Creativity and crafts ı Créativité et artisanat ı Creatividad y artesanía

102 Interview with Airside ı Interview avec Airside ı Entrevista con Airside

124 Interview with Vivek Bhatia (Ico Design Consultancy) ı Interview avec Vivek Bhatia (Ico Design Consultancy) ı Entrevista con Vivek Bhatia (Ico Design Consultancy)

148 Interview with Mike Joyce (Stereotype Design) ı Interview avec Mike Joyce (Stereotype Design) ı Entrevista con Mike Joyce (Stereotype Design)

176 Fashion and beauty ı Mode et beauté ı Moda y belleza

196 Interview with Jeffrey M. Wallace (BorsaWallace) ı Interview avec Jeffrey M. Wallace (BorsaWallace) ı Entrevista con Jeffrey M. Wallace (BorsaWallace)

222 Interview with David Barath (David Barath Design) ı Interview avec David Barath (David Barath Design) ı Entrevista con David Barath (David Barath Design)

248 Interview with Christoph Geppert + Madelyn Postman (Grain Limited + Madomat) ı Interview avec Christoph Geppert + Madelyn Postman (Grain Limited + Madomat) ı Entrevista con Christoph Geppert + Madelyn Postman (Grain Limited + Madomat)

264 Movies and videogames ı Cinéma et jeux vidéo ı Cine y videojuegos

276 Interview with Sebastian Bissinger + Laure Boer (BANK) ı Interview avec Sebastian Bissinger + Laure Boer (BANK) ı Entrevista con Sebastian Bissinger + Laure Boer (BANK)

302 Interview with Carlos Ranedo + Coke Rueda (Shackleton 70mm) ı Interview avec Carlos Ranedo + Coke Rueda (Shackleton 70mm) ı Entrevista con Carlos Ranedo + Coke Rueda (Shackleton 70mm)

318 Additional proposals ı Propositions supplémentaires ı Propuestas adicionales

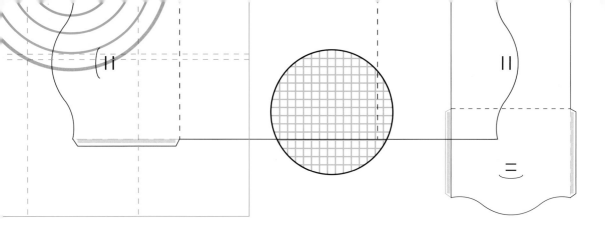

Introduction Introduction Introducción

If you've ever visited Las Vegas you will possibly have come across some bizarre leaflet distributors who attract the attention of passers-by banging or blowing on their wad of leaflets. If you sit near them and watch the reaction of tourists, you will see that the majority, if not virtually all, look at the distributor they blow on their wad. This may seem anecdotal, but there is more to this than first meets the eye: think about how difficult it is to attract passer-by's attention, even if only for a brief second, in a city in which the number of visual and auditory stimuli per second is quite possibly the largest in the world.

Press and promotional kits try to achieve exactly the same function as these distributors: to draw the attention of a potential customer in a stimuli-saturated market. Or, as one of the designers interviewed for this book puts it, "drawing attention to something that might otherwise go unnoticed". Obviously, a kit should not only be attractive, but also make an impact on the recipients, who are mostly journalists, and, also it should be as aesthetically appealing as possible.

The 79 kits included in this book are a representative sample of the latest trends in promotional design. Among these 79 designs, the reader can find what we all identify with the term "press kit", i.e. a box of promotional goodies for a film, video game or a specific product (T-shirts, pins, posters, CDs with press images, one or more information packs), but also non-standard kits. In some cases the kit is the actual product or catalogue of the brand and a promotional item is added. In other cases, the kit does not include press information of any kind and is mere "sample" of the designer's creativity.

The book also includes interviews 10 of the featured designers, plus an additional final chapter including alternative proposals and ideas aimed at graphic designers and communication agencies. Each and every one of the kits also includes a template, or, in cases whereby this is impossible due to the nature or the material used for the kit, a template respecting the spirit of the original design.

Si vous avez déjà visité Las Vegas, vous aurez probablement rencontré quelques distributeurs de prospectus singuliers qui, pour attirer l'attention des passants, crient ou font claquer leur pile de prospectus. Si vous vous restez à côté de l'un d'eux pour observer la réaction des touristes, vous pourrez constater que la majorité d'entre eux, pour ne pas dire la totalité, se retourne quand il fait claquer ses prospectus. Cela peut sembler anodin, mais ce détail a davantage de mérite qu'il n'y paraît : pensez à la difficulté d'attirer l'attention d'un passant, même pour un bref instant, dans une ville où le nombre de stimuli visuels et auditifs par seconde est sans doute le plus élevé du monde.

Les kits de presse et promotionnels remplissent exactement la même fonction que ces distributeurs : attirer l'attention d'un client potentiel dans un marché saturé de stimuli. Ou, comme le dit l'un des designers interviewés dans ce livre, « attirer l'attention sur quelque chose qui aurait pu passer inaperçu ». Mais un kit ne doit pas seulement attirer l'attention, il doit aussi rester gravé dans la mémoire des destinataires, en majorité des journalistes, et, dans la mesure du possible, être esthétiquement attrayant.

Les soixante-dix-neu kits que comprend ce livre sont un échantillon représentatif des dernières tendances en matière de design promotionnel. Parmi ces soixante-dix-neu designs, le lecteur pourra découvrir ce que nous connaissons tous sous le nom de « kit de presse » : une boîte contenant le matériel promotionnel d'un film, d'un jeu vidéo ou d'un produit (des tee-shirts, des pin's, des posters, des CD contenant des images de presse, un ou plusieurs dossiers informatifs), mais également des kits atypiques. Dans certains cas, le kit est le produit lui-même ou le catalogue de la marque, davantage on ajoute un élément promotionnel. Dans d'autres cas, le kit ne comporte aucune information de presse quelle qu'elle soit et ne représente qu'un « échantillon » de la créativité de son designer.

Ce livre contient également les interviews de dix des designers qui y sont mentionnés, ainsi qu'un chapitre supplémentaire dans lequel nous avons intégré des propositions et des idées alternatives à l'attention des designers graphiques et des agences de communication. Chaque kit est accompagné d'un patron ou, dans les cas où le kit, de par sa nature propre ou celle du matériel dont il est fait, ne peut pas être élaboré de manière conventionnelle, d'un patron approximatif respectant l'esprit du design original.

Quien haya visitado Las Vegas se habrá topado con unos peculiares repartidores de publicidad que llaman la atención de los paseantes golpeando o haciendo sonar su taco de folletos. Si se sienta cerca y observa la reacción de los turistas, verá que la mayoría de ellos, por no decir todos, desvían la vista hacia el repartidor. Esto, que puede parecer anecdótico, tiene mucho más mérito de lo que parece si pensamos en la dificultad que entraña atraer a un paseante casual, aunque sólo sea por un instante, en una ciudad en la que el número de estímulos visuales y auditivos por segundo es, muy probablemente, el mayor del mundo.

Los kits de prensa y de promoción cumplen exactamente la misma función que esos repartidores: llamar la atención de un cliente potencial en un mercado saturado de estímulos. O, como dice uno de los diseñadores entrevistados para este libro, «llamar la atención sobre algo que habría podido pasar desapercibido». Un kit no sólo debe resultar llamativo; también debe perdurar en la memoria de su destinatario, periodistas en la mayoría de los casos, y, en la medida de lo posible, resultar estéticamente atractivo.

Los setenta y nueve kits incluidos en este libro son una muestra representativa de las últimas tendencias del diseño promocional. No sólo se recogen ejemplos de aquello que todos identificamos con un kit de prensa, es decir, una caja con material promocional de una película, un videojuego o un producto (camisetas, chapas, pósteres, CD con imágenes de prensa, uno o varios dosieres informativos), sino también kits atípicos. En algunos casos, es el producto mismo o el catálogo de la marca en sí, a los que se ha añadido algún elemento de promoción. En otros, el kit no incluye información de prensa y tan sólo funciona como muestra de la creatividad de su diseñador.

El libro se complementa con entrevistas a diez de los diseñadores cuyos trabajos aparecen en estas páginas, además de con un capítulo con propuestas e ideas alternativas destinadas a diseñadores gráficos y agencias de comunicación. Todos los kits vienen acompañados de su correspondiente plantilla o, en los casos en los que por su naturaleza o por el material con el que están fabricados no puedan reproducirse de la manera convencional, una plantilla aproximada que respeta el espíritu del diseño original.

Icons and captions

The list that the reader will find below explains the meaning of the icons corresponding to the press kits included in this book. These icons will provide the reader with additional information on the most important aspects of the materials and finishes of the mentioned kits.

These symbols, along with the creation of the elements, will give the reader enough information to be able to adapt the designs created by agencies or studios included in this book to their needs. Both the creations and their symbols are guidelines and should be used as a starting point for customizing the elements. They can all be adapted in terms of the materials available, the contents of the kit or their budget.

Icônes et légendes

La liste qui figure ci-dessous détaille la signification des icônes accompagnant les kits de presse inclus dans ce livre. Ces icônes donnent des informations supplémentaires sur les aspects les plus importants des matériaux et des finitions de ces kits.

Ces symboles, ainsi que la création des éléments, apportent au lecteur suffisamment d'indications pour qu'il puisse adapter selon ses besoins les designs créés par les agences ou cabinets inclus dans ce livre. La création et les légendes sont fournis à titre indicatif afin de définir le point de départ de la personnalisation des éléments. Ils sont tous modifiables en fonction des matériaux disponibles, des contenus du kit ou du budget prévu pour leur réalisation.

Iconos y leyendas

La lista que el lector encontrará a continuación detalla el significado de los iconos que acompañan a los kits de prensa incluidos en este libro. Gracias a estos iconos, el lector recibirá información adicional sobre los aspectos más destacables de los materiales y los acabados de los kits.

Estos símbolos, junto con los desarrollos de los elementos, le darán las pistas suficientes para adaptar a sus necesidades los diseños creados por las agencias o los estudios incluidos en este libro. Tanto los desarrollos como su simbología son orientativos y sólo pretenden establecer el punto de partida para la personalización de los elementos. Todos ellos permiten su modificación en función de los materiales disponibles, los contenidos del kit o el presupuesto con el que se cuente.

Cutting line
Ligne de coupe
Línea de corte

Folding/splitting line
Ligne de fente/pliage
Línea de hendido/doblado

Micro-perforated line
Ligne de microperforation
Línea de microperforado

Gluing/pasting area
Zones d'encollage/collage
Zonas de encolado/pegado

Plastic material
Matériel plastique
Material plástico

Sticker/adhesive material
Matériel adhésif/autocollant
Material adhesivo/sticker

Transparent material
Matériel transparent
Material transparente

Translucent/plant/silk/parchment material
Matériel translucide/végétal/de soie/sulfurisé
Material translúcido/vegetal/seda/sulfurizado

Bubble/protective wrap
Papier bulle/de protection
Material de burbujas/protección

Foam/protective material
Matériel en mousse/protection
Material de espuma/protección

Engraving/relief
Gravures/reliefs
Grabados/relieves

Magnet
Aimant
Imán

Varnish/gloss finish
Finition laque/brillance
Acabado barniz/brillo

Stampings
Stampings
Stampings

Textile/lining finish or material
Matériaux ou finitions tissus/
doublures
Materiales o acabados textiles/
forrados

Metal/shiny finish or material
Matériaux ou finitions
métallisés/brillants
Materiales o acabados
metalizados/brillantes

Inflated/air/protective finish
Finition gonflée/air/protection
Acabado inflado/aire/protección

Vacuum-packed
À vide
Al vacío

Elastic material
Matériel élastique
Material elástico

Ribbon/rope
Rubanerie/corde
Cintería/cuerda

Metallic material
Matériel métallique
Material metálico

Velcro
Velcro
Velcro

Eyelet/drill/rivet
Œillet/trou percé/rivure
Ojal/taladro/remachado

Scented material
Matériel aromatisé
Material aromatizado

Stitching/binding finish
Finition cousue/assemblage
Acabado cosido/unión

Special stitching/binding finish
Finition cousue/assemblage spécial(e)
Acabado cosido/unión especial

A box and inside a T-shirt with the product logo, a sample of the product and a CD with high resolution photos and press information, this is the typical press kit that comes to mind when we think of such products. And it is not a bad concept, really (just because it is obvious does not mean it will not work: does a spoon need to be redesigned?) However, the projects featured in this chapter, which promote products or services from all types of companies (restaurants, printers, warehouses, etc.) show that it is possible to go beyond the beaten track, either by using the latest technologies in the field of printing, or adding unusual elements to the kit or converting it into an object of real luxury, into a collector's item worthy of an honorable place on our mantelpiece. Although in the latter case, the danger is that the kit ends up eclipsing the product to be promoted. If we move closer to this boundary without overstepping it, we will have designed, if not the perfect kit, something similar.

Une boîte contenant une chemise avec le logo du produit, un échantillon de celui-ci et un CD avec des photos haute résolution ainsi que des informations de presse : voici le kit de presse conventionnel, celui que nous avons tous à l'esprit quand nous pensons à ce type d'objets. Et ce n'est pas un mauvais concept en réalité (qu'il soit évident ne signifie pas qu'il ne fonctionne pas : la cuillère a-t-elle besoind´être reconçue ?) Toutefois, les projets de ce chapitre, qui font la promotion de produits ou de services d'entreprises en tout genre (restaurants, imprimeries, bars à vin...), démontrent qu'il est possible de s'éloigner des sentiers battus, que ce soit en ayant recours aux dernières technologies en matière d'impression, en ajoutant des éléments atypiques au kit ou en faisant de celui-ci un véritable objet de luxe, une pièce de collection qui mérite une place d'honneur sur nos étagères. Mais, dans ce dernier cas, le risque peut être que le kit finisse par éclipser le produit que l'on cherche à promouvoir. Si nous parvenons à nous approcher de cette frontière sans la franchir, nous aurons conçu, si ce n'est le kit parfait, quelque chose qui s'en approche fortement» por «de très proche.

Una caja y, en su interior, una camiseta con el logotipo del producto, una muestra, y un CD con fotografías en alta resolución e información de prensa. Éste es el kit de prensa convencional, el que todos tenemos en mente. En realidad, no es un mal concepto: que sea obvio no quiere decir que no funcione (¿necesita la cuchara un rediseño?). Sin embargo, los proyectos de este capítulo, que promocionan productos o servicios de empresas de todo tipo (restaurantes, imprentas, bodegas...) demuestran que es posible ir más allá de los caminos trillados, ya sea haciendo uso de las últimas tecnologías en el terreno de la impresión, ya sea añadiendo elementos atípicos al kit o convirtiéndolo en un auténtico objeto de lujo, en una pieza de coleccionista merecedora de un puesto de honor en nuestras estanterías. En este último caso, el peligro es que el kit acabe eclipsando al producto que se pretende promocionar, pero si conseguimos acercarnos a esa frontera sin traspasarla por completo, habremos diseñado, si no el kit perfecto, algo que se le parece bastante.

Products and services

Produits et services

Productos y servicios

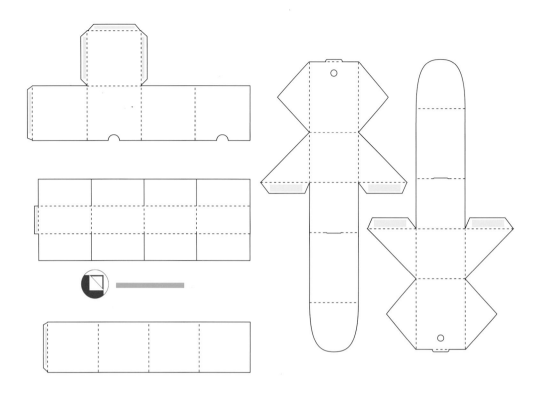

N97 Special Edition Packaging

How do you present and promote a technical gadget in the most spectacular way possible? Madomat chose a case that opens out in several steps. The last step is to open up the semi-hidden compartment that holds all the accessories for Nokia N97 phone. In this sense, the opening of the case practically becomes another sensory experience associated with the product. Inside the case, the phone has been embedded into a soft foam cube which prevents any direct impact and damage.

Quelle est la façon la plus spectaculaire de présenter et de promouvoir un gadget technologique ? Madomat a opté pour une boîte qui s'ouvre en plusieurs étapes dont la dernière, l'ouverture d'un compartiment à moitié caché qui dévoile tous les accessoires du téléphone N97 de Nokia. Ainsi, consiste en un kit devient presque l'une des expériences sensorielles associées au produit. À l'intérieur de la boîte, le téléphone a été placé dans un cube moelleux afin d'éviter tout dommage ou dégât.

¿Cómo presentar y promocionar un *gadget* tecnológico de la manera más espectacular posible? Madomat optó por una caja que se abre en varios pasos hasta llegar a la apertura del compartimento semioculto que alberga todos los complementos del teléfono N97 de Nokia. En este sentido, la apertura de la caja se convierte prácticamente en una más de las experiencias sensoriales asociadas al producto. En el interior de la caja, el teléfono ha sido encajado en un cubo de espuma blanda que evita cualquier tipo de impacto directo y la consiguiente rotura.

Madomat
London, UK_Londres, Royaume-Uni_Londres (Reino Unido)
www.madomat.com ı studio@madomat.com

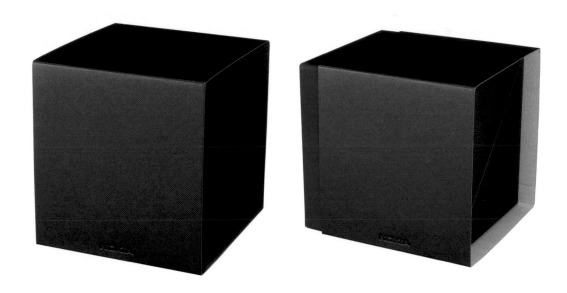

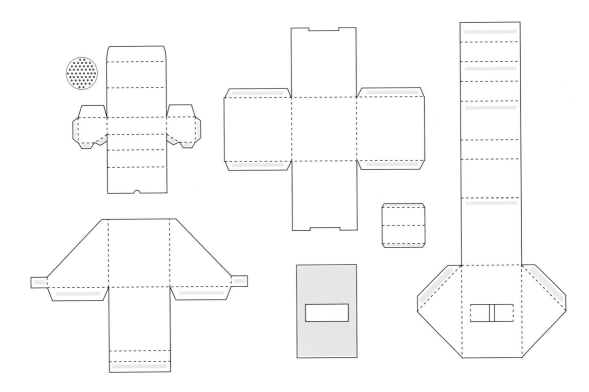

N97 Limited Edition Packaging

Based on the same concept used in the N97 Special Edition Packaging, the N97 Limited Edition Packaging consists of a hand-built wooden case, which can be later used by the client as they wish, rather than being thrown away. Only 30 units of the N97 Limited Edition Packaging were sent to specially selected customers. The black lacquer finish on the case and the engraved Nokia logo convert the case into a real collector's item.

L'édition limitée du N97 reproduit presque trait pour trait le concept du coffret N97 Special Edition Packaging. Il se présente sous forme d'une boîte en bois faite à la main, conçue pour être réutilisée par le client au lieu d'être jetée à la poubelle. Seuls trente exemplaires du N97 Limited Edition Packaging ont été fabriqués et envoyés à des clients choisis avec soin. La finition laquée noire du coffret, ainsi que le logo Nokia gravé dessus en font un véritable objet de collection.

Siguiendo casi paso a paso el mismo concepto de la caja N97 Special Edition Packaging, el N97 Limited Edition Packaging consta de una caja de madera fabricada a mano, destinada a ser utilizada posteriormente por el cliente para cualquier otro uso, en vez de tirarla a la basura. Del N97 Limited Edition Packaging se fabricaron sólo treinta unidades, que fueron enviadas a clientes especialmente seleccionados. El acabado lacado en negro de la caja, así como el logotipo de Nokia grabado en ella, la convierten en un auténtico objeto de coleccionista.

Madomat
London, UK_Londres, Royaume-Uni_Londres (Reino Unido)
www.madomat.com ı studio@madomat.com

N97 Presentation Packaging
"Superbox" - 30 pieces

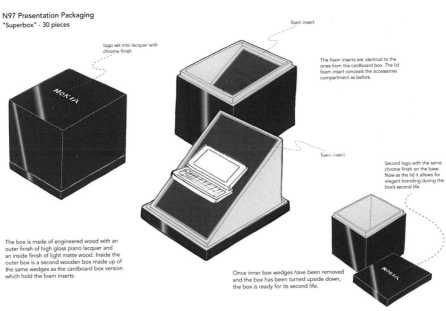

logo set into lacquer with chrome finish

foam insert

The foam inserts are identical to the ones from the cardboard box. The lid foam insert conceals the accessories compartment as before.

foam insert

Second logo with the same chrome finish on the base. Now as the lid it allows for elegant branding during the box's second life.

The box is made of engineered wood with an outer finish of high gloss piano lacquer and an inside finish of light matte wood. Inside the outer box is a second wooden box made up of the same wedges as the cardboard box version which hold the foam inserts.

Once inner box wedges have been removed and the box has been turned upside down, the box is ready for its second life.

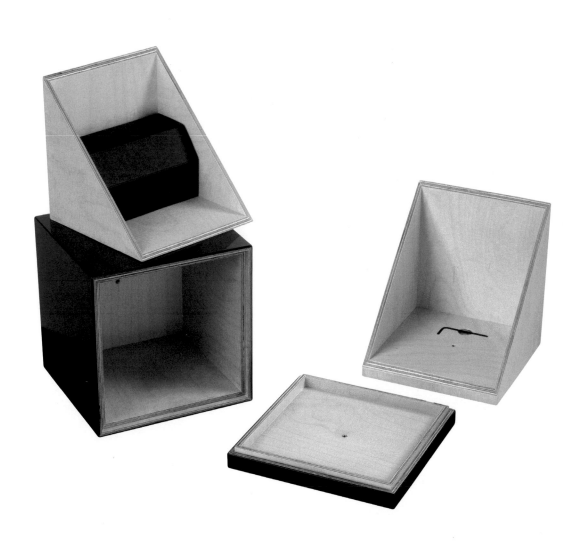

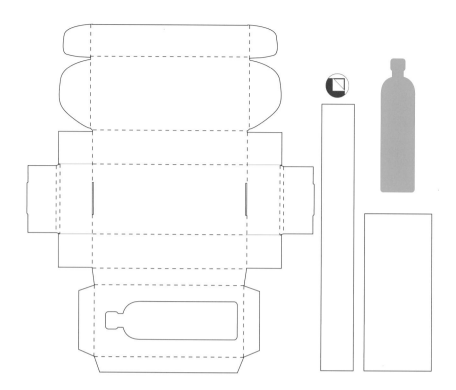

Project 7 kit

Created for Project 7, this box has different uses, including serving as the press and promotional kit. The design had to accommodate both the product (water bottle) and the press kit, and all at a reasonable cost. 29 Agency opted for a box made of eco-friendly and recycled materials that also can be easily personalized. The appearance and layout of the box perfectly match the aesthetics and philosophy of the brand. The printed message changes depending on the recipient of the kit: the general public, press, communication agencies, and so on.

Créée pour Project 7, cette boîte devait pouvoir s'adapter à différents usages, dont celui de kit de presse et de promotion. Le design devait accueillir à la fois le produit (la bouteille d'eau) et le dossier de presse, et tout cela à un coût raisonnable. 29 Agency a opté pour une boîte écologique et durable, fabriquée à partir de matériaux recyclés, et pouvant être facilement personnalisée. L'apparence et le design de la boîte s'accordent parfaitement avec l'esthétique et la philosophie de la marque. De plus, le message imprimé sur le kit change en fonction des personnes à qui il s'adresse : le grand public, la presse, les agences de communication…

Creada para Project 7, esta caja debía poder destinarse a diferentes usos, incluido el de kit de prensa y promoción. El diseño necesitaba dar cabida tanto al producto (la botella de agua) como al dosier de prensa, y todo ello a un coste razonable. Los creativos de 29 Agency optaron por una caja ecológicamente sostenible fabricada con materiales reciclados y que permite una fácil individualización. La apariencia y el diseño de la caja se ajustan perfectamente a la estética y la filosofía de la marca. Además, el mensaje impreso cambia en función del destinatario del kit: el público general, la prensa, las agencias de comunicación…

29 Agency
Southlake, USA_Southlake, États-Unis_Southlake (Estados Unidos)
www.29agency.com ɪ info@29agency.com

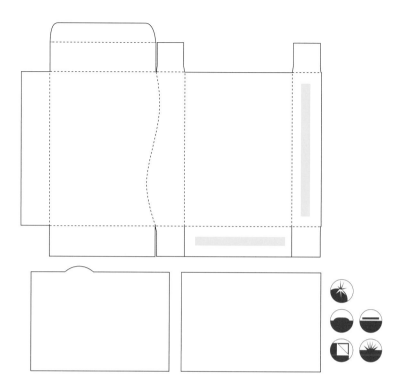

Colours in Motion. Istragrafika press kit

Istragrafika is a printers specializing in high quality printing. Bruketa & ZinicOM was asked to design a promotional kit for the opening of the new Istragrafika production center. The kit should be an example of the client's work and the potential of its technology. Therefore, the kit shows a wide variety of colors, and an irregular and winding silhouette that not all printers can create. Inside, the recipient will find several sheets each made with a special type of paper and a range of completely different printing techniques.

Istragrafika est une imprimerie spécialisée dans l'impression de haute qualité. Bruketa&ZinicOM s'est vu confier le design d'un kit promotionnel à l'occasion de l'ouverture du nouveau centre de production Istragrafika. Le kit devait être un aperçu du travail du client et des possibilités qu'offre sa technologie. Ainsi, il comprend un large éventail de couleurs formant une figure singulière et sinueuse que toutes les imprimeries ne peuvent pas réaliser. À l'intérieur, le destinataire découvre plusieurs planches ; chacune est élaborée à partir d'un type de papier spécial et imprimée selon une technique complètement différente.

Istragrafika es una imprenta especializada en la impresión de alta calidad. Bruketa&ZinicOM recibió el encargo de diseñar un kit promocional con ocasión de la apertura del nuevo centro de producción de Istragrafika. El kit debía ser un ejemplo del trabajo del cliente y de las posibilidades que ofrece su tecnología. Por ello, el kit muestra una amplia variedad de colores y una silueta peculiar y sinuosa que no todas las imprentas pueden realizar. En su interior, el destinatario encuentra varias láminas, cada una fabricada con un tipo de papel especial e impresa con una técnica completamente diferente a la de las demás.

Bruketa&ZinicOM
Zagreb, Croatia_Zagreb, Croatie_Zagreb (Croacia)
www.bruketa-zinic.com ı bruketa-zinic@bruketa-zinic.com

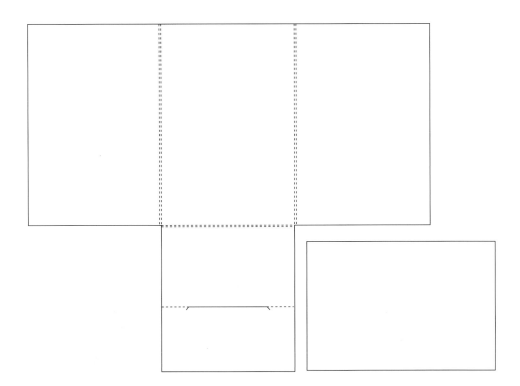

Promotional gift packaging and press kit

Oyuna is a company that manufactures accessories, household goods and clothing for women. For the brand's press campaign, Oyuna wanted the design studio Grain not only to design the press kit but also a promotional gift mainly targeting the Japanese market. This gift should be cheap but impressive, and strongly focused on the satisfaction of opening a gift. The solution was a box carefully closed with a ribbon in Oyuna's corporate color with an interior pocket to store the CD with all the press information about the brand.

Oyuna est une entreprise qui fabrique des accessoires, des articles de maison et des vêtements pour femmes. Pour la campagne de presse de la marque, Oyuna a souhaité que le studio Grain conçoive non seulement le kit de presse, mais également un cadeau promotionnel spécialement conçu pour le marché japonais. Ce cadeau devait être bon marché mais spectaculaire, et s'inspirer notamment de la satisfaction que l'on ressent en déballant un cadeau. La solution qu'ils ont trouvée a donc été de fabriquer un coffret soigneusement fermé avec un ruban de la couleur corporative de Oyuna et d'y placer une pochette renfermant le CD et toute la documentation de presse relative à la marque.

Oyuna es una empresa que fabrica accesorios, productos para el hogar y ropa para mujer. Para la campaña de prensa de la marca, quiso que el estudio Grain diseñara no sólo el kit de prensa, sino también un regalo promocional especialmente dirigido al mercado japonés. Este regalo debía ser barato pero espectacular, y centrarse sobre todo en la satisfacción que se experimenta al abrir un regalo. La solución consistió en una caja cuidadosamente cerrada con una cinta del color corporativo de Oyuna, que cuenta en su interior con un bolsillo en el que guardar el CD con toda la información de prensa sobre la marca.

Grain
London, UK_Londres, Royaume-Uni_Londres (Reino Unido)
www.graincreative.com ı **studio@graincreative.com**

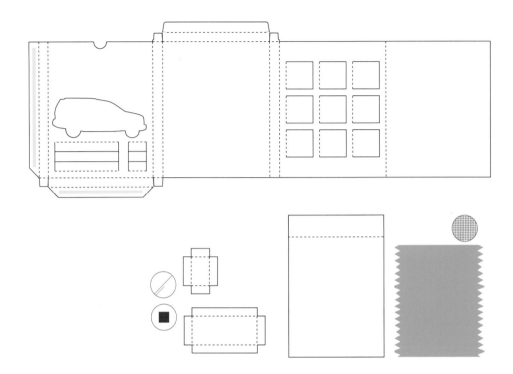

Yes Essentials

Yes Essentials manufactures stain and odor-resistant fabrics and carpets for cars. The brand's demonstration kit includes, besides all the usual technical information about the product and a sample of the product, several sachets and containers filled with some of the products that usually stain the car upholstery and carpets (ketchup, for example). The goal is for the recipient of the kit to stain the Yes Essentials carpet sample with these products to see first hand its qualities and the accuracy of information provided by the manufacturers.

Yes Essentials fabrique des tissus et des tapis anti-odeurs et anti-taches pour voitures. Le kit de démonstration de la marque comporte, en plus de toutes les informations techniques relatives à la marchandise et d'un échantillon de celle-ci, plusieurs sachets et récipients remplis de produits qui peuvent habituellement tacher les tissus et les tapis d'une voiture (le ketchup, par exemple). L'objectif est que le destinataire du kit promotionnel essaie de tacher l'échantillon de moquette Yes Essentials avec les produits qui lui sont donnés afin de se rendre compte par lui-même des vertus de la marchandise et de la véracité des informations divulguées par ses fabricants.

Yes Essentials fabrica tapizados y moquetas para coches resistentes a las manchas y a los olores. El kit de demostración de la marca incluye, además de toda la información técnica habitual sobre el producto y una muestra de éste, varias bolsitas y recipientes rellenos de algunos de los productos que suelen manchar la tapicería y las alfombras de los coches (kétchup, por ejemplo). El objetivo es que el receptor del kit promocional manche la muestra de la moqueta de Yes Essentials con dichos productos para comprobar de primera mano sus virtudes y la veracidad de la información proporcionada por sus fabricantes.

BorsaWallace
New York, USA_New York, États-Unis_Nueva York (Estados Unidos)
www.borsawallace.com ı info@borsawallace.com

Evelio Mattos

How should the perfect promotional kit be?
The promo kit's impact should be instantaneous. You want every person that handles it to know exactly what you or your company does and clearly understand how well you do it.

What's (or what should be) its objective?
The objective for every promo kit is to find new clients, create buzz, and leave a lasting positive impression of what or who is being promoted.

What's the main difficulty when designing a promotional kit?
Money. Hands down, the biggest obstacle is the immediate cost of doing a well produced piece.

And what's the easiest thing about it?
Concepting. If you have a clear understanding of the message and a successful piece constitutes, developing concepts on how to execute this message becomes the easiest, and most fun, aspect of a project. When you have too many ideas you are trying to promote at

Comment devrait être le kit promotionnel parfait ?
L'impact du kit promotionnel devrait être immédiat, chaque personne qui l'a en main doit comprendre exactement ce que vous ou votre société fait et être conscient que vous le faites bien.

Quel est (ou quel devrait être) son objectif ?
L'objectif de chaque kit promotionnel est d'attirer de nouveaux clients, faire du buzz et laisser une impression positive durable de ce qu'est l'objet de la promotion.

Quelle est la principale difficulté lors de la conception d'un kit promotionnel ?
L'argent. C'est bien le problème, le plus gros obstacle est le coût immédiat d'un travail bien fait.

Et qu'est-ce qui est le plus facile ?
La conception. Si vous avez bien compris le message et ce qui constitue un travail réussi, l'élabotation de concepts sur la manière de faire passer ce message constitue la partie facile, et la plus amusante, d'un projet. Si vous avez trop d'idées et que vous essayez de les met-

¿Cómo debería ser el kit promocional perfecto?
El impacto de un kit promocional debe ser inmediato: quieres que cada persona que lo vea sepa exactamente lo que haces tú o tu empresa y sea consciente de lo bien que lo haces.

¿Cuál es (o cuál debería ser) su objetivo?
El objetivo de los kits promocionales es captar nuevos clientes, levantar rumores y dejar un sabor de boca positivo de lo que o de quien hace la promoción.

¿Cuál es la principal dificultad cuando se diseña un kit promocional?
El dinero. Sin duda, el mayor obstáculo es el coste inmediato de crear un buen producto.

¿Y qué parte del proceso de diseño es la más fácil?
Buscar los puntos clave. Si entiendes correctamente el mensaje y lo que es un producto con éxito, desarrollar conceptos sobre cómo trasladar el mensaje es fácil y es también el aspecto más divertido de un proyecto. Cuando tienes

Creative director at Design Packaging Scottsdale, USA
www.designpackaginginc.com
evelio@designpackaginginc.com
Project on page 140

Directeur créatif de Design Packaging Scottsdale, États-Unis
www.designpackaginginc.com
evelio@designpackaginginc.com
Projet sur la page 140

Director creativo de Design Packaging Scottsdale (Estados Unidos)
www.designpackaginginc.com
evelio@designpackaginginc.com
Proyecto en la página 140

once, it becomes too difficult to develop successful concepts, Promo kits need to be pointed and carry a clear message.

What do you most enjoy about designing a promotional kit?
Aside from the concepting, I love working with new materials and printing methods.

In your opinion, what kind of clients/ brands should make use of promotional or press kits?
Everybody should have one. Just as everyone has a website these days, it is imperative for businesses to have a promotional piece that clearly defines who they are.

How do you check or test the effectiveness of your work and designs, and more specifically your press kits? Do you receive any kind of feedback from the client or the consumer?
Yes. The first thing we hear in regards to Design Packaging's promo kit, is "I can't believe the interior is lined in suede. We lined the interior of our outer sleeve in suede to allow the inner box to slide out

tre toutes en oeuvre, il est difficile de développer un concept correctement. Les kits promotionnels doivent avoir un objectif bien défini et transmettre un message clair.

Qu'est-ce que vous plaît le plus dans la conception d'un kit promotionnel ?
Mise à part la conception, j'adore travailler avec de nouveaux matériaux et de nouvelles méthodes d'impression.

À votre avis, quel genre de clients/ marques devraient utiliser les kits promotionnels ou de presse ?
Tout le monde devrait en avoir un, tout comme de nos jours tout le monde a un site Internet. Il est impératif que les entreprises aient un élément promotionnel qui définisse clairement ce qu'elles sont.

Comment vérifiez-vous l'efficacité de votre travail et de vos designs et, plus précisément, de vos kits de presse ? Recevez-vous un feedback de la part du client ou du consommateur ?
Oui. La première chose que nous entendons concernant le kit de promotion du packaging, c'est « je ne peux pas croire

muchas ideas e intentas expresarlas todas de una sola vez, es demasiado complicado desarrollar un concepto correctamente. Los kits promocionales deben tener un objetivo definido y transmitir un mensaje claro.

¿Con qué disfrutas más cuando diseñas un kit promocional?
Además de con el proceso de búsqueda del concepto, me gusta trabajar con nuevos materiales y nuevos métodos de impresión.

Para ti, ¿qué tipo de clientes/marcas deberían utilizar kits promocionales o carpetas de prensa?
Todo el mundo debería tener uno. Al igual que a día de hoy todo el mundo tiene una página web, para un negocio es esencial tener un kit promocional que lo defina claramente.

¿Cómo compruebas o mides la efectividad de un trabajo o un diseño y, especialmente, de un kit de prensa? ¿Recibes *feedback* de los clientes o los consumidores?
Sí. Lo primero que oímos de los kits pro-

smoothly, and create a sensual feeling that you normally do not receive from packaging. The materials are top of the line and the craftsmanship is impeccable. Concept, materials, and craftsmanship are the top three things that are commented on by clients.

What are your favorite materials for a promotional kit? Why?
As a packaging company, we have an endless variety of materials to work with. Our sourcing office sends us new materials weekly. But I am more about new constructions than materials per se unless the medium is the message. My focus is the user experience.

Do you need to "like" the product you're helping to promote to do a good job with it? Be sincere.
You don't have to like the product, but it really helps if you are able to see the value in the product or service you are promoting.

How will new technologies and the fast evolution of the net affect it?
The intertwining of new technologies

que l'intérieur soit doublé en daim » car nous avons doublé l'intérieur de notre chemise extérieure en daim afin que la boîte intérieure sorte doucement, créant ainsi une impression sensuelle que vous n'avez pas en temps normal avec un packaging. Les matériaux sont haut de gamme et le travail est impeccable. Le concept, les matériaux et le travail sont les trois choses que les clients commentent le plus.

Quels sont vos matériaux favoris pour un kit promotionnel ? Pourquoi ?
En tant que société spécialisée dans le packaging, nous avons une variété infinie de matériaux à travailler. Nous recevons toutes les semaines de nouveaux matériaux de la part de notre bureau d'approvisionnement. Cependant, je préfère les nouvelles constructions plutôt que les matériaux en eux-mêmes, sauf si le média est le message, et je suis axé sur l'expérience utilisateur.

Pour faire un bon travail, devez-vous « aimer » le produit dont vous assurez en partie la promotion ? Répondez sincèrement.

mocionales de Design Packaging es: «No puedo creer que el interior esté forrado de ante». Forramos el interior de la funda exterior de ante para que la caja interior salga con mayor suavidad y crear así un tacto atractivo que no suelen tener otros embalajes. Los materiales son de primera calidad y los acabados son impecables. El diseño, los materiales y los acabados son los tres factores que más comentan nuestros clientes.

¿Cuáles son tus materiales favoritos para un kit promocional? ¿Por qué?
Como somos una empresa de embalajes, trabajamos con infinidad de materiales: nuestra oficina de suministros nos envía materiales nuevos todas las semanas. Yo prefiero nuevos diseños a los materiales en sí, salvo si el medio es el mensaje. Para mí lo esencial es la experiencia del usuario.

¿Necesitas que te guste el producto que estás promocionando para hacer una buena promoción? Sé sincero.
No es imprescindible que te guste el producto, pero ayuda mucho ver el valor del producto o del servicio que promocionas.

into mass produced promo pieces will become more common as these technologies become cheaper and more commonly used. I feel that now more than ever promo kits have a deeper impact due to the heavy use of web based promotions. It is so rare to receive a promo kit that stops you in your tracks, so when you do receive one the message resonates beyond anything web-based.

What's the best promotional work you've ever seen, and what product was it related to? Why do you like it? Did you buy the product or did you hire the service just because of its promotional work?

There are many. I love to receive pieces that are hand made pieces of art. Not mass produced slick promo pieces. I see those every day. I want something that I may just keep the promo piece for myself even if I don't buy the product.

What weight and importance do you give to the briefing of the client, when it doesn't fit your ideas?

You always have to take the client's perspective into consideration. You should

Vous n'avez pas à aimer le produit mais cela aide vraiment si vous pouvez voir la valeur dans le produit ou service dont vous faites la promotion.

Comment les nouvelles technologies et l'évolution rapide du réseau vont-ils l'affecter ?

La combinaison des nouvelles technologies et des éléments de promotion produits en masse va s'intensifier de jour en jour car ces technologies deviennent moins chères et sont plus fréquemment utilisées. Je pense que les kits promotionnels ont désormais, plus que jamais, un impact plus profond, du fait de l'utilisation importante de promotions sur Internet. Il est tellement rare de recevoir un kit promotionnel qui vous interpelle que, lorsque vous en voyez un, le message a davantage de retentissement que tout ce qu'il peut y avoir sur Internet.

Quel est le meilleur travail promotionnel que vous ayez jamais vu et de quel produit s'agit-il ? Pourquoi vous a-t-il plu ? Avez-vous acheté le produit ou loué le service juste pour son travail promotionnel ?

¿Cómo influirán las nuevas tecnologías y la rápida evolución de la Red?

El uso conjunto de las nuevas tecnologías para promociones a gran escala será cada vez mayor conforme esas tecnologías vayan siendo más baratas y más utilizadas. Creo que, ahora más que nunca, los kits tienen un impacto mayor por el amplio uso de promociones on-line. Es tan extraño recibir un kit promocional que te asombre que, cuando ves uno, el mensaje resuena más allá de la Red.

¿Cuál es el mejor trabajo de promoción que has visto? ¿Qué promocionaba? ¿Por qué te gustó? ¿Compraste el producto o contrataste el servicio sólo por el trabajo promocional?

Hay muchos. Me gusta recibir objetos hechos a mano que son auténticas obras de arte y no elementos fabricados en serie. Ésos los veo todos los días. Quiero algo que pueda guardar para mí mismo, aunque después no compre el producto.

¿Qué peso y qué importancia das al *briefing* del cliente cuando no piensa lo mismo que tú?

Siempre hay que tener en cuenta la pers-

also be able to voice your opinions, and have discussions before creating anything. The days of the designer being the all-knowing creator who knows more than their clients are over. These days, clients are more educated now in marketing than they have ever been. Development of anything should be a collaborative effort.

What's the promotional kit you would like to design and why?
Channel. They understand the value of quality materials, and the cost of craftsmanship.

Where do you look for new ideas?
Wherever I am: Argentina, Italy, Hong Kong, New York, Arizona... Everywhere you are there is something you haven't seen and it can inspire you. You just have to look for it.

Name the items, personal objects and tools you absolutely could not work without.
Last.fm, my Mac. That's pretty much it.

Describe your average working day.
Testing, mocking up, sourcing materials, checking color, prepping proofs, and reviewing pre-press. That's just in the first hour! Followed by research, sketching, testing, blogging, checking SEO, and creating.

Describe the perfect client.
Someone who is not afraid to allow you to push them past their comfort zone.

Il y en a beaucoup, j'aime recevoir des éléments qui sont des objets d'art faits à la main. Pas des éléments de promotion superficiels, produits en masse, ceux que je vois tous les jours. Je veux quelque chose qui me permette de conserver l'élément de promotion, même si je n'achète pas le produit.

Quelle importance donnez-vous au briefing du client lorsqu'il ne partage pas vos idées ?
Vous devez toujours tenir compte du point de vue du client et vous devriez aussi pouvoir exprimer vos opinions et discuter avant de créer quoi que ce soit. Les temps où le designer était un créateur omniscient qui en savait plus que ses clients sont révolus. De nos jours, les clients en savent nettement plus sur le marqueting qu'avant et tout développement devrait être le fruit d'une collaboration.

Quel kit promotionnel aimeriez-vous concevoir et pourquoi ?
Chanel. Ils sont conscients la valeur des matériaux de qualité et du coût du travail.

Où cherchez-vous de nouvelles idées ?
À l'endroit où je me trouve, Argentine, Italie, Hong-Kong, New York, Arizona, où que vous soyez, il y a quelque chose que vous n'avez pas vu et qui peut vous inspirer. Il vous suffit de le chercher.

Quels sont les éléments, les objets personnels et les outils dont vous ne pourriez absolument pas vous passer pour travailler ?
Last.fm, mon Mac et voilà.

Décrivez-nous une journée de travail.
Tester, faire des maquettes, m'approvisionner en matériaux, tester des couleurs, préparer des essais, revoir la préimpression, tout ça pendant la première heure ! Ensuite, rechercher, ébaucher, tester, bloguer, vérifier le SEO (optimisation pour les moteurs de recherche) et créer.

Décrivez le client parfait.
Quelqu'un qui n'a pas peur de vous laisser l'emmener en dehors de sa zone confortable.

pectiva del cliente. También debes ser capaz de plantearle tus opiniones y discutir el proyecto antes de crear nada. Los días en los que el diseñador era un creativo omnisciente que sabía más que el cliente pasaron a la historia. Actualmente, los clientes saben mucho más de *marketing* que nunca, por lo que cualquier proyecto debe hacerse de forma conjunta.

¿Qué kit promocional te gustaría diseñar y por qué?
Channel. Entiende el valor de los materiales de calidad y el coste de los trabajos manuales.

¿Dónde buscas nuevas ideas?
Dondequiera que esté: Argentina, Italia, Hong Kong, Nueva York, Arizona... Siempre hay algo que no has visto que puede inspirarte; sólo tienes que buscarlo.

Nombra las cosas, los objetos personales y las herramientas sin las que te sería imposible trabajar.
Last.fm y mi Mac. Son esenciales.

Describe un día de trabajo normal.
Probar, hacer maquetas, obtener materiales, probar colores, preparar pruebas y revisar preprensas... ¡y eso sólo en la primera hora! Después toca investigar, hacer bocetos, investigar, probar, bloquear, comprobar el posicionamiento en buscadores y crear.

Describe al cliente perfecto.
Alguien que no tiene miedo de permitirte llevarle más allá de su zona de confort.

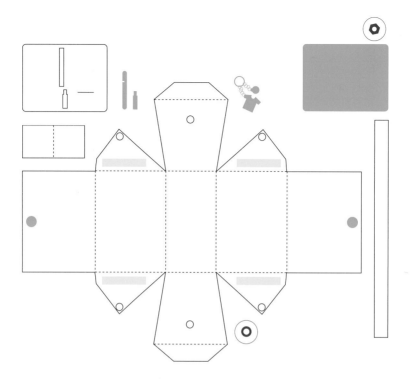

Tide to Go

Tide to Go is a small marker that can remove any stain on clothes. The product's promotional kit includes, in a rectangular metal box, a small container with a liquid with which the user has to stain their clothing, and a Tide to Go pen accompanied by instructions for use. The kit also includes a key ring with several pins featuring designs relating to the product (its logo, a T-shirt…) and a leather pouch to store the pen. The kit box, decorated with the logo of the brand, has a handle.

Tide to Go est un petit stylo capable d'enlever n'importe quelle tache sur un vêtement. Le kit promotionnel du produit comporte, à l'intérieur d'une boîte rectangulaire en métal, un petit récipient rempli d'un liquide avec lequel le destinataire est censé tacher ses vêtements, ainsi qu'un stylo Tide to Go accompagné de son mode d'emploi. Le kit contient également un anneau auquel sont accrochés plusieurs porte-clefs avec le design du produit (son logo, un tee-shirt…) et un étui destiné à contenir le stylo. La boîte du kit, décorée avec le logo de la marque, est transportable grâce à sa anse.

Tide to Go es un rotulador de pequeño tamaño capaz de eliminar cualquier tipo de mancha sobre la ropa. El kit promocional del producto contiene, dentro de una caja metálica rectangular, un pequeño recipiente con un líquido con el que el usuario ha de manchar su ropa y un rotulador Tide to Go acompañado de las instrucciones de uso. El kit incluye además un llavero del que cuelgan varias chapas con diseños referentes al producto (su logotipo, una camiseta…) y una funda de piel en la que guardar el rotulador. La caja del kit, decorada con el logotipo de la marca, puede ser transportada gracias a su asa.

BorsaWallace
New York, USA_New York, États-Unis_Nueva York (Estados Unidos)
www.borsawallace.com ɪ **info@borsawallace.com**

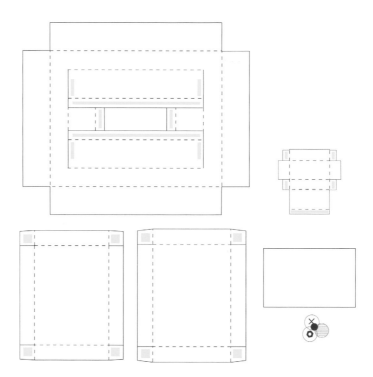

Think Tank

The promotional kit designed by Airside for the packaging company Think Tank includes a game and a book. Its aim is to give as much information as possible about the company. Both elements, the game and the book, feature different print finishes to illustrate the wide range of techniques and materials used by Think Tank. The game, based on the traditional Misfits, consists of several cards made with different materials, including velvet and metal. The pages of the book illustrate the different types of finishes that the company offers.

Le kit promotionnel conçu par Airside pour l'entreprise de packaging Think Tank comprend un jeu et un livre. Son objectif est de transmettre le plus d'informations possible sur l'entreprise. Ces deux éléments présentent diverses finitions d'impression illustrant la vaste gamme de techniques et de matériaux utilisés par Think Tank. Le jeu s'inspire du classique Misfits et se compose de plusieurs cartes faites à partir de différents matériaux comme le velours ou le métal. Les pages du livre illustrent les différents types de produits finis avec lesquels l'entreprise

El kit promocional diseñado por Airside para la compañia de *packaging* Think Tank incluye un juego y un libro. Su objetivo es transmitir la mayor información posible sobre la empresa. Ambos elementos, el juego y el libro, tienen diferentes acabados de impresión para ejemplificar la amplia gama de técnicas y materiales que utiliza Think Tank. El juego, basado en el tradicional Misfits, se compone de varias tarjetas fabricadas con diferentes materiales, incluidos el terciopelo y el metal. Las páginas del libro muestran los distintos tipos de acabados con los que trabaja la empresa.

Airside
London, UK_Londres, Royaume-Uni_Londres (Reino Unido)
www.airside.co.uk ı studio@airside.co.uk

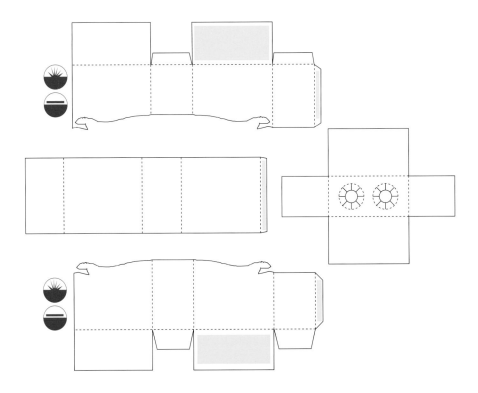

Sebeka

Sebeka is a South African wine whose philosophy is based on the spirit of "exploration and discovery". Based on this, BorsaWallace has chosen for its press kit a black box (the color of the mystery) on which several details (such as the brand logo) have been printed in bright ink. The box has been stamped with the silhouette of a cheetah, which refers, of course, to the African origin of the brand, and it is exposed when the lid is raised. The box, manufactured from high density foam, has been designed with the objective of protecting the bottles inside and preventing them from breaking,

Sebeka est un vin sud-africain dont la philosophie repose sur l'esprit de « recherche et découverte ». À partir de là, BorsaWallace a conçu son kit de presse en optant pour une boîte de couleur noire (la couleur du mystère) sur laquelle plusieurs détails, comme le logo de la marque, ont été imprimés à l'encre brillante. Une silhouette de guépard a été découpée dans la boîte, pour rappeler les origines africaines de la marque, que l'on ne peut découvrir qu'en soulevant le couvercle. La boîte, fabriquée à partir d'une mousse très dense, a été conçue de façon à protéger les bouteilles et à éviter qu'elles ne se cassent.

Sebeka es un vino sudafricano cuya filosofía se basa en el espíritu de «exploración y descubrimiento»; de ahí que BorsaWallace haya optado para su kit de prensa por una caja de color negro (el color del misterio) sobre la que se han impreso varios detalles, como el logotipo de la marca, en tinta brillante. La caja ha sido troquelada con la silueta de un guepardo, que hace referencia al origen africano de la marca y que queda al descubierto cuando se levanta la tapa. La caja, fabricada con espuma de alta densidad, ha sido diseñada con el objetivo de proteger las botellas de su interior y evitar su rotura accidental.

Jason Davis, Rebecca Marshall/BorsaWallace
New York, USA_New York, États-Unis_Nueva York (Estados Unidos)
www.borsawallace.com ı info@borsawallace.com

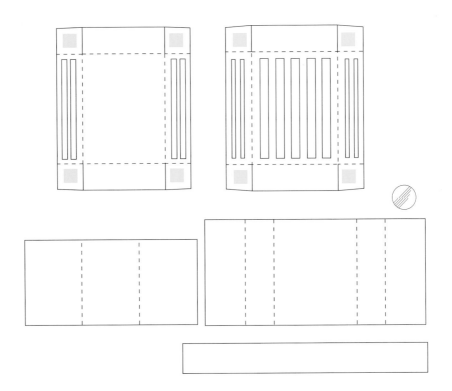

Foods of Québec

As a culinary Mecca that mixes the oldest culinary traditions with new trends, the province of Quebec proposed to increase demand for its products among US consumers, and particularly among restaurateurs, distributors in the food industry and food specialist business owners. A campaign was launched that began with a series of promotional postcards showing some of the Quebecois culinary secrets, and ended with the sending of a wooden box containing samples of products from the region.

En véritable Mecque de la cuisine, alliant les traditions culinaires les plus anciennes aux nouvelles tendances, la province de Québec a décidé d'augmenter la demande de ses produits chez les consommateurs américains, et notamment chez les restaurateurs, distributeurs du secteur alimentaire et propriétaires de commerces spécialisés. Pour cela, elle a lancé une campagne en commençant par envoyer une série de cartes postales promotionnelles qui dévoilaient quelques secrets culinaires québécois et qui étaient accompagnées d'une boîte en bois contenant des échantillons de produits de la région.

Como meca culinaria que mezcla la cocina tradicional con las nuevas tendencias, la provincia de Quebec se propuso incrementar la demanda de sus productos entre los consumidores estadounidenses, y muy especialmente entre los restauradores, los distribuidores del ramo de la alimentación y los propietarios de comercios especializados. Para ello, lanzó una campaña, que empezó con una serie de postales promocionales que mostraban algunos de los secretos culinarios quebequeses y concluyó con el envío de una caja de madera que contenía muestras de productos de la región.

Jason Davis, Cecilia Molina/BorsaWallace
New York, USA_New York, États-Unis_Nueva York (Estados Unidos)
www.borsawallace.com ı info@borsawallace.com

You'll wonder how we ever kept it a secret...

FOODS OF QUÉBEC "IS BUILT ON A
FOUNDATION OF TRADITIONAL HAUTE
CUISINE, TIMELESS QUÉBÉCOIS RECIPES,
AND THE HAPPY PROLIFERATION OF
INGREDIENTS THAT ARE RAISED,
CULTIVATED, OR MADE IN THE PROVINCE..."

GOURMET MAGAZINE, MARCH 2006

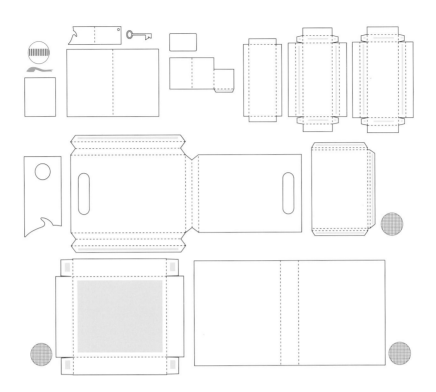

Background

Dolphin House is the promotional apartment complex in Dolphin Square. In order to capture the potential public of boutique hotels, Ico was commissioned to create promotional materials that reflect the quality of the apartments. Purple was chosen as the main color, which is also the color in the suites advertised. Ico designed several elements: a flyer, the website, the invitation to the opening night and promotional pack which guests receive on arrival including a key-card and its case, the labels for luggage and a laundry bag.

Dolphin House sont des appartements promotionnels faisant partie du complexe Dolphin Square. Afin de capter l'attention des potentiels clients des hôtels-boutiques, Ico s'est vu confier la création d'un matériel promotionnel reflétant la qualité des appartements. Pour cela, le pourpre, que l'on retrouve dans les suites qui y sont mentionnées, a été choisi comme couleur dominante. Ico a conçu plusieurs éléments : une brochure publicitaire, la page Web, l'invitation à l'inauguration et le pack promotionnel avec lequel les clients sont accueillis. Ce dernier comporte une carte-clé et son étui, des étiquettes à bagages et un sac de blanchisserie.

Dolphin House son los apartamentos promocionales pertenecientes al complejo Dolphin Square. Con el objetivo de captar al público potencial de los hoteles *boutique*, Ico recibió el encargo de crear material promocional que reflejara la calidad de los apartamentos. Para ello, se optó por el púrpura como color principal, que es también el de las *suites* publicitadas. El estudio diseñó varios elementos: un folleto publicitario, la página web, la invitación al acto inaugural y el *pack* de promoción con el que se recibe a los clientes, que incluye una llave-tarjeta y su funda, las etiquetas para las maletas y una bolsa para la lavandería.

Ico Design Consultancy
London, UK_Londres, Royaume-Uni_Londres (Reino Unido)
www.icodesign.co.uk ı info@icodesign.co.uk

50

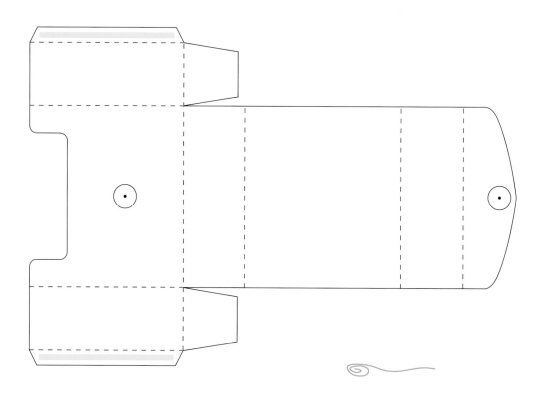

Get in Bed with Us!

The press kit Get in Bed with Us! was designed to internationally promote the Virgin label catalog of artists. Inspired by the ad sections of newspapers, the kit features new artists from the label and recalls the old. The kit has been designed for recruitment agencies and advertisers seeking artists to promote their customer's products. In the words of the designers, "this is how the old songs that talk about injecting heroin end up promoting pleasure cruises".

Le kit de presse Get in Bed with Us! a été conçu pour promouvoir le catalogue d'artistes du label de musique Virgin à l'échelle internationale. Le kit s'inspire des petites annonces de journaux pour présenter les nouveaux artistes de la maison de disques et rappeler les anciens. Les destinataires du kit sont les agences de recrutement et de publicité qui sont à la recherche d'artistes pour promouvoir les produits de leurs clients. Pour reprendre les mots des designers, « c'est comme ça que les vielles chansons qui parlent de s'injecter de l'héroïne finissent par promouvoir des croisières de loisirs ».

El kit de prensa Get in Bed with Us! fue diseñado para promocionar a escala internacional el catálogo de artistas de la discográfica Virgin. Inspirado por las secciones de anuncios por palabras de los diarios, el kit presenta a los nuevos artistas del sello y rememora a los viejos. Sus destinatarios son las agencias de contratación y publicidad que buscan artistas para promocionar los productos de sus clientes. En palabras de los propios diseñadores, «así es como las viejas canciones que hablan de inyectarse heroína acaban promocionando cruceros de placer».

Mike Joyce/Stereotype Design
New York, USA_New York, États-Unis_Nueva York (Estados Unidos)
www.stereotype-design.com ɪ **mike@stereotype-design.com**

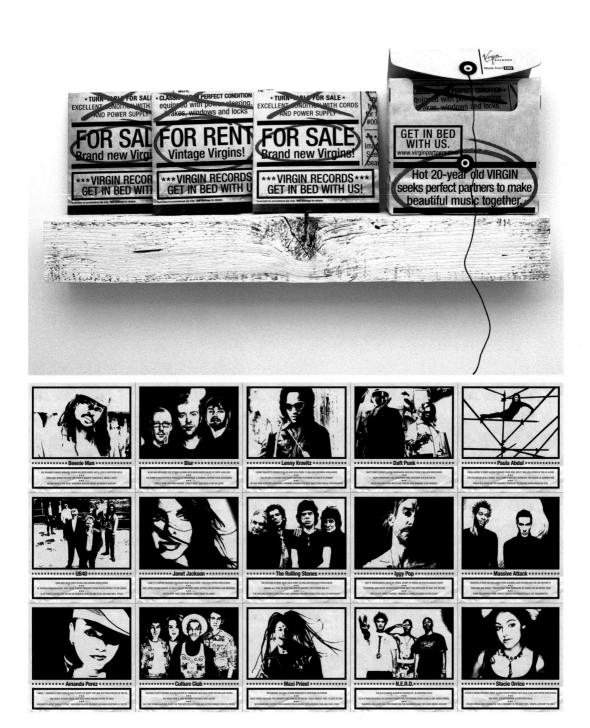

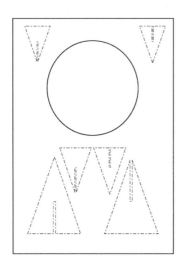

Alexander Pelikan Chair

The Dutch designer Alexander Pelikan is the creator of Clicfurniture, a line of furniture made from Trespa, a material consisting of high-pressure laminated panels. One of these pieces is the Monolounge, a detachable chair made from four sheets of material that can be slotted together. For the press kit, Marjolijn Stappers decided to build a smaller version of the chair that the recipients can build by themselves. The same sheet which contains the four pieces that make the mini-Monolounge also includes the CD with the commercial information about its creator and the rest of his products.

Le designer hollandais Alexander Pelikan est l'auteur de Clicfurniture, une ligne de meubles fabriqués avec des produits Trespa, des matériaux composés de panneaux de résine thermostables, de haute pression, que l'on emploie dans l'architecture et l'aménagement intérieur. L'un de ces meubles est la Monolounge, une chaise pliante formée de quatre planches qui s'emboîtent. Pour le kit de presse, Marjolijn Stappers a décidé de construire une version miniature de cette chaise que le destinataire doit monter lui-même. Les quatre pièces qui composent la chaise sont issues du même panneau en cartonet contiennent le CD comportant toutes les informations commerciales sur le créateur et le reste de ses produits.

El diseñador holandés Alexander Pelikan es el autor de Clicfurniture, una línea de mobiliario fabricado con Trespa, un material compuesto por unas placas de resina de alta presión termoestables que se emplea en arquitectura e interiorismo. Uno de esos muebles es la Monolounge, una silla desmontable formada por cuatro láminas que encajan por medio de pestañas. Para el kit de prensa, Marjolijn Stappers optó por una versión reducida de la silla que el destinatario del kit debe montar. La misma lámina de la que se han de extraer las cuatro piezas que forman la mini-Monolounge alberga el CD con toda la información comercial sobre su creador y el resto de sus productos.

Marjolijn Stappers
Amsterdam, the Netherlands_Amsterdam, Pays-Bas_Ámsterdam (Países Bajos)
www.typolectro.nl ı info@typolectro.nl

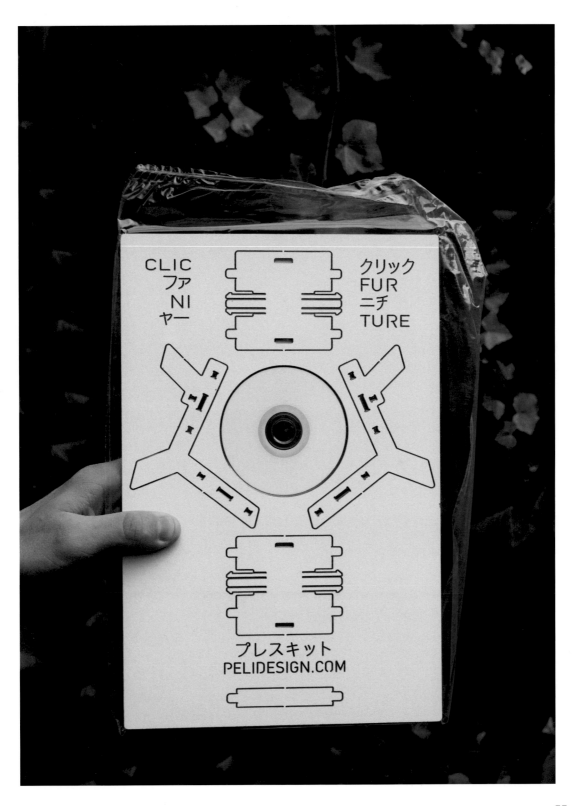

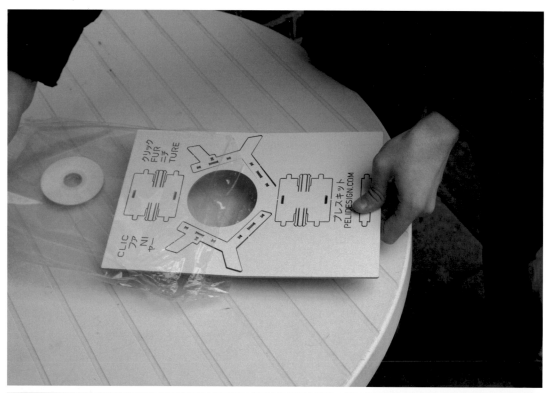

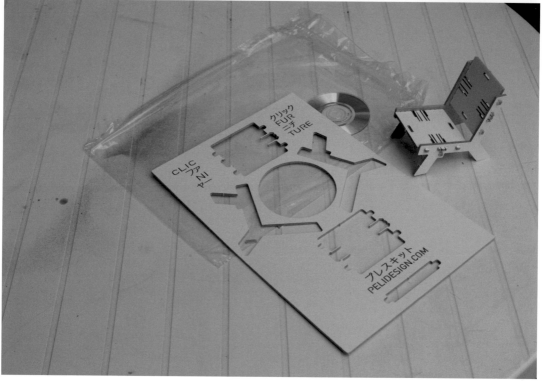

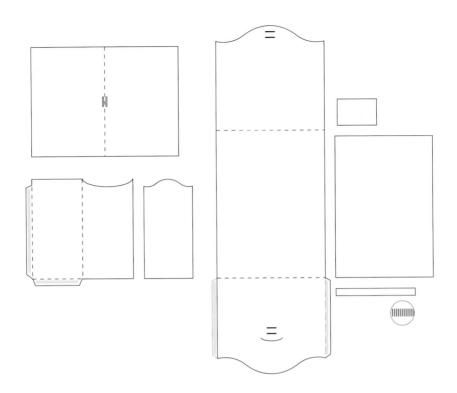

Webster House press kit

Webster House is both a shop, a restaurant and an event space. The press kit for the new Webster House redesigned by the Design Ranch studio was sent to all kinds of publications, hotels, wedding planners, agencies and individual clients. The kit consists of a folded that closes with a tie. Inside, the recipient can find two information packs, writing paper and a card. The inspiration for the press kit came from traditional crafts. The photography, meanwhile, focuses on close-ups to emphasize the exquisite details of pieces from Webster House.

Webster House est à la fois une boutique, un restaurant et une salle de réception. Le kit de presse de la nouvelle Webster House remaniée par le studio Design Ranch a été envoyé à des publications en tout genre, à des hôtels, à des agences d'organisation de mariages et à des clients particuliers. Ce kit consiste en un dossier fermé par un nœud. À l'intérieur, le destinataire peut trouver deux dossiers d'information, du papier à lettre et une carte. Le design du kit de presse s'inspire de l'artisanat traditionnel. Les photographies, quant à elles, mettent l'accent sur les détails raffinés de la Webster House grâce à des gros plans.

Webster House es al mismo tiempo una tienda, un restaurante y un espacio para eventos. El kit de prensa de la nueva Webster House rediseñada por el estudio Design Ranch se envió a hoteles, a agencias de organización de bodas, a clientes individuales y a publicaciones de todo tipo. El kit consiste en una carpeta plegada que se cierra con un lazo. En su interior, el destinatario puede encontrar dos dosieres informativos, papel de carta y una tarjeta. La inspiración para el diseño del kit de prensa surgió de la artesanía tradicional. La fotografía, por su lado, se centra en los planos cortos para enfatizar los detalles exquisitos de las piezas de la Webster House.

Design Ranch
Kansas City, USA_Kansas City, États-Unis_Kansas City (Estados Unidos)
www.design-ranch.com ı info@design-ranch.com

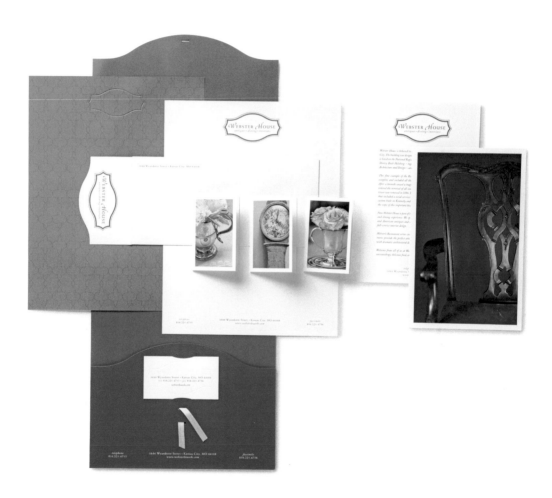

${\cal I}$NTRODUCTION

Welcome to Kansas City's historic Webster House, one of the finest shopping and dining experiences in the Midwest. We are proud to share this award-winning and lovingly restored, 19th century school with the public. Whether you drop in for a bite to eat, or to browse our five distinct shops with their breathtaking displays of antiques, gifts, and interior accessories, our house is always your home.

${\cal G}$IFTS

A gift from one of the other three Webster House shops is like a memento from far-away travels. Our buyers search globally so you can explore locally. Whether you are being generous at a moment's notice or turning a quiet day into a shopping adventure, Necessary Luxuries, The Decorative Home, and The Book Club will create memorable impressions.

Private Parties

At Webster House, we believe life is worth celebrating. So we open our doors for all your family milestones and holidays – the grand and the intimate. Because we design parties that realize your vision, your guests experience delicious cuisine, imaginative themes, and gracious atmosphere. For our expert planners, the only goal is your comfort and success. The result is parties that people remember forever.

There is only one meaning of life, the act of living itself.
ERICH FROMM

Art directors of Bruketa&ZinicOM
Zagreb, Croatia
www.bruketa-zinic.com
bruketa-zinic@bruketa-zinic.com
Project on page 22

Directeurs artistiques de Bruketa&ZinicOM
Zagreb, Croatie
www.bruketa-zinic.com
bruketa-zinic@bruketa-zinic.com
Projet sur la page 22

Directores artísticos de Bruketa&ZinicOM
Zagreb (Croacia)
www.bruketa-zinic.com
bruketa-zinic@bruketa-zinic.com
Proyecto en la página 22

How should the perfect promotional kit be?

Primarily it should be designed with a sense of purpose, and then it should be creative and properly produced in terms of quality.

What's the main difficulty when designing a promotional kit?

Trying to find something special about the client, something that makes them stand out from others in the same category.

In your opinion, what kind of clients/ brands should make use of promotional or press kits?

It's best to create something physical, a sample that represents the client and its possibilities. For some companies and brands it is simply better to use on-line promotion. All depends on what the company/client produces, what they are trying to present and communicate.

How do you check or test the effectiveness of your work and designs, and more specifically your press kits? Do you receive any kind of feedback from the client or the consumer?

Comment devrait être le kit promotionnel parfait ?

Tout d'abord, il devrait être conçu avec un objectif clair tout en étant créatif et correctement produit en termes de qualité.

Quelle est la principale difficulté lors de la conception d'un kit promotionnel ?

D'essayer de trouver quelque chose de spécial chez le client, quelque chose qui le distingue des autres de la même catégorie.

À votre avis, quel genre de clients/ marques devraient utiliser les kits promotionnels ou de presse ?

Il vaut mieux créer quelque chose de physique, un échantillon représentant le client et ses possibilités. Cependant, pour certaines sociétés et certaines marques, il vaut mieux utiliser la promotion en ligne mais cela dépend de ce que l'entreprise/client produit, de ce qu'il essaye de présenter et de communiquer.

Comment vérifiez-vous l'efficacité de votre travail et de vos designs et, plus précisément, de vos kits de presse ?

¿Cómo debería ser el kit promocional perfecto?

Para empezar, debería diseñarse teniendo muy claro el objetivo. Además, debe ser creativo e impecable en cuanto a calidad.

¿Cuál es la principal dificultad cuando se diseña un kit promocional?

Intentar encontrar algo especial en el cliente, algo que lo diferencie de la competencia.

Para vosotros, ¿qué tipo de clientes/ marcas deberían utilizar kits promocionales o carpetas de prensa?

Lo mejor es diseñar algo físico, una muestra que represente al cliente y sus posibilidades. Para algunas empresas y marcas simplemente es mejor una promoción *on-line*, pero depende de lo que produzca la empresa/cliente, lo que intente presentar y comunicar.

¿Cómo comprobáis o medís la efectividad de un trabajo o un diseño y, especialmente, de un kit de prensa? ¿Recibís *feedback* de los clientes o los consumidores?

Sí, recibimos el *feedback* de los clientes,

Imelda Ramovic + Mirel Hadzijusufovic

Yes, we receive feedback from clients, reactions from the public as well as the specific numbers from the market.

What's your working method when designing a promotional kit? Is there a particular path you follow?
There is no special method that differs from the other work we do. First, we research and try to get to know the client/brand/market, then the idea comes and then we try to find the best way to represent the idea.

Do you need to "like" the product you're helping to promote to do a good job with it? Be sincere.
We try to approach every project professionally and search for a new challenge each time. We think that's the point of all we do: to find the best way to communicate what is relevant for the client and the consumer in a situation where you don't necessarily have to like or dislike what you are communicating. What you have to like and be satisfied with is the solution you create.

What weight and importance do you give to the briefing of the client when

Recevez-vous un feedback de la part du client ou du consommateur ?
Oui, nous recevons des feedbacks des clients, des réactions du public, ainsi que des chiffres précis du marché.

Quelle est votre méthode de travail lors de la conception d'un kit promotionnel ? Suivez-vous un processus particulier ?
Nous n'avons pas de méthode spéciale qui varie par rapport aux autres travaux que nous effectuons. Nous commençons par faire des recherches afin de savoir ce que le client/marque/marché veut, puis l'idée vient et nous essayons de trouver la meilleure manière de la présenter.

Pour faire un bon travail, devez-vous « aimer » le produit dont vous assurez en partie la promotion ? Répondez sincèrement.
Nous essayons d'aborder chaque projet d'un point de vue professionnel et nous cherchons de nouveaux défis à chaque fois. Nous considérons que c'est l'objectif de tout ce que nous faisons, c'est-à-dire chercher la meilleure manière de communiquer ce qui est important pour

las reacciones del público y, además, cifras concretas del mercado.

¿Qué método de trabajo seguís cuando diseñáis un kit promocional? ¿Os basáis en algunas pautas en concreto?
No tenemos ningún método concreto diferente del resto de trabajo que realizamos. Primero, investigamos y tratamos de conocer al cliente/marca/mercado; después, surge la idea e intentamos encontrar el mejor medio para mostrarla.

¿Necesitáis que os guste el producto que estáis promocionando para hacer una buena promoción? Sed sinceros.
Intentamos plantear todos los proyectos de forma profesional y buscamos constantemente nuevos retos. Creemos que ésta es la clave de todo lo que hacemos: buscar la mejor forma de comunicar lo que es importante para el cliente y para el consumidor en una situación en la que no tienes que estar necesariamente de acuerdo o en desacuerdo con lo que estás promocionando. Lo que tiene que gustarte y con lo que tienes que estar satisfecho es con la solución que diseñas.

it doesn't fit your ideas? How do you match these two opposite views?
A good briefing is certainly 50% of the work, but the truth is we don't get this kind of briefing often. Then we try to ask additional questions.

Name the items, personal objects and tools you absolutely could not work without.
Here we would like to use Bruce Mau as a reference: "Don't clean your desk. You might find something in the morning that you can't see tonight".

le client et le consommateur dans une situation où vous n'avez pas forcément à aimer ou pas l'objet dont vous faites la promotion. Ce que vous devez aimer et qui doit vous satisfaire, c'est la solution que vous trouvez.

Quelle importance donnez-vous au briefing du client lorsqu'il ne partage pas vos idées ? Comment conciliez-vous ces deux points de vue opposés ?
Un bon briefing représente certainement 50 % du travail mais il faut reconnaître que nous n'en avons pas souvent. Nous essayons ensuite de poser d'autres questions.

Quels sont les éléments, les objets personnels et les outils dont vous ne pourriez absolument pas vous passer pour travailler ?
Nous aimerions citer Bruce Mau comme référence : « Ne faites pas le vide sur votre bureau. Vous pourriez y trouver quelque chose le matin que vous n'avez pas vu la veille ».

¿Qué peso y qué importancia dais al *briefing* del cliente cuando no piensa lo mismo que vosotros? ¿Cómo conseguís encontrar un punto medio para dos puntos de vista diferentes?
Sin duda alguna, unas buenas directrices suponen el 50% del trabajo, pero lo cierto es que no solemos contar a menudo con este tipo de directrices. Después, intentamos plantear más preguntas.

Nombrad las cosas, los objetos personales y las herramientas sin las que os sería imposible trabajar.
Aquí nos gustaría citar a Bruce Mau, quien dijo: «No limpies tu escritorio. Puedes encontrar algo por la mañana que no puedes ver ahora».

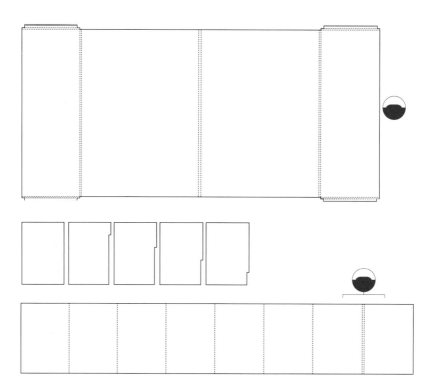

Christmas at Liberty

StudioThomson designed the 2007 Christmas campaign for the Liberty department stores, which tries to fuse both items of luxury and fantasy. StudioThomson drew inspiration from crystal chandeliers, candles and carnival-related paraphernalia. To make the press kit, they used embossed and bas-relief printing techniques to give the kit a heightened tactile experience. The silver front page features images of the products on sale in the stores. The cards correspond to the Liberty Fabric project, which shows the patterns designed by the Liberty textile department.

En 2007, StudioThomson a conçu la campagne de Noël des magasins Liberty, qui prétendait conjuguer les concepts de luxe et de fantaisie. Pour cela, StudioThomson s'est inspiré à la fois des chandeliers en cristal, des bougies, et de tout l'attirail associé au carnaval. Pour la réalisation du kit de presse, les designers ont opté pour des techniques spéciales d'impression qui lui procurent un intérêt tactile (comme l'impression en bas-relief). Sur la couverture argentée, la gravure fait référence aux produits qui sont en vente dans les magasins. Les cartes correspondent au projet Liberty Fabric, qui présente les patrons confectionnés par le département de design textile de Liberty.

StudioThomson diseñó la campaña navideña de 2007 de los almacenes Liberty, que pretendía fusionar los conceptos de lujo y fantasía. Para ello, se inspiró en los candelabros de cristal, las velas y la parafernalia asociada al carnaval. Para la realización del kit de prensa se optó por técnicas especiales de impresión que añadían interés táctil, como el estampado en bajorrelieve. En la portada, plateada, se ha grabado un patrón de flores, que remite visualmente a la estética de los productos a la venta en los almacenes. Las tarjetas corresponden al proyecto Liberty Fabric, que muestra los patrones diseñados por el departamento de diseño textil de Liberty.

StudioThomson
London, UK_Londres, Royaume-Uni_Londres (Reino Unido)
www.studiothomson.com ı info@studiothomson.com

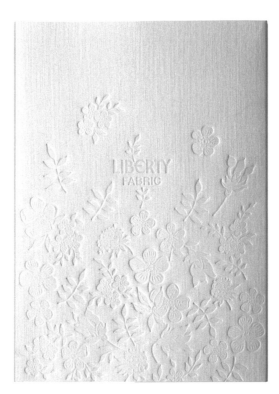

**LIBERTY FABRIC
SPRING SUMMER 2009
COLLECTION**

Liberty's exquisitely printed fabrics are amongst the world's finest and have been at the forefront of textile design since the 1880s.
The Liberty Fabric Spring Summer 2009 collection continues the tradition of creating innovative designs that set trends in fashion and textiles, expertly mixing high colour prints with more subtle creations.
A timeless vision of colour, design and cloth.

A collection of design and colour created with original photography, drawing, painting and reworking of historical archival documents, acknowledging contemporary and historical lifestyle trends in fashion.

CITY BLUE

TOWN BRIGHTS

VILLAGE GREEN

SOFT BEACH

ECO NATURAL

ROCK STAR

SURF

CHILDREN'S CHOICE

CITY VIBES

COUNTRY SOCIETY

**LIBERTY FABRIC
SPRING SUMMER 2009
COLLECTION**

DESIGN
An original design story inspired by an eclectic mix of society, appreciating certain styles and choices and sitting perfectly with colour for this season, a lifestyle range we can all relate or aspire to.
Research was based on local 'County' ladies, City workers, Children and their Mothers, a Free Sports commentator, and Rock Star event organisers and directors.

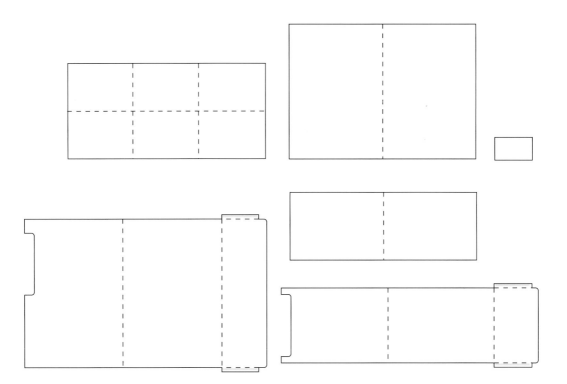

Tin Tab promotion campaign

Tin Tab is a company that designs and manufactures furniture. The Aloof studio was asked to design and implement their image and brand identity, logo, all graphic and promotional elements, and their website. Aloof was also in charge of drafting the texts and taking the photographs to illustrate these elements. The results are radically contemporary and minimalist promotional items that convey a modern image and that show several of Tin Tab's projects in recent years.

Tin Tab est une entreprise qui se consacre au design et à la fabrication de meubles. Le studio Aloof s'est chargé de concevoir et d'élaborer son image de marque, son identité, son logo, tous ses éléments graphiques et promotionnels, ainsi que son site Web. Aloof a également rédigé les textes et réalisé toutes les photos qui illustrent ces différents éléments. Résultat : des objets promotionnels au design minimaliste et totalement contemporain qui transmettent une image moderne et présentent plusieurs des projets réalisés par Tin Tab au cours des dernières années.

Tin Tab es una empresa dedicada al diseño y la fabricación de muebles. El estudio Aloof fue el encargado de diseñar e implementar su imagen e identidad de marca, el logotipo, todos los elementos gráficos y promocionales, y la página web. Además, redactó los textos y realizó todas las fotografías que ilustran dichos elementos. El resultado es un material promocional de diseño minimalista y radicalmente contemporáneo que transmite una imagen moderna y que muestra varios de los proyectos realizados por Tin Tab a lo largo de los últimos años.

Aloof Design
Lewes, UK_Lewes, Royaume-Uni_Lewes (Reino Unido)
www.aloofdesign.com ı sam@aloofdesign.com

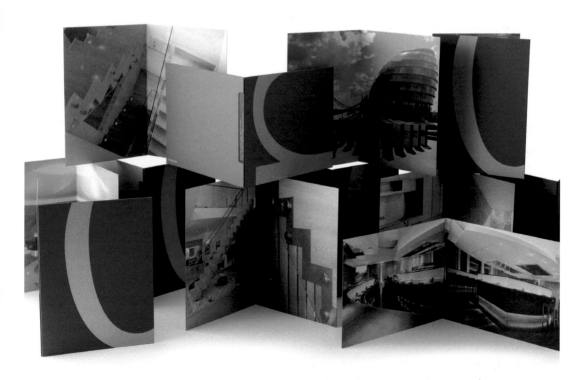

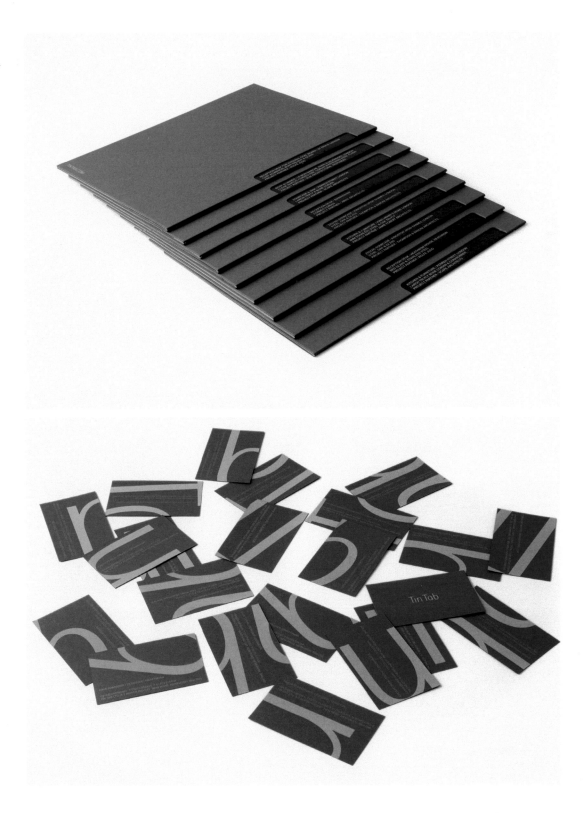

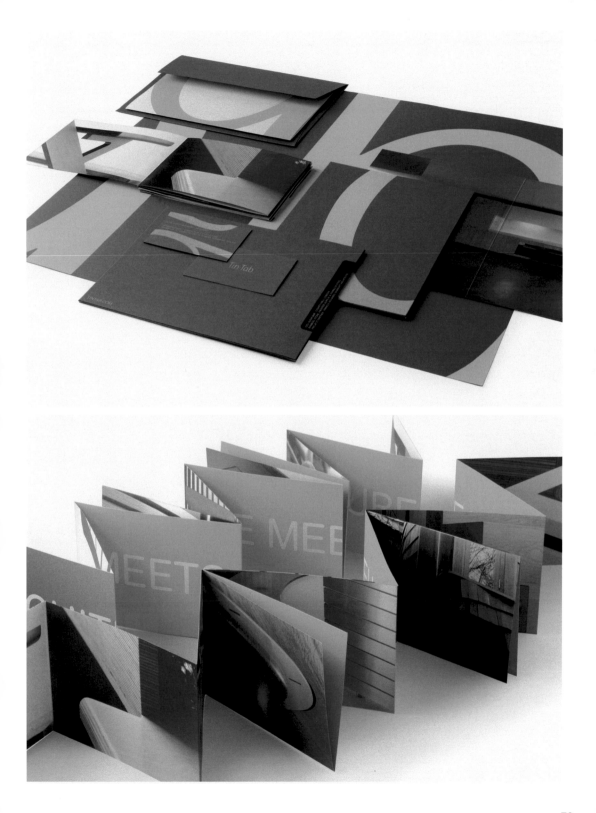

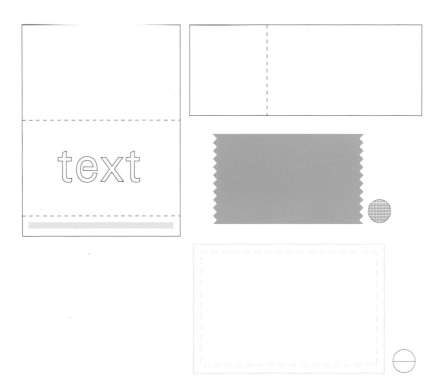

Textus media kit

The objective of this press kit was to achieve the perfect balance between minimizing costs and maximizing visual impact. Aimed at publishers and interior design magazines, the kit reveals the new upholstery factory collection The Gradient Collection. As the fabrics are designed from highly saturated colors, one of these fabrics was shown through the Textus logo cut-out on a single sheet of folded paper. The kit contains the mentioned fabric sample, an information booklet and a press CD, among other elements, and was sent out inside a vacuum-sealed transparent food bag.

L'objectif de ce kit de presse était de parvenir à trouver l'équilibre parfait entre un coût minimum et un impact visuel maximum. Créé à l'intention des éditeurs et des revues de design, le kit annonce la nouvelle collection de tissus pour revêtements, The Gradient Collection. Comme les tissus ont été conçus avec des couleurs très saturées, les designers ont choisi de montrer l'un de ces tissus à travers le logo de Textus découpé dans une simple feuille de papier pliée en deux. Le kit contient l'échantillon de tissu, un dépliant et un CD de presse, entre autres. Il a été envoyé sous vide dans un sac en plastique transparent.

El objetivo de este kit de prensa era conseguir el equilibrio perfecto entre costes mínimos e impacto visual máximo. Destinado a editores y revistas de diseño, el kit anuncia la nueva colección de tejidos para tapizados The Gradient Collection. Como las telas han sido diseñadas a partir de colores muy saturados, se optó por mostrar uno de dichos tejidos a través del logotipo de Textus recortado en una simple hoja de papel plegada. El kit contiene la mencionada muestra de tela, un folleto informativo plegado y un CD de prensa, entre otros elementos, y se envió en el interior de una bolsa de comida transparente sellada al vacío.

Cory Grosser Design and Strategy
Los Angeles, USA_Los Angeles, États-Unis_Los Ángeles (Estados Unidos)
www.corygrosser.com ι info@corygrosser.com

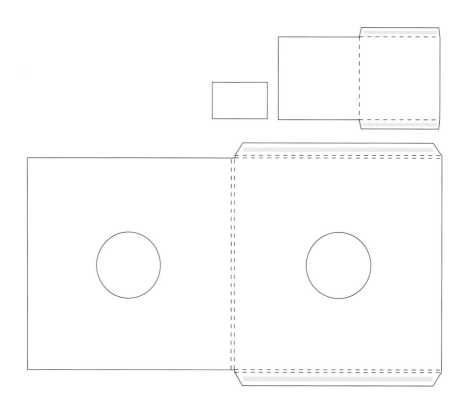

Neuropa Records

Created in 2005, Neuropa Records is an experimental industrial music label based in the city of Aalst, Belgium. To design its identity and all its promotional materials, the designer Nikolay Saveliev chose a simple palette of three colors (red, black and white) and repeated three slogans that perfectly define the label's philosophy. A red vinyl, a few pins representing musical influences and Neuropa Records aesthetics, the press CD and a business card complete the promotional kit.

Créé en 2005, Neuropa Records est un label de musique industrielle et expérimentale, basé à Aalst, en Belgique. Pour la conception de son identité visuelle et de tous ses éléments promotionnels, le designer Nikolay Saveliev a opté pour une palette simple de trois couleurs (rouge, noir et blanc) et pour la répétition de trois slogans qui définissent à la perfection la philosophie du label. Un vinyle rouge, quelques badges qui font référence aux influences musicales et esthétiques de Neuropa Records, le CD de presse et une carte de visite viennent compléter le kit promotionnel.

Creado en 2005, Neuropa Records es un sello discográfico de música industrial experimental de la ciudad de Aalst, en Bélgica. Para el diseño de su identidad y de todos sus elementos promocionales, el diseñador Nikolay Saveliev optó por una sencilla paleta de tres colores (rojo, negro y blanco) y por la repetición de tres eslóganes que definen a la perfección la filosofía del sello. Un vinilo rojo, unas cuantas chapas que hacen referencia a las influencias musicales y estéticas de Neuropa Records, el CD de prensa y una tarjeta de visita completan el kit promocional.

Nikolay Saveliev
New York, USA_New York, États-Unis_Nueva York (Estados Unidos)
nikolaysaveliev.com, www.hugoandmarie.com ı nikolay@nikolaysaveliev.com

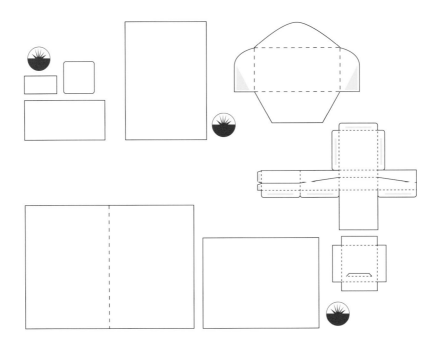

The Prime Society

The Prime Society is an informal restaurant that humorously tries to be an old fraternity dedicated to the search for the perfect steak washed down with the finest wine. The venue, a former army barracks, combines colonial beauty with contemporary chic. For the opening of the restaurant, AC2 International asked the Asylum studio to design the opening kit, including all the details of the premises as well as promotional items: menus, coasters with the club's commandments, VIP medals, and so on. A Victorian style was chosen for the fonts and images.

The Prime Society est un restaurant informel qui, avec humour, se fait passer pour une vieille confrérie se consacrant à la recherche du bifteck parfait et à la dégustation du meilleur alcool. Le local, des anciennes baraques de l'armée, conjugue une esthétique coloniale et un style contemporain chic. Pour l'inauguration du restaurant, AC2 International a confié au studio Asylum le design du kit inaugural qui contient toute la documentation relative au local, ainsi que des éléments promotionnels : menus, dessous-de-verre avec les commandements du club, médailles VIP, etc. Pour la typographie et les images, les designers ont opté pour un style victorien.

The Prime Society es un restaurante informal que pretende, jocosamente, ser una vieja fraternidad dedicada a la búsqueda del bistec perfecto y la degustación del mejor alcohol. El local, unos antiguos barracones militares, combina la estética colonial con el estilo chic contemporáneo. Para la apertura del restaurante, AC2 International encargó al estudio Asylum el diseño del kit inaugural, que incluía toda la papelería relacionada con el local, además de los elementos promocionales: menús, posavasos con los mandamientos del club, medallas vip… Para ello, se optó por la estética victoriana en tipografías e imágenes.

Asylum
Singapore_Singapour_Singapur (República de Singapur)
www.theasylum.com.sg ı info@theasylum.com.sg

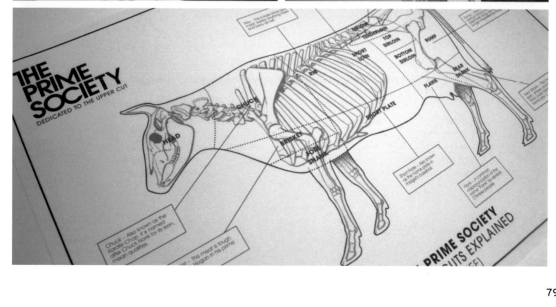

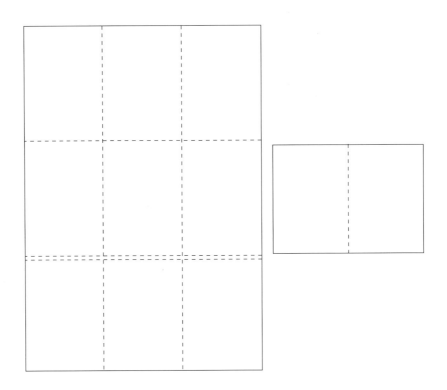

All-in-One Design Challenge

The city council of Aarhus hired the design agency Hello Monday to design the visual concept and identity of the new local magazine and Christmas greeting card. By converting the traditional Christmas card into a giant poster, this serves four distinct functions: Christmas greeting card, decorative poster, envelope, and wrapper for the aforementioned magazine. In short, a way just like any other (but especially imaginative) to kill four birds with one stone.

La mairie de la ville d'Aarhus a engagé l'agence de design Hello Monday pour élaborer le concept et l'identité visuelle de la nouvelle revue municipale et de sa carte de Noël. Transformée en affiche géante, la carte traditionnelle de Noël peut remplir quatre fonctions différentes : carte de Noël, affiche décorative, enveloppe et emballage de la revue précédemment mentionnée. En résumé, une façon comme une autre (bien que imaginative) de faire d'une pierre quatre coups.

El Ayuntamiento de la ciudad de Aarhus contrató a la agencia de diseño Hello Monday para que creara el concepto y la identidad visual de la nueva revista municipal y de la tarjeta de felicitación navideña. Al convertir la postal tradicional en un cartel gigante, cumple cuatro funciones distintas: tarjeta navideña, cartel decorativo, sobre y envoltorio para la citada revista. En resumen, una manera como otra cualquiera (aunque especialmente imaginativa) de matar cuatro pájaros de un tiro.

Hello Monday
New York, USA; Aarhus and Copenhagen, Denmark
New York, États-Unis ; Aarhus et Copenhague, Danemark
Nueva York (Estados Unidos), Aarhus y Copenhague (Dinamarca)
www. hellomonday.com ı hello@hellomonday.net

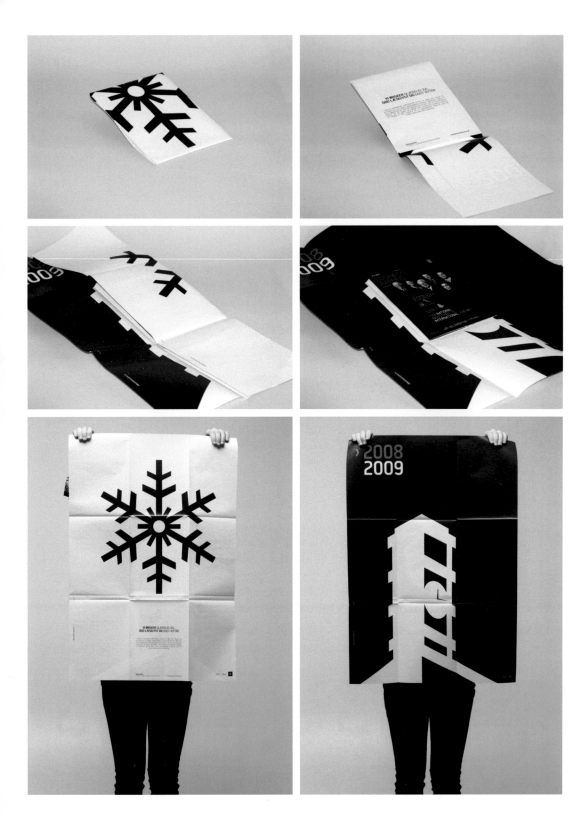

The kits in this chapter have been created by design agencies to promote their services or by all classes of creative teams, artists and unorthodox beings to publicize their work or activity. What makes these kits different from the others featured in this book is that these objects have been designed with total freedom, without any restrictions apart from the obvious, i.e. the budget and the actual imagination of the creator. These press kits also can be used as catalogs of the agencies work, so they must combine their practical function with pure and simple advertising. In this context, a kit demonstrating only the work of the agency or the artist is no different to a student's portfolio, while a kit without added information and that only tries to attract the attention of the recipients would not last more than a minute on their table, or however long it takes for the visual impact to wear off.

Les kits de ce chapitre ont été conçus par des agences de design afin de promouvoir leurs services ou par des créateurs, artistes et anticonformistes de tout genre dans le but de faire connaître leur œuvre ou leurs activités. À la différence des autres kits de ce livre, ceux-ci ont été conçus en toute liberté, sans restriction aucune, mis à part celles que supposent évidemment le budget et l'imagination même du créateur. En général, ces kits de presse servent également de catalogues des travaux des agences et doivent donc allier l'aspect pratique et l'aspect publicitaire pur et dur. En ce sens, un kit qui ne ferait que montrer les travaux de l'agence ou de l'artiste ne serait en rien différent d'un book d'étudiant, alors qu'un kit sans informations supplémentaires, qui ne chercherait qu'à attirer l'attention de son destinataire, ne resterait pas plus d'une minute sur le bureau de celui-ci, le temps que le premier impact visuel se dissipe.

Los kits de este capítulo han sido creados por agencias de diseño para promocionar sus servicios, o por creativos, artistas y heterodoxos de todo tipo con el objetivo de dar a conocer su obra o su actividad. Lo que los diferencia del resto de los kits incluidos en este libro es que se trata de objetos diseñados con total libertad, sin ceñirse a ninguna otra restricción que las impuestas por el presupuesto y la propia imaginación del creativo. Estos kits de prensa suelen funcionar también como catálogos de los trabajos de las agencias, por lo que deben combinar su función práctica con la de reclamo puro y duro. En este sentido, un kit que sólo mostrara los trabajos de la agencia o del artista no se distinguiría en nada del book de un estudiante, mientras que un kit sin información añadida y que sólo pretendiera llamar la atención del destinatario no duraría sobre la mesa más de un minuto o lo que tardara en disiparse el efecto del primer impacto visual.

Creativity and crafts

Créativité et artisanat

Creatividad y artesanía

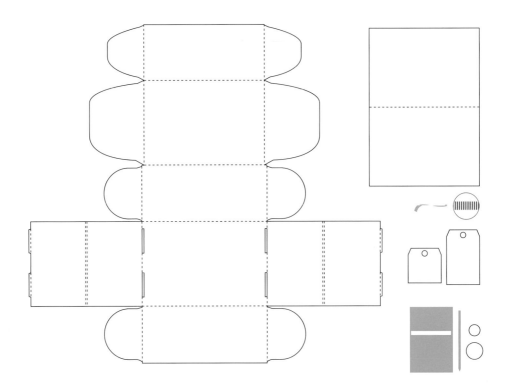

Bacon across America

In 2008, the Bacon family spent a sabbatical year visiting all 50 states in the USA for 50 weeks. During this adventure, the Bacon family distributed promotional T-shirts with a map of America made up of slices of bacon, with the (double meaning) logo "Bacon Across America". These T-shirts were intended to publicize and promote their journey among the media and to attract visits to their website. Each kit includes, besides the aforementioned T-shirt (in a tray of food), a travel journal, a pencil and a press kit.

En 2008, la famille Bacon a pris une année sabbatique pour visiter les 50 états des États-Unis en 50 semaines. Au cours de son aventure, la famille Bacon a distribué des tee-shirts promotionnels sur lesquels on pouvait voir une carte des États-Unis en tranches de bacon, avec le slogan (à double sens) « Bacon across America » (Bacon en Amérique). Ces tee-shirts avaient pour objet de faire connaître et de promouvoir leur voyage dans les médias et, ainsi, d'inciter les gens à visiter leur page Web. Chaque kit comportait, en plus du tee-shirt (dans un plateau-repas), un journal de voyage, un crayon et un dossier de presse.

En 2008, la familia Bacon se tomó un año sabático y visitó los cincuenta estados que componen Estados Unidos durante cincuenta semanas. Durante su aventura, los Bacon repartieron camisetas promocionales en las que podía verse un mapa del país formado por lonchas de bacón y el lema (de doble sentido) *Bacon across America* (Bacon por toda América). Estas camisetas tenían como objetivo dar a conocer y promocionar su viaje entre los medios de prensa y así atraer visitas a su página web. Cada kit incluye, además de la mencionada camiseta (en una bandeja de comida), un diario de viaje, un lápiz y un dosier de prensa.

Corianton Hale/Sleep Op
Seattle, USA_Seattle, États-Unis_Seattle (Estados Unidos)
www.sleepop.com ɪ **corianton@sleepop.com**

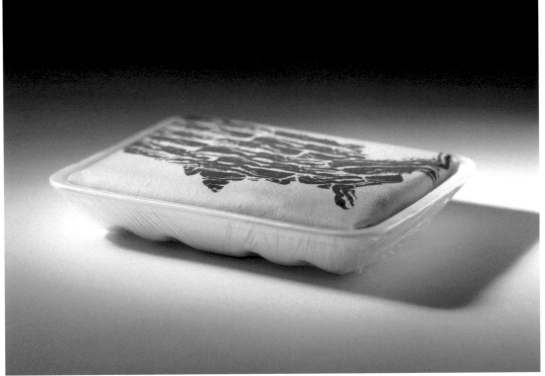

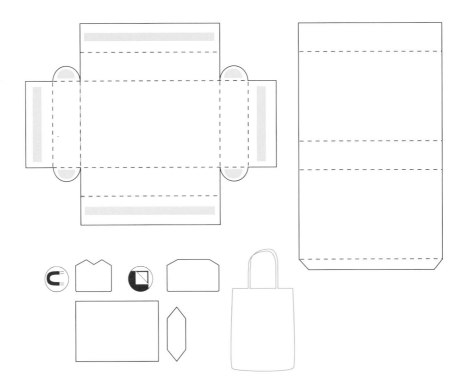

A-Glow-Glow Macro Interactive Media Arts Exhibition

Organized by Microwave in April 2008, the *A-Glow-Glow* exhibition converted Hong Kong into the nerve center of innovation in the field of art. Milkxhake was in charge of designing the identity of the event, including stationery and the webpage, as well as limited edition promotional products to be handed out at the exhibition. The box included event promotional stickers, T-shirts, bags, and other common promotional items. Cyan and purple were chosen as the colors for the identity of the event symbolizing the luminosity of the art installations of the exhibition.

Organisée par Microwave en avril 2008, l'exposition *A-Glow-Glow* a fait de Hong Kong le centre névralgique de l'innovation dans le domaine de l'art. C'est Milkxhake qui s'est occupé de concevoir l'identité de l'événement, ce qui impliquait aussi bien le support papier que des éléments comme sa page Web ou les produits promotionnels d'édition limitée distribués pendant l'exposition. Le kit promotionnel comportait des autocollants, des tee-shirts, des sacs et d'autres éléments promotionnels habituels. Les couleurs choisies pour l'identité de l'événement étaient le cyan et le pourpre, en référence à la luminosité des installations artistiques de l'exposition.

Organizada por Microwave en abril de 2008, la exposición *A-Glow-Glow* convirtió Hong Kong en el centro neurálgico de la innovación en el terreno del arte. Milkxhake fue el encargado de diseñar la identidad del evento, lo que incluía tanto sus elementos de papelería como la página web o los productos promocionales de edición limitada que se distribuían en la exposición. La caja incluía pegatinas, camisetas, bolsas y demás elementos de promoción habituales. Los colores escogidos para la identidad del evento fueron el cian y el púrpura, en referencia a la luminosidad de las instalaciones artísticas de la muestra.

Milkxhake
Hong Kong, China_Hong Kong, Chine_Hong Kong (China)
www.milkxhake.org ı mix@milkxhake.org

Microwave X Buddha Machine Limited Edition

Thanks to the annual festival organized in Hong Kong, Microwave has become one of the leading platforms for promoting art. In the 2007 Luminous Echo festival, fluorescent pink was chosen as the hallmark of this edition and was added to the traditional corporate orange used by Microwave in all promotional materials. One of the promotional goods was a limited edition of the Microwave X Buddha Machine, a small loop music player. The Buddha Machine was presented in clear plastic fluorescent orange wrap, designed by Milkxhake in collaboration with FH3 artists from Beijing.

Grâce au festival annuel organisé par la ville de Hong Kong, Microwave est devenu l'une des plate-formes les plus réputées pour la promotion artistique. Le rose fluo était la couleur dominante de l'édition 2007 du festival Luminous Echo et a donc été ajouté à l'orange de l'entreprise Microwave sur tous ses éléments promotionnels. L'un d'eux était une édition limitée de la Microwave X Buddha Machine, une petite boîte à musique de chants bouddhistes. La Buddha Machine était présentée dans un emballage en plastique transparent de couleur orange fluo, réalisé par Milkxhake en collaboration avec les artistes de FH3 de Pékin.

Gracias al festival anual que organiza en Hong Kong, Microwave se ha convertido en una de las plataformas de promoción del arte más destacadas. Para la edición de 2007 del Luminous Echo, se escogió como color distintivo el rosa fluorescente y se añadió al tradicional naranja corporativo de Microwave en todos los elementos promocionales. Uno de ellos era una edición limitada de la Microwave X Buddha Machine, un pequeño reproductor de *loops* de cantos budistas. La Buddha Machine se presentaba dentro de un envoltorio de plástico transparente de color naranja fluorescente, realizado por Milkxhake en colaboración con los artistas FH3 de Pekín.

Milkxhake
Hong Kong, China_Hong Kong, Chine_Hong Kong (China)
www.milkxhake.org ı mix@milkxhake.org

MICROWAVE X BUDDHA MACHINE
Limited Edition

0013

**The Buddha Machine
is a little plastic box that
PLAYS MUSIC**

Specifically, FM3 constructed nine drones, varying from two seconds to 42 seconds, which repeat endlessly in the listener's ear until the "track" is switched to the next drone (or the two AA batteries run out). The machine has its own built-in speaker, but there is also a headphone jack for more personal meditative experiences. There is a switch on the side that allows for reversal of the tracks, and a DC jack (though an adapter is not included) for those who would like the Buddha Machine experience be truly endless.

About FM3

Founded in 1999 by Christiaan Virant and Zhang Jian, two active members of the Beijing music scene, FM3 are considered pioneers of electronic music in China. Known for dedicating prime space for "live" aspects within their work, FM3 produces mysterious, meditative and minimalist soundscapes, while subtly adding elements of Chinese folk tradition into a universe abundant in micro-sounds and synthetic glitches.

"An extraordinary piece of sound art"
(The Wire)

Beautifully useless
(New York Times)

microwave
www.microwavefest.net
www.thebuddhamachine.com

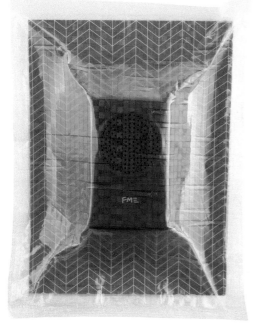

MICROWAVE X BUDDHA MACHINE
Limited Edition

0013

**The Buddha Machine
is a little plastic box that
PLAYS MUSIC**

Specifically, FM3 constructed nine drones, varying from two seconds to 42 seconds, which repeat endlessly in the listener's ear until the "track" is switched to the next drone (or the two AA batteries run out). The machine has its own built-in speaker, but there is also a headphone jack for more personal meditative experiences. There is a switch on the side that allows for traversal of the tracks, and a DC jack (though an adapter is not included) for those who would like the Buddha Machine experience be truly endless.

About FM3

Founded in 1999 by Christiaan Virant and Zhang Jian, two active members of the Beijing music scene, FM3 are considered pioneers of electronic music in China. Known for dedicating prime space for "live" aspects within their work, FM3 produces mysterious, meditative and minimalist soundscapes, while subtly adding elements of Chinese folk tradition into a universe abundant in micro-sounds and synthetic glitches.

"An extraordinary piece of sound art"
(The Wire)

Beautifully useless
(New York Times)

microwave
www.microwavefest.net
www.fm3buddhamachine.com

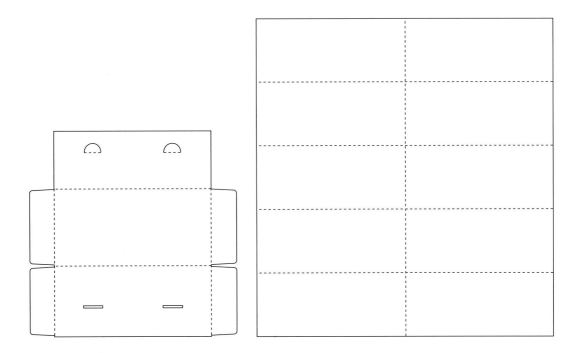

R.Godá. Escrituras & Filigranas exhibition

R. Godá is a young Brazilian painter and sculptor. Before designing his promotional kit, the creative team from the Mopa studio visited the Godá studio to take some photographs of his work. After the visit they decided that a simple brochure was not the way to present and promote his work. Not only because of its limited size, but also because it would be hard to appreciate the detail of his work in a conventional brochure. Finally, they decided on fold-out posters that were made as large as possible. The posters were then placed into a cardboard envelope that closes with tabs.

R. Godá est un jeune peintre et sculpteur brésilien. Avant de concevoir son kit promotionnel, les créateurs du studio Mopa ont visité le studio de Godá pour prendre quelques photos de son travail. Après quoi, ils ont décidé qu'une simple brochure n'était pas l'idéal pour présenter et promouvoir son œuvre. En effet, une brochure conventionnelle serait non seulement trop petite mais elle ne ferait pas non plus justice au détail que présente l'œuvre de cet artiste. Finalement, ils ont opté pour une affiche dépliante la plus grande possible. Les affiches ont ensuite été glissées dans des enveloppes en carton qui se ferment avec des languettes.

R. Godá es un joven pintor y escultor brasileño. Antes de diseñar su kit promocional, los creativos del estudio Mopa visitaron el estudio de Godá para tomar algunas fotografías de su trabajo. Tras la visita decidieron que un simple folleto no era lo más adecuado para presentar y promocionar su obra, no sólo por su limitado tamaño, sino también porque el grado de detalle de su obra es difícilmente visible en un folleto convencional. Finalmente se optó por unos carteles plegados del mayor tamaño posible. Los carteles fueron introducidos posteriormente en un sobre de cartón que se cierra con pestañas.

Mopa
Brasilia, Brazil_Brasilia, Brésil_Brasilia (Brasil)
www.estudiomopa.com ı info@estudiomopa.com

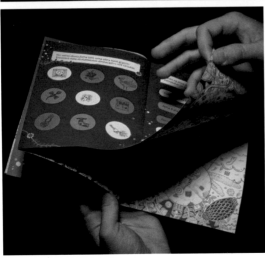

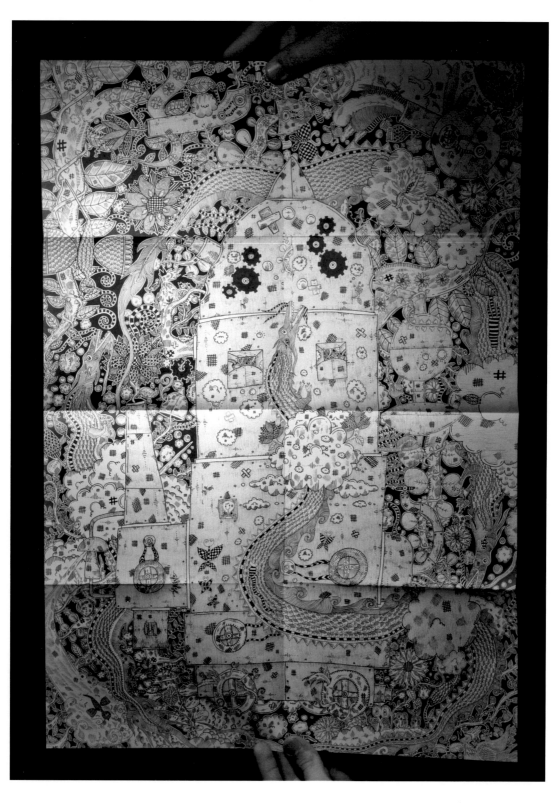

Weetu

Created for the Chicago-based interior design agency Weetu (goweetu.com), this press kit is intended to reflect the personality and philosophy of the customer and provide the recipients of the kit detailed information about its work. Fluorine colors, different-sized covers and several humorous texts written by the designers themselves have been used for the kit, along with a few photographs they have taken themselves. The end result is an interesting press kit that could be considered as a collector's item.

Réalisé par l'agence de design et d'aménagement d'intérieur de Chicago Weetu (goweetu.com), ce kit a pour objet de refléter la personnalité et la philosophie du client, et de donner des informations détaillées sur son travail. Pour cela, les designers ont utilisé des couleurs fluo, des couvertures de différentes tailles et enfin, mais pas des moindres, divers textes humoristiques qu'ils ont eux-mêmes écrits ainsi que des photos de leurs mains. Le résultat obtenu est un kit de presse ayant suffisamment d'intérêt pour être considéré comme un objet de collection à part entière.

Realizado para la agencia de diseño e interiorismo de Chicago Weetu (goweetu.com), este kit de prensa tiene como objetivos reflejar la personalidad y la filosofía del cliente y proporcionar a sus destinatarios una información detallada sobre su trabajo. Para ello se han usado colores flúor, tamaños distintos para las diferentes portadas y varios textos humorísticos escritos por los mismos diseñadores, además de algunas fotografías de sus manos. El resultado es un kit de prensa con el suficiente interés como para ser considerado, por sí mismo, un objeto de coleccionismo.

TNOP™ Design
Chicago, USA; Bangkok, Thailand_Chicago, États-Unis ; Bangkok, Thaïlande_Chicago (Estados Unidos) y Bangkok (Tailandia)
www.tnop.com ı info@tnop.com

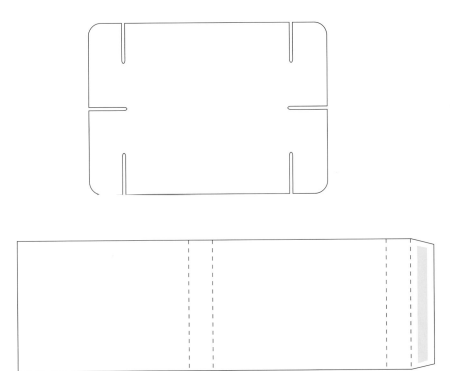

Re:Creation. National Creativity Awards

As an extension of the work carried out to document the contemporary creativity in the field of music, film, art, fashion and design, the magazine *Dazed & Confused* joined forces with Topshop to create a road exhibition showing examples of this creativity. The tour coincided with a series of Re:Creation events with seminars in six British cities. All posters and press and promotional items were created by Form studio, which was inspired by the groundbreaking and avant-garde aesthetic of *Dazed & Confused* and Topshop. Hence the wide palette of colors used and the strident fonts chosen.

Tel un prolongement du travail réalisé pour documenter la créativité contemporaine dans les domaines de la musique, du cinéma, de l'art, de la mode et du design, le magazine *Dazed & Confused* a collaboré avec la marque Topshop pour créer une exposition itinérante illustrant créativité. La tournée a coïncidé avec une série de fêtes Re:Creation et avec des séminaires dans six villes britanniques. Toutes les affiches et autres éléments de presse et promotionnels ont été créés par le studio Form qui s'est inspiré des styles avant-gardistes de *Dazed & Confused* et de Topshop. D'où la vaste palette de couleurs et les typographies tape-à-l'œil.

Como una extensión de la labor realizada para documentar la creatividad contemporánea en el terreno de la música, el cine, el arte, la moda y el diseño, la revista *Dazed & Confused* se unió a la marca Topshop para crear una exposición itinerante que exhibiera ejemplos de dicha creatividad. La gira coincidió con una serie de fiestas Re:Creation y con seminarios en seis ciudades británicas. Todos los carteles y los elementos de prensa y de promoción fueron creados por el estudio Form, que se inspiró en las estéticas rompedoras y vanguardistas de *Dazed & Confused* y Topshop; de ahí la amplia paleta de colores utilizada y las estridentes tipografías escogidas.

Paul West, Nick Hard/Form
London, UK_Londres, Royaume-Uni_Londres (Reino Unido)
www.form.uk.com ı studio@form.uk.com

London, UK
www.airside.co.uk
info@airside.co.uk
Project on page 40

Londres, Royaume-Uni
www.airside.co.uk
info@airside.co.uk
Projet sur la page 40

Londres (Reino Unido)
www.airside.co.uk
info@airside.co.uk
Proyecto en la página 40

How should the perfect promotional kit be?

The perfect promotional kit should grab your attention immediately. You should hold it in your hands and think, "wow, what is this?" While it doesn't have to have a strictly hard sell attitude, the recipient should know exactly what the point of the promotion was by the time they are finished with the kit. Finally it should have longevity. A good promotion kit should be something that people will want to keep, whether it's on display on a shelf above their desk or even bring it home. Even if the recipient looks at the kit, and then they proceed to throw it away, it's not a truly successful kit.

What's (or what should be) its objective?

The objective should be exactly what the client wants to achieve, whether that is more sales or awareness of their product or service. From a design point of view, it is about using design skills and tools to demonstrate these products or services in as clear and interesting a way as possible. At Airside

Comment devrait être le kit promotionnel parfait ?

Un kit promotionnel parfait doit attirer votre attention immédiatement. Vous devez le prendre et vous dire : « Ouah ! Qu'est-ce que c'est ? » Bien que le kit ne soit pas strictement créé pour la vente, le destinataire devrait savoir exactement quel était l'objectif de la promotion au moment où il voit le kit. Finalement, il doit durer. Un bon kit promotionnel doit être quelque chose que les gens souhaitent conserver, exposé sur une étagère au-dessus de leur bureau, où même emporter à la maison. Même si le destinataire examine le kit sous toutes les coutures mais qu'il le jette ensuite, ce n'est pas un kit réussi.

Quel est (ou quel devrait être) son objectif ?

L'objectif devrait être exactement ce que le client veut obtenir, que ce soit plus de ventes ou une sensibilisation à ses produits ou services. Du point de vue du design, il s'agit d'utiliser des talents et des outils de conception pour présenter ces produits ou services de la manière la plus claire et intéressante possible. Chez

¿Cómo debería ser el kit promocional perfecto?

Un kit promocional perfecto debería captar la atención inmediatamente. Deberías cogerlo y pensar: «Madre mía, pero ¿qué es esto?». Aunque no es necesario que aparente estar creado por y para la venta, el destinatario debe saber exactamente el objetivo de la promoción cuando haya visto el kit. Por último, debe ser duradero. Un buen kit promocional debería ser algo que la gente quiere guardarse, ya sea para colocarlo en una estantería encima de su escritorio o para llevárselo a casa. Si el destinatario le echa un vistazo y lo tira después a la papelera, el kit no está totalmente logrado.

¿Cuál es (o cuál debería ser) su objetivo?

El objetivo debe ser exactamente lo que el cliente quiere conseguir, que puede ir desde un incremento de las ventas hasta el aumento de la popularidad del producto o servicio. Desde el punto de vista del diseño, el objetivo es utilizar habilidades y herramientas de diseño para mostrar esos productos o servicios de la forma más clara y atractiva posible. En Airside

Airside

we also like to inject a sense of fun into everything we do. A perfect promotional kit doesn't have to be fun, but that's how we like it.

What's the main difficulty when designing a promotional kit?
It depends. Sometimes it's difficult trying to get your head around the clients and what they do and what they want to achieve. Other times, that part is easy, but it's hard to figure out how best to explain it. For the Think Tank job it was probably both. We had to understand all the different processes and techniques they offered and then work out a way to promote them so that the result was more than a straightforward catalog.

In your opinion, what kind of clients/ brands should make use of promotional or press kits?
I suppose everyone should use promotional or press kits. Probably most people do, though few will actually go to the trouble of producing something really great. So in a lot of cases they are just wasting their time and money.

Airside, nous voulons ajouter une touche d'humour dans tout ce que nous faisons. Bien sûr, un kit promotionnel parfait ne doit pas nécessairement être amusant mais nous aimons qu'il le soit.

Quelle est la principale difficulté lors de la conception d'un kit promotionnel ?
Cela dépend. Parfois, il vous est difficile de comprendre le client, ce qu'il fait et ce qu'il veut obtenir. À d'autres moments, cette partie est facile mais il est difficile de l'exprimer. Pour le travail du Think Tank, ça a probablement été les deux. Nous devions comprendre tous les différents processus et techniques qui sont proposés et ensuite trouver au-delà du catalogue comment faire leur promotion.

À votre avis, quel genre de clients/ marques devraient utiliser les kits promotionnels ou de presse ?
Je pense que tout le monde devrait utiliser les kits promotionnels ou de presse. Il est probable que la plupart des gens le font même si peu d'entre eux osent produire quelque chose de vraiment fantastique. Et dans la plupart des cas, ils ne

también nos gusta añadir un toque de humor en todo lo que hacemos. A ver, un kit promocional perfecto no necesita ser gracioso, pero nos gusta que lo sea.

¿Cuál es la principal dificultad cuando se diseña un kit promocional?
Depende. A veces, es difícil saber qué le pasa por la cabeza al cliente, lo que hace y lo que quiere conseguir. Otras veces, esto es sencillo y la dificultad es conseguir explicarlo. En el trabajo para Think Tank, posiblemente se presentaban estos dos problemas. Teníamos que comprender los diferentes procesos y técnicas que ofrecían y luego buscar una forma de promocionarlos que fuera más allá de un simple catálogo.

¿Qué tipo de clientes/marcas deberían utilizar kits promocionales o carpetas de prensa?
Creo que todos deberían tener un kit promocional o kits de prensa. De hecho, posiblemente la mayoría de la gente tiene, pero son pocos los que se atreven a tirarse a la piscina y producir algo realmente bueno. Por lo tanto, en muchos casos sólo están perdiendo tiempo y dinero. Si

If you've got a great product or service that people will want to hear about, a promotional kit is a good idea. You just have to be willing to put in the effort to make something a little special so it doesn't end up in next week's recycling.

How do you check or test the effectiveness of your work and designs, and more specifically your press kits? Do you receive any kind of feedback from the client or the consumer?

We tend to stay in touch with our clients and talk about the work we did for them as long as it is relevant. Unless the kit features a specific way of measuring interest like a unique weblink or discount code, you tend to rely on empirical evidence. From our chats with Think Tank, they were very happy with the kit and noticed an increase in enquiries and sales that coincided with the distribution of the kit. It goes to show that paying good money for good design can be an investment in your business. Oh, and the Think Tank kit won a HOW International Design Award.

font que dépenser du temps et de l'argent. Si vous avez un excellent produit ou service et que les gens vont vouloir en entendre parler, c'est une bonne idée de faire un kit promotionnel. Vous devez seulement être disposé à faire l'effort de fabriquer quelque chose de spécial afin qu'il ne finisse pas à la poubelle à la fin de la semaine.

Comment vérifiez-vous l'efficacité de votre travail et de vos designs et, plus précisément, de vos kits de presse ? Recevez-vous un feedback de la part du client ou du consommateur ?

Nous avons tendance à rester en contact avec nos clients et à parler du travail que nous avons fait. Sauf si le kit dispose d'un moyen spécifique pour mesurer l'intérêt comme un lien internet ou un code de remise unique, nous avons tendance à nous fier à une preuve empirique. D'après nos conversations avec le Think Tank, ils étaient ravis du kit et ils ont observé une augmentation des demandes et des ventes, qui a coïncidé avec la distribution du kit. Cela démontre que payer pour un bon design peut être un investissement pour votre société. Ah, et puis le

tienes un buen producto o servicio que la gente quiere conocer, un kit promocional es una buena ida. Sólo necesitas estar dispuesto a esforzarte por hacer algo especial que no termine en la papelera de reciclaje al cabo de una semana.

¿Cómo comprobáis o medís la efectividad de un trabajo o un diseño y, especialmente, de un kit de prensa? ¿Recibís *feedback* de los clientes o los consumidores?

Solemos seguir en contacto con nuestros clientes durante un tiempo y hablamos sobre el trabajo que hicimos para ellos. Salvo en caso de que el kit cuente con un medio específico para medir el interés mediante, por ejemplo, un *link* o un código de descuento, sueles confiar en los datos empíricos. Durante nuestras charlas, en Think Tank nos comentaron que estaban muy contentos con el kit y que habían constatado un aumento de las solicitudes de información y de las ventas que coincidía con la distribución del kit. Y todo esto para decir que pagar por un buen diseño puede ser una inversión para su negocio. Ah, y el kit de Think Tank ganó un HOW International Design Award.

Do you need to "like" the product you're helping to promote to do a good job with it? Be sincere.
Obviously it helps to like the product, but it doesn't have to be a necessity. In some ways it's the mark of a good designer to be able to successfully promote something you have no interest in. Ultimately it is probably more important to have respect for the product, or at least the client. Fortunately for us, we liked Think Tank as people and for what services they provided.

How will promotional kit design evolve along the upcoming years? How will new technologies and the fast evolution of the net affect it?
No doubt, physical objects will become rarer as people deal more in digital communication. However, this will mean that physical objects will have more impact for their rarity. In terms of digital stuff, the possibilities are huge and ever changing. However, the sheer volume of communication that exists currently makes its harder for your voice to be heard. But this is

kit du Think Tank a remporté le Prix de Design International HOW.

Pour faire un bon travail, devez-vous « aimer » le produit dont vous assurez en partie la promotion ? Répondez sincèrement.
Bien évidemment, si nous aimons le produit, cela aide mais ce ne doit pas être une nécessité. Parfois, c'est la marque d'un bon designer d'être capable de faire une promotion réussie de quelque chose qui ne l'intéresse pas. Il est sans doute plus important d'avoir du respect pour le produit ou pour au moins le client. Heureusement pour nous, nous apprécions le Think Tank aussi bien en tant que personnes que pour les services qu'ils fournissent.

Comment la conception de kits promotionnels va-t-elle évoluer dans les années qui viennent ? Comment les nouvelles technologies et l'évolution rapide du réseau vont-ils l'affecter ?
Il ne fait aucun doute que les objets physiques vont devenir plus rares, les gens utilisant de plus en plus les communications numériques. Cela signifie cepen-

¿Necesitáis que os guste el producto que estáis promocionando para hacer una buena promoción? Sed sinceros.
Obviamente, ayuda que te guste el producto, pero no es imprescindible. En cierto modo, es el distintivo de un buen diseñador, aquel que puede promocionar con éxito algo que no le interesa. En última instancia, posiblemente sea más importante respetar el producto o, como mínimo, al cliente. Afortunadamente para nosotros, nos gustaba Think Tank tanto por su gente como por los servicios ofrecidos.

¿Cómo evolucionará el diseño de los kits promocionales en los próximos años? ¿Cómo influirán las nuevas tecnologías y la rápida evolución de la Red?
No cabe duda de que los objetos físicos van a perder terreno conforme la gente se vaya familiarizando más con las nuevas tecnologías digitales de comunicación. No obstante, esto conlleva también que los objetos físicos tendrán un impacto mayor por su carácter poco común. Y, en términos de abanico de posibilidades digitales, las perspectivas son enormes y están en continua evolución. Sin embar-

the great challenge: to continually be heard against the background noise.

What weight and importance do you give to the briefing of the client, when it doesn't fit your ideas? How do you match these two opposite views?
You've always got to give primary weight and importance to the client's brief. After all, it's the whole point of you doing the work. There is room for design for design sake if you want to invest your own time and money, but once someone is paying you to do something, their needs take priority. Obviously your ideas count – after all that's why they approached you – and we would always try and convince a client to go with an idea that we felt strongly about. But ultimately it's their call, and if they are not buying it they won't be able to sell it. If you reach the stage where you can't reconcile your work with the client's attitude, perhaps you need to consider whether you should be working with them at all. Either get out or shut up and take the money.

dant que les objets physiques auront un plus gros impact du fait de leur rareté. En termes de matériaux numériques, les possibilités sont énormes et en évolution perpétuelle. Cependant, le volume en soi de communications qui existe aujourd'hui ne facilite pas la promotion. Voilà le grand réussir à faire entendre sa voix dans le brouhaha.

Quelle importance donnez-vous au briefing du client lorsqu'il ne partage pas vos idées ? Comment conciliez-vous ces deux points de vue opposés ?
Vous devez toujours donner une importance capitale aux indications du client. Il s'agit, après tout, du travail que vous allez avoir à faire. Vous pouvez toujours faire du design pour le design si vous souhaitez y consacrer votre temps et votre argent mais, une fois que quelqu'un vous paye pour faire quelque chose, ses besoins deviennent la priorité. Bien évidemment, vos idées aussi et c'est pour cela d'ailleurs que le client s'adresse à vous. Nous essaierons toujours de le convaincre de suivre une idée si nous y croyons fermement. Cependant, c'est lui qui a le dernier mot et s'il n'y souscrit

go, la mera magnitud de la comunicación dificulta la difusión de la promoción. Pero ése es el gran reto: conseguir que tu voz se escuche a pesar de todo el ruido de fondo.

¿Qué peso y qué importancia dais al briefing del cliente cuando no piensa lo mismo que vosotros? ¿Cómo conseguís encontrar un punto medio para dos puntos de vista diferentes?
Siempre debes conceder un peso primordial a las indicaciones del cliente. Al fin y al cabo, es él quien te está solicitando un trabajo. Siempre hay un lugar para el diseño por el diseño si quieres invertir tu propio tiempo y dinero, pero cuando alguien te está pagando por hacer algo, sus necesidades son prioritarias. Por supuesto, te vienen muchas ideas; al fin y al cabo, por eso se han puesto en contacto contigo, y siempre intentamos convencer al cliente de optar por la idea que nos parece más adecuada. Pero ellos tienen la última palabra, y si no creen en la promoción, no podrán venderla. Si llegas a un punto en el que no puedes alcanzar un elemento común entre tu trabajo y la opinión del cliente,

Name the items, personal objects and tools you absolutely could not work without.
Give me a Mac, a Wacom tablet and a steaming mug of tea and I will give you a happy designer.

pas, il ne sera pas capable de la défendre. Si vous arrivez au stade où vous ne pouvez pas concilier votre travail avec les intentions du client, il vous faudra peut-être envisager de ne pas travailler du tout avec lui. Soit vous partez soit vous vous taisez et vous prenez l'argent.

Quels sont les éléments, les objets personnels et les outils dont vous ne pourriez absolument pas vous passer pour travailler ?
Donnez-moi un Mac, une tablette Wacom et une tasse de thé bien chaude et je serai content.

tienes que plantearte si debes seguir trabajando con él. Puedes salir del proyecto o callarte y coger el dinero.

Nombrad las cosas, los objetos personales y las herramientas sin las que os sería imposible trabajar.
A mí, dame un Mac, una tableta Wacom y una taza de té bien caliente y seré feliz.

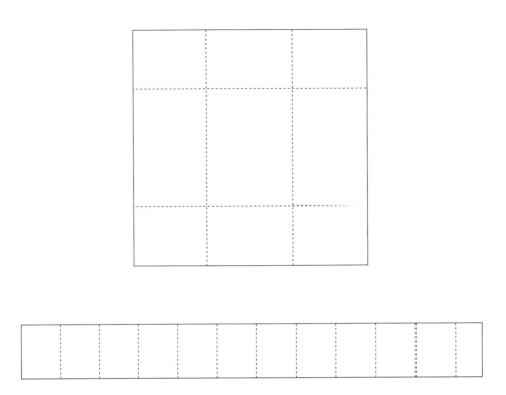

Zita Elze promotional campaign

Zita Elze is a well-known London florist. Zita asked the Aloof studio to promote her work among corporate circles and the general public. To do this, Aloof created an innovative marketing concept, known as "painting with flowers", which used photographs to reproduce the process of putting together a bouquet of flowers such as those she makes for her clients. The original packaging of the promotional kit, a sheet of paper folded several times, reinforces the idea that it tries to express: the boundless originality and creativity of the handcrafted work of Zita Elze.

Zita Elze est une célèbre fleuriste londonienne. Elle a fait appel au studio Aloof pour promouvoir son travail au sein d'organisations corporatives et du grand public. Pour cela, Aloof a créé un concept de marketing innovant, « peindre avec des fleurs ». À l'aide de photos, il a reproduit le processus de création d'un bouquet de fleurs comme ceux que réalise sa cliente. L'emballage original du kit promotionnel, une feuille de papier pliée plusieurs fois, renforce l'idée qu'il est censé transmettre : celle de l'originalité et de la créativité sans limite du travail artisanal de Zita Elze.

Zita Elze es una conocida florista londinense. Zita encargó al estudio Aloof promocionar su trabajo entre clientes corporativos y el público general. Para ello, Aloof creó un innovador concepto de *marketing*, que bautizó como «pintura con flores», para lo que usó fotografías que reproducían el proceso de creación de un ramo de flores como los que elabora su clienta. El original envoltorio del kit promocional, un lámina de papel plegada varias veces sobre sí misma, refuerza la idea que se pretende transmitir: la de la originalidad y la creatividad sin límites del trabajo artesanal de Zita Elze.

Aloof Design
Lewes, UK_Lewes, Royaume-Uni_Lewes (Reino Unido)
www.aloofdesign.com ι sam@aloofdesign.com

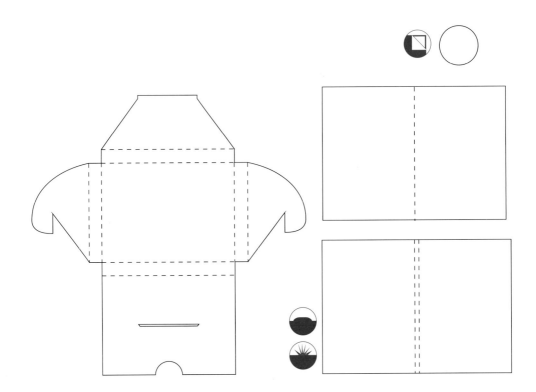

CCW Prospectus

The promotional document designed by This Is Studio for CCW (Camberwell College of Art, Chelsea College of Art and Design and Wimbledon College of Art) reflects the identity of the three faculties, and distances itself from standard university brochures. Ten students received a camera, a user guide and 10 words that should inspire them to photograph the scenes that will then feature in the brochure. The end product includes three booklets, a sticker and individual envelopes, printed with vegetable inks on recycled paper. The covers were printed with the colors of each of the faculties.

Le document promotionnel conçu par This Is Studio pour le CCW (Camberwell College of Art, Chelsea College of Art and Design et Wimbledon College of Art) reflète l'identité des trois facultés et est très loin des brochures universitaires ordinaires. Pour son élaboration, dix étudiants se sont vu attribuer un appareil photo, un guide d'utilisation et dix mots dont ils devaient s'inspirer pour prendre les photos qui apparaîtraient ensuite dans la brochure. Le produit final comporte trois livrets, un autocollant et des enveloppes individuelles, imprimés à l'encre végétale sur du papier recyclé. Sur chaque couverture, on retrouve la couleur caractéristique de chacune des facultés.

El documento promocional diseñado por This Is Studio para el CCW (Camberwell College of Art, Chelsea College of Art and Design y Wimbledon College of Art) refleja la identidad de las tres facultades y se distancia de los folletos universitarios convencionales. Para su realización, diez estudiantes recibieron una cámara de fotos, una guía de uso y diez palabras que debían inspirarles para fotografiar las escenas que luego aparecerían en el folleto. El producto final consta de tres prospectos, una pegatina y sobres individuales impresos con tintas vegetales sobre papel reciclado. Las portadas se grabaron con el color característico de cada facultad.

This Is Studio
London, UK_Londres, Royaume-Uni_Londres (Reino Unido)
www.thisisstudio.com ı info@thisisstudio.com

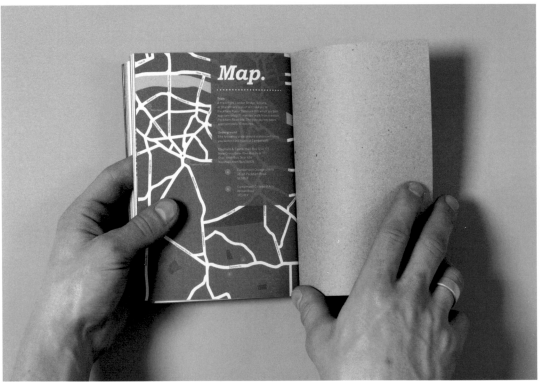

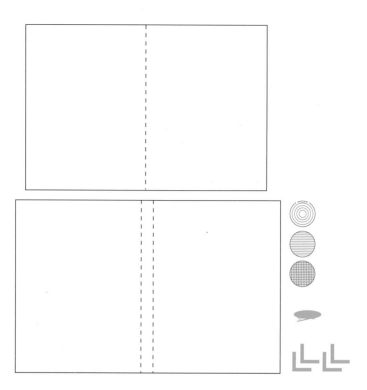

Kristian Kozul

These books-objects have been designed as promotional kits by the artist Kristian Kozul, who works with the emotions of the spectators caused by the individual interpretation of recently-made customized objects. The kit is not just a catalogue of his works, but a reinterpretation of them. There are three different editions, all with different covers: the first has been covered with black velvet, the second in red velvet, and the third is a limited edition white faux fur to which old pins have been stuck.

Ces livres-objets ont été conçus comme kits promotionnels de l'œuvre de l'artiste Kristian Kozul, qui travaille avec les émotions que l'interprétation individuelle d'objets récemment conçus et personnalisés suscitent chez les spectateurs. Le kit est non seulement un catalogue de ses œuvres, mais également une réinterprétation de celles-ci. Il existe trois éditions différentes du livre-kit, chacune avec une couverture différente : la première a été recouverte de velours noir, la deuxième, de velours rouge, et la troisième est une édition limitée en cuir synthétique blanc recouvert de vieux pin's.

Estos libros-objeto han sido diseñados como kits promocionales de la obra del artista Kristian Kozul, que trabaja con las emociones que despierta en los espectadores la interpretación individual de objetos recién hechos y personalizados. El kit no es sólo un catálogo de sus obras, sino también una reinterpretación de ellas. Existen tres ediciones distintas, todas con diferentes portadas: la primera ha sido forrada con terciopelo negro, la segunda con terciopelo rojo y la tercera es una edición limitada de piel artificial blanca en la que se han clavado viejos pins.

Laboratorium
Zagreb, Croatia_Zagreb, Croatie_Zagreb (Croacia)
www.laboratorium.hr ɪ ivana@laboratorium.hr

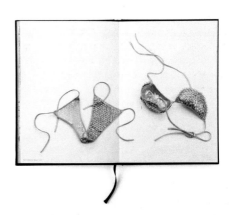

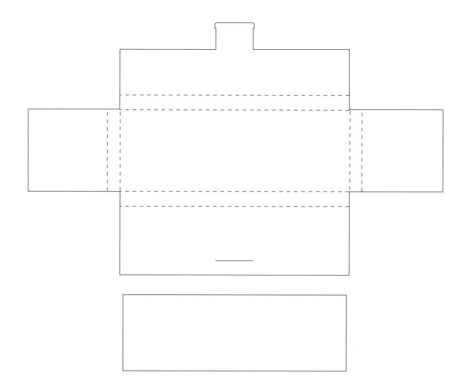

La parole brûlée

Eve Schütz is a poet. When Eve asked the designer Fabien Barral to create a visual interpretation of some of her poems, the result was this promotional book-object consisting of a cardboard box the size of a book that contains several cards with extracts of her work. The book is aimed to become a real collectible for fans of the poet. The images that adorn and decorate the cards are actually photographs by anonymous authors found in the trash and were about to be burnt.

Eve Schütz est poète. Quand Eve a demandé au designer Fabien Barral une interprétation visuelle de certains de ses poèmes, celui-ci a créé ce livre-objet promotionnel. Il consiste en une boîte en carton de la taille d'un livre, dans laquelle se trouvent plusieurs cartes où sont imprimés certains de ses poèmes. Le livre a été créé pour devenir un véritable objet de collection pour les admirateurs de la poète. Les images qui ornent les cartes sont en réalité des photographies d'auteurs anonymes trouvées dans une poubelle alors qu'elles étaient sur le point d'être brûlées.

Eve Schütz es poetisa. Cuando Eve le pidió al diseñador Fabien Barral una interpretación visual de algunos de sus poemas, el resultado fue este libro-objeto promocional, que consiste en una caja de cartón del tamaño de un libro y en cuyo interior se pueden encontrar varias tarjetas en las que se han impreso algunos de sus textos. El libro está destinado a convertirse en un auténtico objeto de coleccionismo para los seguidores de la poetisa. Las imágenes que lo adornan y con las que se han decorado las tarjetas son en realidad fotografías de autores anónimos encontradas en la basura y que estaban a punto de ser quemadas.

Fabien Barral
Auvergne, France_Auvergne, France_Auvergne (Francia)
www.fabienbarral.com ׀ ecrire@fabienbarral.com

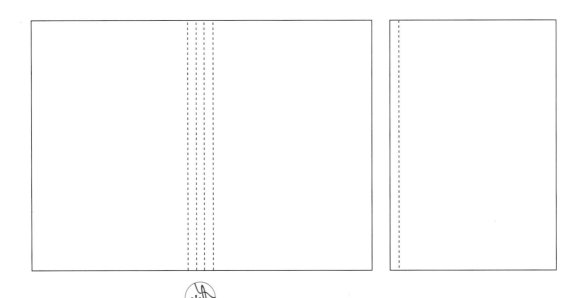

Movement Anatomy

Movement Anatomy is a curious promotional kit designed by the Swedish designer based in Sydney Malin Holmström for the movie production company Movement Production, which pays tribute to the so-called Seventh Art. It is a flipbook that features photographs of two models who gesticulate and make four of the most basic human facial movements: chewing, laughing, yawning and sneezing. The flipbook imitates the optical illusion of movement caused by the rapid succession of stills in movie screens. By flipping the pages quickly, the recipient of the kit can see the models "in action".

Movement Anatomy est un kit promotionnel atypique réalisé par le designer suédois Malin Holmström, établit à Sydney, pour l'entreprise de production cinématographique Movement Production, en hommage à ce que l'on appelle le septième art. Il s'agit d'un *flipbook* comportant les photos de deux mannequins qui gesticulent et effectuent quatre des mouvements faciaux les plus basiques de l'être humain : mâcher, rire, bâiller et éternuer. Le *flipbook* imite l'illusion de mouvement provoquée par la succession rapide des photogrammes sur les écrans de cinéma. En tournant rapidement les pages, le destinataire du kit peut voir les mannequins « en action ».

Movement Anatomy es un kit promocional atípico realizado por el diseñador sueco afincando en Sídney Malin Holmström para la productora cinematográfica Movement Production, y que homenajea al llamado «séptimo arte». Se trata de un *flipbook* que muestra las fotografías de dos modelos que gesticulan y realizan cuatro de los movimientos faciales más básicos del ser humano: masticar, reír, bostezar y estornudar. El folioscopio juega con la ilusión óptica de movimiento provocada por la rápida sucesión de las imágenes, como en el cine. Al pasar las páginas rápidamente, el destinatario del kit puede ver a los modelos «en acción».

Malin Holmström
Sydney, Australia_Sydney, Australie_Sídney (Australia)
www.malinholmstrom.com ı hello@malinholmstrom.com

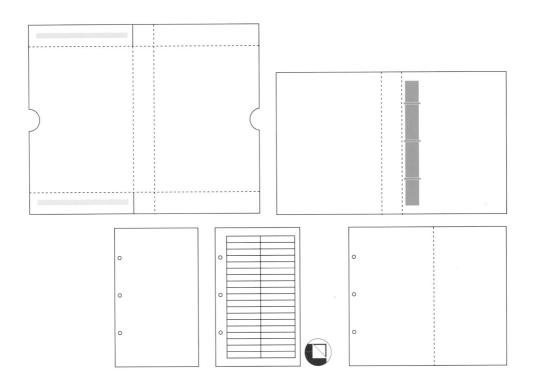

Restart/Rethink

The Hong Kong-based company Antalis, dedicated to the manufacturing and marketing of paper, each year writes a New Year's journal. The 2006 edition that we can see in these pages consists of a box with the diary inside that also serves as a notebook, and it is based on the concepts of "restart" and "rethink". The box also contains a series of stickers so that customers can stick them to any everyday object, spreading and disseminating the message of the company.

L'entreprise Antalis, située à Hong Kong, se consacre à la fabrication et à la commercialisation du papier et élabore chaque année un carnet pour le nouvel an. Celui de l'année 2006, que vous pouvez voir ici, consistait en une boîte dans laquelle se trouvait le carnet, qui pouvait également servir d'agenda ; il tournait autour des concepts de « recommencer » (restart) et de « repenser » (rethink). La boîte comportait également une série d'autocollants que les clients pouvaient coller sur des objets d'usage quotidien, ce qui permettait de répandre et de transmettre le message de l'entreprise.

La empresa Antalis, de Hong Kong, dedicada a la fabricación y la comercialización de papel, elabora cada año nuevo un diario. El de 2006, que podemos ver en estas páginas, consistía en una caja en cuyo interior los clientes podían encontrar el mencionado diario (que también cumplía las funciones de agenda de notas), basado en los conceptos «comenzar de nuevo» (restart) y «repensar» (rethink). La caja contenía, además, una serie de pegatinas para que los clientes las colocaran en cualquier objeto de uso cotidiano, expandiendo y difundiendo así el mensaje de la compañía.

Milkxhake
Hong Kong, China_Hong Kong, Chine_Hong Kong (China)
www.milkxhake.org ı mix@milkxhake.org

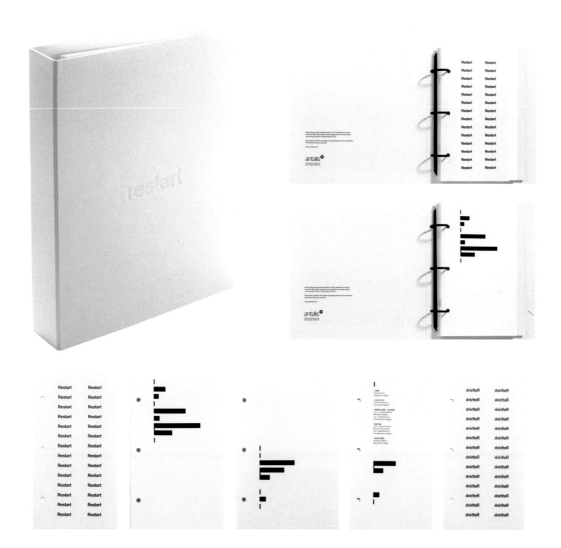

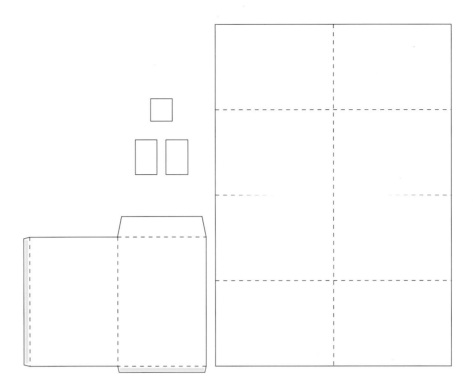

All of the Above

The four posters you can see on these pages are part of a series of self-promotional items by the Dutch studio Almost Modern. In them, the designers have symbolically reflected several themes that occupied their minds at this time. The slogans or phrases printed on the posters are used by the studio as a starting point for their work in typography or design. The Almost Modern designers have screen-printed posters on newsprint so that over time they turn yellow, leaving the mark of time on them.

Les quatre affiches ici présentées font partie d'une série d'envois auto-promotionnels du studio Almost Modern. Les designers y ont exprimé le reflet symbolique des divers thèmes qu'ils pouvaient avoir à l'esprit à ce moment. Les slogans ou phrases imprimés sur les affiches sont utilisés par le studio comme point de départ de leurs travaux typographiques ou de design. Les designers de Almost Modern ont créé eux-mêmes les affiches avec du papier journal afin qu'elles jaunissent en vieillissant et portent ainsi la marque du temps qui passe.

Los cuatro carteles que pueden verse en estas páginas forman parte de una serie de envíos autopromocionales del estudio neerlandés Almost Modern. En ellos, los diseñadores han reflejado simbólicamente varios de los temas que ocupan sus mentes en este momento. Las frases y los lemas impresos en los carteles son usados por el estudio como punto de partida para sus trabajos tipográficos o de diseño. Los mismos diseñadores de Almost Modern han serigrafiado los carteles sobre papel de periódico para que el paso del tiempo los amarillee y deje en ellos su huella.

Almost Modern
Rotterdam, the Netherlands_Rotterdam, Pays-Bas_Róterdam (Países Bajos)
almostmodern.com ı mail@almostmodern.com

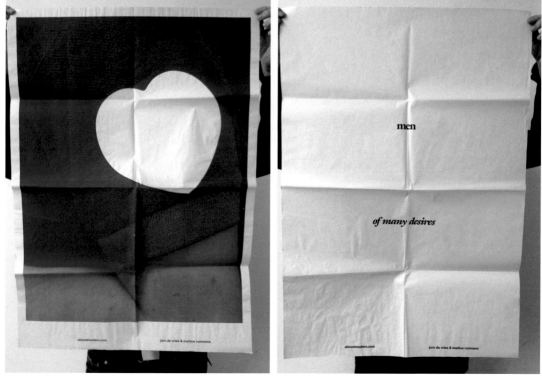

Senior designer at Ico Design Consultancy
London, UK
www.icodesign.co.uk
viv.bhatia@icodesign.co.uk
Project on page 48

Designer senior de Ico Design Consultancy
Londres, Royaume-Uni
www.icodesign.co.uk
viv.bhatia@icodesign.co.uk
Projet sur la page 48

Diseñador sénior de Ico Design Consultancy
Londres (Reino Unido)
www.icodesign.co.uk
viv.bhatia@icodesign.co.uk
Proyecto en la página 48

How should the perfect promotional kit be?

Consistency and flexibility are the key aspects. Consistent so that everything hangs together yet flexible enough that individual items remain interesting.

What's (or what should be) its objective?

Like any good design, communication is the key objective; even a logo on a page can communicate the positioning of a brand through the use of color and material.

What's the main difficulty when designing a promotional kit?

Often this is getting the balance right between consistency and doing something that doesn't look like something else.

And what's the easiest thing about it?

Once the core idea and the look are established, rolling it out over different applications becomes easier.

What do you most enjoy about designing a promotional kit?

It's always satisfying to create a whole greater than the sum of its parts.

Comment devrait être le kit promotionnel parfait ?

La cohérence et la flexibilité sont les aspects clés. Cohérent pour que tout concorde et néanmoins suffisamment flexible pour que les éléments individuels restent intéressants.

Quel est (ou quel devrait être) son objectif ?

Comme pour tout bon design, la communication est l'objectif clé ; un logo sur une page peut transmettre le positionnement d'une marque par l'utilisation d'une couleur ou un matériau.

Quelle est la principale difficulté lors de la conception d'un kit promotionnel ?

Il s'agit souvent d'obtenir le bon équilibre entre la cohérence et le fait de faire quelque chose qui ne ressemble à rien d'autre.

Et qu'est-ce qui est le plus facile ?

Une fois établis l'idée centrale et l'aspect, les introduire dans différentes applications devient plus facile.

¿Cómo debería ser el kit promocional perfecto?

Consistencia y flexibilidad son los aspectos clave. Consistencia, para que todo cuadre, y, a la vez, la suficiente flexibilidad como para que los elementos individuales sigan siendo interesantes.

¿Cuál es (o debería ser) su objetivo?

Como en cualquier buen diseño, la comunicación es clave: incluso un logotipo en una página puede comunicar el posicionamiento de una marca por medio del color y del material.

¿Cuál es la principal dificultad cuando se diseña un kit promocional?

A menudo, equilibrar la balanza entre la consistencia y hacer algo que no se parezca a otra cosa.

¿Y qué parte es la más fácil?

Cuando la idea y el aspecto principal están definidos, bascular hacia otras aplicaciones resulta más fácil.

¿Con qué disfrutas más cuando diseñas un kit promocional?

Siempre es satisfactorio crear un todo mayor que la suma de sus partes.

Vivek Bhatia

In your opinion, what kind of clients/ brands should make use of promotional or press kits?
This is dependent on the individual client, but the key to good branding is individuality and consistency, so all brands wanting to promote themselves effectively could make use of a press kit given the right circumstances.

How do you check or test the effectiveness of your work and designs, and more specifically your press kits? Do you receive any kind of feedback from the client or the consumer?
Client/consumer feedback is always a good indicator of how well you've done the job. Without feedback it's often difficult to gauge. You know you've done a good job if the client gives you more work!

What's your working method when designing a promotional kit? Is there a particular path you follow?
The starting point for any project is really understanding the client's needs and what they hope to achieve, followed by research. This is often followed by a range of ideas that are then put to the

Qu'aimez-vous le plus dans la conception d'un kit promotionnel ?
J'adore créer un ensemble plus grand que la somme de ses parties.

À votre avis, quel genre de clients/ marques devraient utiliser les kits promotionnels ou de presse ?
Cela dépend du client individuel mais la clé d'une bonne marque est l'individualisme et la cohérence. Toutes les marques qui souhaitent faire leur promotion avec efficacité pourraient utiliser un kit de presse étant donné les bonnes circonstances.

Comment vérifiez-vous l'efficacité de votre travail et de vos designs et, plus précisément, de vos kits de presse ? Recevez-vous un feedback de la part du client ou du consommateur ?
Le feedback du client/consommateur est toujours un bon indicateur de votre niveau de réussite. Sans feedback, il est difficile de juger. Vous savez si vous avez fait un bon travail si le client vous en donne d'autres !

Quelle est votre méthode de travail

Para ti, ¿qué tipo de clientes o marcas deberían utilizar kits promocionales o carpetas de prensa?
Depende del cliente, pero la clave de un buen *branding* se basa en la individualidad y la consistencia, así que todas las marcas que quieran promocionarse podrían hacer uso de un kit de prensa si se dan las circunstancias adecuadas.

¿Cómo compruebas o mides la efectividad de un trabajo o un diseño y, especialmente, de un kit de prensa? ¿Recibes *feedback* de los clientes o los consumidores?
El *feedback* del cliente o del consumidor siempre es un buen indicador de si lo has hecho bien. Sin *feedback*, a menudo es difícil juzgar. Pero ¿sabes que has hecho un buen trabajo cuando el cliente te da más trabajo!

¿Qué método de trabajo sigues cuando diseñas un kit promocional? ¿Te basas en algunas pautas en concreto?
El punto de partida para cualquier proyecto realmente reside en entender las necesidades del cliente y lo que espera conseguir y, después, el trabajo de in-

test. The best ones are then presented to the client.

Do you need to "like" the product you're helping to promote to do a good job with it? Be sincere.
It obviously helps if you like the product or identify with its benefits. If you are the target market you're naturally more interested/passionate about the project. That doesn't mean you can't do a good job for a product or service that doesn't interest or you don't know much about. It's more a case of it's a bonus when you do.

What's the difference between designing a promotional kit and designing any other kind of work?
Each area of design has its own challenges and nuances; a book is obviously a very different task to tackling a website but the aim is the same: to try and do something interesting that answers the brief and that you're proud of.

How will promotional kit design evolve along the upcoming years? How will new technologies and the fast evolution of the net affect it?

lors de la conception d'un kit promotionnel ? Suivez-vous un processus particulier ?
Le point de départ de tout projet est de comprendre vraiment les besoins du client et ce qu'il espère obtenir, suivi de la recherche. Une série d'idées arrivent souvent après et elles sont ensuite testées. Les meilleures sont présentées au client.

Pour faire un bon travail, devez-vous « aimer » le produit dont vous assurez en partie la promotion ? Répondez sincèrement.
Il est évident que cela aide si vous aimez le produit ou identifiez ses bénéfices. Si vous êtes le marché cible, vous êtes naturellement plus intéressé/passionné par le projet. Cela ne veut pas dire que vous ne pouvez pas faire un bon travail pour un produit ou un service qui ne vous intéresse pas ou que vous ne connaissez pas beaucoup, c'est plutôt un avantage si c'est le cas.

Quelle différence y-a-t-il entre la conception d'un kit promotionnel et celle d'un autre genre de travail ?
Chaque secteur du design a ses propres défis et nuances ; la conception d'un

vestigación. Esto suele venir seguido de una prueba de las ideas propuestas. Y al cliente se le presentan las mejores.

¿Necesitas que te guste el producto que estás promocionando para hacer una buena promoción? Sé sincero.
Obviamente, ayuda si te gusta el producto o lo identificas con sus beneficios. Si formas parte del mercado objetivo, naturalmente estás más interesado o entusiasmado con el proyecto. Eso no significa que no puedas hacer un buen trabajo para un producto o un servicio que no te interese o del que no sabes mucho; se trata más bien de un punto a tu favor.

¿Cuál es la diferencia entre diseñar un kit promocional y diseñar otro tipo de trabajo?
Cada área del diseño tiene sus propios retos y matices. Un libro es, obviamente, una tarea diferente a la de enfrentarse a una página web, pero el objetivo es el mismo: intentar y conseguir hacer algo interesante, que responda a las indicaciones del cliente y de lo que te sientas orgulloso.

The internet has changed everything. Communicating through new avenues of social media, blogs as well as traditional websites means being able to target people in new and innovative ways. But it still rests in the pursuit of good ideas followed by consistency of the brand.

What's the best promotional work you've ever seen, and what product was it related to? Why do you like it? Did you buy the product or did you hire the service just because of its promotional work?
I can only comment on what's fresh in my mind at the moment. One thing I've always liked is the graphics for the food chain Leon. They use distinct bold, retro style graphics on a range of recycled materials that feels quite unique amongst other fast food eateries in the United Kingdom.
Also Kessels Kramer's promotion of Amsterdam's worst hotel springs to mind. Instead of trying to promote the positives they focused on exactly what the hotel offered: awful accommodation. One of their promotional ploys was to

livre est évidemment une tâche très différente de celle du traitement d'un site Internet mais l'objectif est le même, essayer et faire quelque chose d'intéressant répondant aux critères du client et dont vous êtes fier.

Comment la conception de kits promotionnels va-t-elle évoluer dans les années qui viennent ? Comment les nouvelles technologies et l'évolution rapide du réseau vont-ils l'affecter ?
Internet a tout changé. La communication au travers des nouveaux réseaux sociaux, des blogs, ainsi que des sites Internet traditionnels, signifie qu'il est possible de cibler des gens de différentes manières nouvelles et innovantes. Cependant, le défi reste la recherche de bonnes idées ainsi que de la cohérence de la marque.

Quel est le meilleur travail promotionnel que vous ayez vu et de quel produit s'agissait-il ? Pourquoi vous a-t-il plu ? Avez-vous acheté le produit ou loué le service juste pour son travail promotionnel ?
Je ne peux commenter que ce qui est encore frais dans mon esprit actuellement. J'ai

¿Cómo evolucionará el diseño de los kits promocionales en los próximos años? ¿Cómo influirán las nuevas tecnologías y la rápida evolución de la Red?
Internet lo ha cambiado todo. Comunicarse a través de redes sociales, *blogs* y páginas web tradicionales significa ser capaz de llegar hasta la gente de formas innovadoras. Pero el reto sigue siendo perseguir buenas ideas que vayan acompañadas de la consistencia de la marca.

¿Cuál es el mejor trabajo de promoción que has visto? ¿Qué promocionaba? ¿Por qué te gustó? ¿Compraste el producto o contrataste el servicio sólo por el trabajo promocional?
Sólo puedo comentar lo que tengo fresco en la cabeza ahora mismo. Una cosa que siempre me ha gustado son los gráficos de la cadena de restaurantes Leon. Utilizan diferentes negritas y gráficos de estilo *retro* en un abanico de materiales reciclados que llama la atención y destaca entre otros restaurantes de comida rápida del Reino Unido. También me viene ahora a la cabeza la promoción de Kessels Kramer del peor hotel de Ámsterdam. En vez de intentar promocionar

stick flags bearing the hotels name in dog faeces around Amsterdam. The hotel now has a hardcore following of student back-packers that stay there.

The new branding for Casa da Musica in Lisbon by Stefan Sagmeister is an interesting take on how to execute an identity in a different way. The identity is dynamic and constantly changing. Its shape is based on different views of the building and colour derived from the colour of the image. The end result veers on the ugly, but that's no bad thing as it doesn't look like anything else.

What weight and importance do you give to the briefing of the client when it doesn't fit your ideas? How do you match these two opposite views?

This is often the hardest thing and is the holy grail in design. A good client is one where the project becomes a collaboration, a not so good one is one where the brief is unclear or changes during the project. So clarifying the brief is fundamental to everything.

If you have generated good ideas that you're passionate about, it's always easier to convince the client even if it's

toujours aimé le graphisme de la chaîne de restauration Leon ; ils utilisent un graphisme différent, gras, de style rétro sur une série de matériaux recyclés, qui donne l'impression d'être assez unique parmi les autres établissements de restauration rapide en Grande Bretagne.

De même, la promotion de Kessel Kramer du pire hôtel d'Amsterdam me vient à l'esprit. Au lieu d'essayer de faire la promotion des points positifs, ils se sont simplement axés sur ce que l'hôtel propose : un logement affreux. Un de leurs stratagèmes publicitaires était de planter des drapeaux portant le nom de l'hôtel dans des crottes de chiens dans Amsterdam. L'hôtel a désormais un groupe inconditionnel de routards étudiants qui y séjournent.

La nouvelle marque pour la Casa da Música de Lisbonne de Stefan Sagmeister est un point de vue intéressant sur la manière de mettre en œuvre une identité de manière différente. L'identité est dynamique et change perpétuellement. Sa forme se base sur différentes vues du bâtiment et la couleur provient de la couleur de l'image. Le résultat final vire à la laideur mais ce n'est pas une mauvaise chose car cela ne ressemble à rien d'autre.

los aspectos positivos, se centraron exclusivamente en lo que el hotel ofrecía: un alojamiento penoso. Uno de sus argumentos promocionales fue poner banderas con el nombre del hotel en heces de perros por todo Ámsterdam. Ahora el hotel tiene un grupo de estudiantes mochileros incondicionales que se alojan allí. La nueva marca de Casa da Música en Lisboa de Stefan Sagmeister es una muestra interesante de cómo crear una identidad de un modo diferente. La identidad es dinámica y está en constante cambio. Su forma se basa en diferentes visiones del edificio y en el color derivado del color de la imagen. El resultado final tiende hacia algo feo, pero no es malo, ya que no tiene aspecto de ninguna otra cosa.

¿Qué peso y qué importancia das al *briefing* del cliente cuando no piensa lo mismo que tú? ¿Cómo consigues encontrar un punto medio para dos puntos de vista diferentes?

Esto suele ser lo más duro y el Santo Grial del diseño. Un buen cliente es aquel cuyo proyecto se convierte en una colaboración. Uno no tan bueno es aquel cu-

challenging to them. The hardest thing is often to keep the ideas from being compromised when the client feels more comfortable with something ordinary.

Quelle importance donnez-vous au briefing du client lorsqu'il ne partage pas vos idées ? Comment conciliez-vous ces deux points de vue opposés ?

C'est souvent le plus difficile et constitue le saint graal en design. Un bon client est celui dont le projet devient une collaboration, un moins bon est celui dont les indications ne sont pas claires ou qui réalise des changements pendant le projet. Il est donc capital de clarifier les indications pour tout le reste.

Si vous avez généré de bonnes idées qui vous plaisent, il est toujours plus facile de convaincre le client, même si c'est un défi pour lui. Le plus difficile est souvent d'empêcher de transiger sur les idées quand le client se sent plus à l'aise avec quelque chose plus ordinaire.

yas instrucciones no están claras o que realiza cambios durante el proyecto. Por lo tanto, definir claramente las instrucciones es fundamental para todo. Si has generado buenas ideas y éstas te gustan, siempre es más fácil convencer al cliente, incluso si esas opciones suponen un reto para él. A menudo, lo más complicado es mantener ideas comprometidas cuando sabes que el cliente se siente más cómodo con algo ordinario.

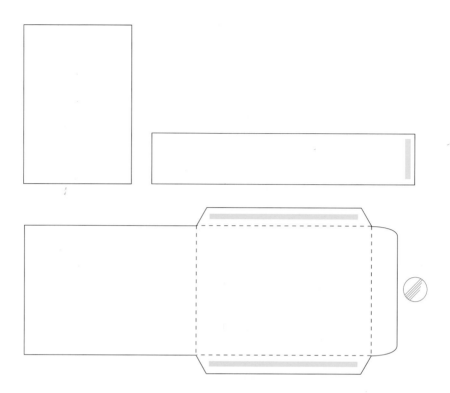

Lisa Grue promotional accordion card

This kit was designed by the illustrator along with her own agency, CWC International, to be sent to clients and friends. The aim was to create a pleasant and playful object to showcase and promote the work of Lisa Grue, and in particular her work which focuses on fashion and graphic patterns. Ten of the best designs from the artist were chosen and printed on both sides of very thick paper, combining the colors black and purple on one side and black and pink on the other. The accordion card with the information about the artist, along with the cards featuring her work, were introduced later in a clear envelope.

Ce kit a été conçu par l'illustratrice et son agence, CWC International, afin d'être envoyé à des clients et à des amis. Il s'agissait de créer un objet agréable et ludique pour présenter et promouvoir le travail de Lisa Grue, notamment celui qui se rapporte à la mode et aux modèles graphiques. Pour cela, dix des meilleures créations de l'artiste ont été choisies et imprimées recto verso sur un papier très épais, conjugant le noir et le pourpre d'un côté, et le noir et le rose de l'autre. Le bandeau contenant des informations sur l'artiste est ensuite été glissé dans une enveloppe transparente avec les cartes présentant son travail.

Este kit fue diseñado por la propia ilustradora junto con su agencia, CWC International, para enviarlo a clientes y amigos. El objetivo era crear un objeto agradable y divertido que mostrara y promocionara el trabajo de Lisa Grue, y especialmente el que se centra en la moda y los patrones gráficos. Para ello se escogieron diez de los mejores diseños de la artista y se imprimieron a doble cara en un papel de mucho grosor, combinando los colores negro y púrpura en una cara, y negro y rosa en la otra. La faja con la información sobre la artista y las tarjetas con su trabajo se introdujeron después en un sobre transparente.

Lisa Grue, CWC International
Copenhagen, Denmark_Copenhague, Danemark_Copenhague (Dinamarca)
www.underwerket.dk ı mail@underwerket.dk

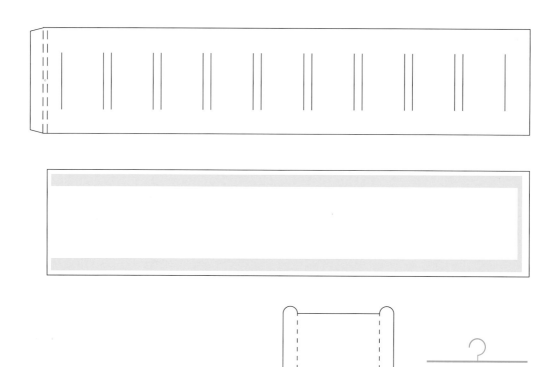

10 Years

Disturbance is a small South African design studio set up in 1997 by Richard and Susie Hart. For its 10 year anniversary, the Disturbance designers decided to design a promotional pack of 10 T-shirts, one for each year of the studio's life, to give to their customers. The pack is presented in a bedroll similar to those used by soldiers during military campaigns, and hangs from a coat-hanger for added customer convenience. Each of the 10 T-shirts has been screen printed with a different design representing in one way or another the work of the studio.

Disturbance est un petit studio de design sud-africain créé en 1997 par Richard et Susie Hart. Pour célébrer le dixième anniversaire, les designers de Disturbance ont décidé de concevoir un pack promotionnel avec dix tee-shirts, un pour chaque année de vie du studio, à offrir à leurs clients. Le pack se présente sous forme d'un sac, similaire à celui qu'utilisent les soldats au cours des campagnes militaires, et se suspend à un cintre pour offrir une plus grande commodité. La sérigraphie des dix tee-shirts est différente mais toujours en rapport, d'une manière ou d'une autre, avec le travail du studio.

Disturbance es un pequeño estudio de diseño sudafricano creado en 1997 por Richard y Susie Hart. Para celebrar sus diez años de vida, los integrantes de Disturbance decidieron diseñar un *pack* promocional de diez camisetas, una por cada año del estudio, para regalar a sus clientes. El lote se presentaba en un petate similar al que utilizan los soldados durante las campañas militares, y se cuelga de una percha para mayor comodidad. Cada camiseta ha sido serigrafiada con un diseño diferente relacionado de una forma u otra con el trabajo del estudio.

Disturbance
Durban, South Africa_Durban, Afrique du Sud_Durban (Sudáfrica)
www.disturbance.co.za ı cindene@disturbance.co.za

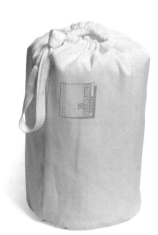

1997 01

1998 02

1999 03

2000 04

2001 05

2002 06

2003 07

2004 08

2005 09

2006 10

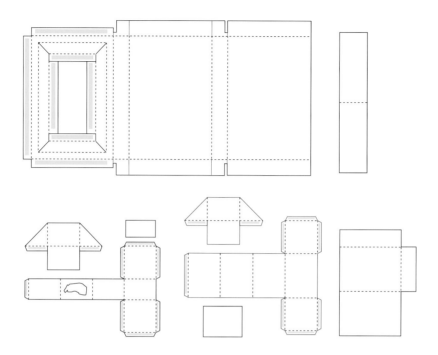

Town of Insecurities. Flat City

This self-promotional design by the young graphic designer Brittany Harriman is a 3D paper town built around the idea of "insecurity". The Town of Insecurities can be rebuilt again and again with different buildings. Each of these buildings or houses exemplifies the personality of its owner both on the outside and inside. The different types of furniture found inside the buildings represent the different personalities, while the exterior of the building represents the human body.

Cette conception auto-promotionnelle de la jeune designer graphique Brittany Harriman consiste en une ville en papier en 3D, construite autour de la notion d'« insécurité ». La Ville des Insécurités (Town of Insecurities) peut être reconstruite à maintes reprises avec différents bâtiments. Chaque bâtiment ou maison reflète la personnalité de son propriétaire, tant à l'intérieur qu'à l'extérieur. Les différents types de mobilier que l'on trouve à l'intérieur incarnent diverses personnalités, alors que l'extérieur des constructions représente le corps humain.

Este diseño autopromocional de la joven diseñadora gráfica Brittany Harriman consiste en una ciudad de papel en 3D construida en torno a la idea de la inseguridad. La Ciudad de las Inseguridades (Town of Insecurities) se puede reconstruir una y otra vez con edificios diferentes. Cada uno de esos edificios o casas muestra la personalidad de su propietario tanto en su exterior como en su interior. Los diferentes tipos de mobiliario que pueden verse dentro de los edificios representan distintas personalidades, mientras que el exterior de las construcciones representa el cuerpo humano.

Brittany Harriman
Sarasota, USA_Sarasota, États-Unis_Sarasota (Estados Unidos)
www.brittanyharriman.com ı bh@brittanyharriman.com

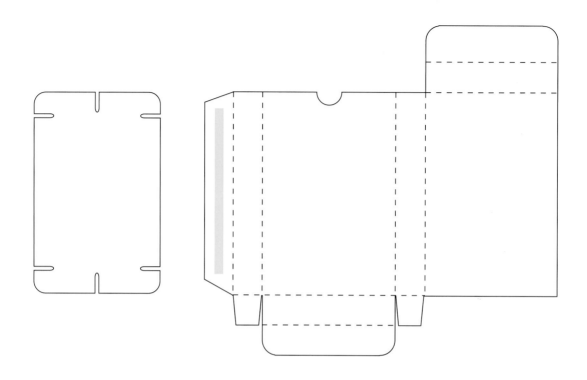

Voll's Card-Box

Voll's Card-Box is a set of 50 cards with six small slots, printed in full color and with a glossy finish, inspired by the famous House of Cards designed by the Eames Office. Each card features a pattern, a graphic design or illustration created by Voll Design and Communication. The Voll's Card-Box with the 50 cards was sent out with a personalized letter to the studio's clients as a gift and collectible, but primarily it is actually an informal sales catalog for the company.

Voll's Card-Box est un ensemble de cinquante cartes brillantes et hautes en couleurs, comportant chacune six petites fentes. Elles s'inspirent de la célèbre House of Cards conçue par la Eames Office. Chaque carte présente un patron, un design graphique ou une illustration réalisés par Voll Design and Communication. La Voll's Card-Box et ses cinquante cartes ont été envoyées avec une lettre personnalisée aux clients du studio, comme cadeau et objet de collection, mais, en réalité, elles font office de catalogue commercial officieux de l'entreprise.

Voll's Card-Box es un set de cincuenta cartas troqueladas con seis pequeñas ranuras, impresas a todo color y con un acabado brillante, inspiradas en la famosa House of Cards diseñada por la Eames Office. Cada carta muestra un patrón, un diseño gráfico o una ilustración realizada por Voll Design and Communication. La Voll's Card-Box con las cincuenta cartas se envió junto con una misiva personalizada a los clientes del estudio como detalle de cortesía y objeto de coleccionismo, aunque en realidad funciona básicamente como catálogo comercial oficioso de la compañía.

Huschang Pourian
Hong Kong, China_Hong Kong, Chine_Hong Kong (China)
www.pourian.com ı huschang@pourian.com

Sustainable press kit

The designer Changzhi Lee believes that packaging designers are obliged to protect their environment by respectfully using the materials they need for their creations. To create the self-promotional kit that can be seen in these pages, and that Changzhi Lee sends out to potential customers, the designer opted for a paper tree made from leftover materials from previous designs. The aim is to symbolically show the philosophy of Lee Changzhi's work: sustainability, originality and sound craftsmanship.

Selon le designer Changzhi Lee, les designers de packaging se doivent de respecter l'environnement en utilisant à bon escient les matériaux dont ils se servent pour leurs créations. Pour la réalisation du kit auto-promotionnel ci-contre que Changzhi Lee a envoyé à des clients potentiels, le designer a opté pour un arbre en papier fabriqué à partir de surplus de matériaux d'autres créations. L'objectif était de faire connaître, de manière symbolique, la philosophie de travail de Changzhi Lee : durabilité, originalité et résistance artisanale.

El diseñador Changzhi Lee cree que los diseñadores de *packaging* tienen la obligación de cuidar de su entorno haciendo un uso respetuoso de los materiales que utilizan para sus creaciones. Para la realización del kit auto-promocional que puede verse en estas páginas, y que Changzhi Lee envía a potenciales clientes, el diseñador optó por un árbol de papel realizado a partir de materiales sobrantes de anteriores diseños. El objetivo es dar a conocer, simbólicamente, su filosofía de trabajo: la sostenibilidad, la originalidad y la solidez artesanal.

Changzhi Advertising & Design
Singapore_Singapour_Singapur (República de Singapur)
www.leechangzhi.com
leechangzhi@gmail.com

139

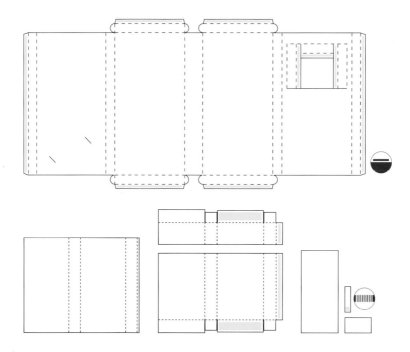

Design Packaging

The Design Packaging kit is a commercial and promotional tool that shows the different creative techniques, finishes and materials used by the company. A simple color palette allows the bright details of the box stand out on a matte background. The tactile velvet ribbon that closes the kit makes it similar to a promotional sleeve for a bestseller. The box has internal pockets which hold cards and sheets, printed in five colors. These sheets feature a number of noteworthy projects carried out by Design Packaging in recent years.

Le kit de Design Packaging est un outil promotionnel et commercial qui présente les différentes techniques de construction, les finitions et les matériaux utilisés. Une palette de couleurs simple permet de faire ressortir les détails brillants de la boîte sur un fond mat. Le ruban de velours qui ferme le kit ajoute un élément tactile similaire aux bandeaux promotionnels des *bestsellers*. La boîte possède des poches intérieures dans lesquelles on a glissé des cartes et des feuilles imprimées en cinq couleurs. Ces feuilles illustrent quelques-uns des projets marquants réalisés par Design Packaging au cours des dernières années.

El kit de la empresa Design Packaging es una herramienta promocional y comercial que muestra las diferentes técnicas de fabricación, acabados y materiales que emplea. Una paleta de colores sencilla permite que los detalles brillantes de la caja resalten sobre un fondo mate. El detalle táctil lo pone la cinta de terciopelo que cierra el kit, similar a las fajas promocionales de los *best sellers*. La caja cuenta con ranuras interiores en las que se han colocado algunas tarjetas y láminas impresas en cinco colores. Dichas láminas presentan varios de los proyectos destacados realizados por Design Packaging durante los últimos años.

Evelio Mattos
Scottsdale, USA_Scottsdale, États-Unis_Scottsdale (Estados Unidos)
www.designpackaginginc.com ı evelio@designpackaginginc.com

designpackaging

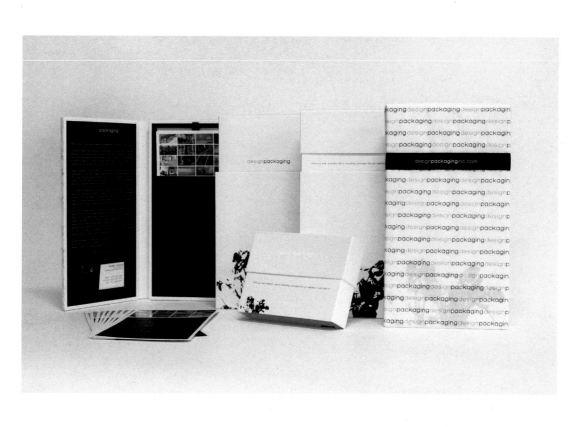

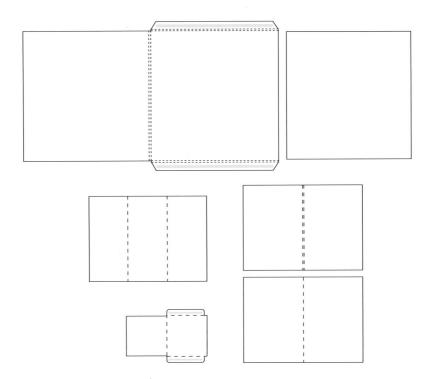

La Coopérative de Mai

La Coopérative de Mai is the concert hall in the city of Clermont-Ferrand where top current bands perform. Every two months, Fabien Barral designs the cover of the playbill and other promotional items. The current logo of the hall is a truck, hence the repeated use of it in the press kit. The programme, about 40 pages long, has been designed by Fabien Barral along with the Mediafix studio team. A limited edition screen-printed poster (only 100 copies) completes the set of promotional elements for the concert hall.

La Coopérative de Mai est la salle de concert de la ville de Clermont-Ferrand qui accueille régulièrement les meilleurs groupes du moment. Tous les deux mois, Fabien Barral conçoit la couverture de son programme ainsi que d'autres éléments promotionnels. Le logo actuel de la salle est un camion, d'où son utilisation répétée dans le kit de presse. Le programme, d'environ quarante pages, a été conçu par Fabien Barral avec l'équipe du studio Mediafix. Parmi les éléments promotionnels de la salle, on trouve une affiche en édition limitée (à peine cent exemplaires).

La Coopérative de Mai es la sala de conciertos de la ciudad de Clermont-Ferrand en la que suelen tocar las mejores bandas del momento. Cada dos meses, Fabien Barral diseña la imagen de portada de su programa, así como otros elementos promocionales. El logotipo actual de la sala es un camión, y de ahí su uso repetitivo en el kit de prensa. El programa, de unas cuarenta páginas, ha sido diseñado por Barral junto con el equipo del estudio Mediafix. Un cartel serigrafiado de edición limitada (apenas cien copias) completa el conjunto de elementos promocionales de la sala.

Fabien Barral
Auvergne, France_Auvergne, France_Auvergne (Francia)
www.fabienbarral.com ı ecrire@fabienbarral.com

147

Mike Joyce

How should the perfect promotional kit be?

First and foremost it should be attractive and eye-catching. There are so many advertising, marketing, and promotional pieces out there that you really need to find a way to make it stand out from the crowd. So whether it is super simple or loud and garish, it needs to grab your attention in some kind of way. I also think that the best promotional pieces have some kind of concept behind them. The simplest idea or design element can really make a kit memorable.

What's the main difficulty when designing a promotional kit?

To make it memorable and to create something the recipient is going to want to keep and not throw away with the trash.

What do you most enjoy about designing a promotional kit?

Probably the challenge of creating something new and interesting. One thing I love about being a graphic designer is the variety of projects I get to work on. I might be working on albums for Morphine and Katy Perry while at the same time design-

Comment devrait être le kit promotionnel parfait ?

Il doit tout d'abord et surtout être séduisant et accrocheur. Il y a tellement d'éléments publicitaires, marketing et promotionnels partout que vous devez trouver une manière de vous distinguer de la foule. Par conséquent, qu'il soit super simple ou voyant et tapageur, il doit attirer votre attention d'une manière ou d'une autre. Je pense que les meilleurs éléments promotionnels ont une sorte de concept derrière. Une idée simple ou un élément de design peuvent rendre un kit inoubliable.

Quelle est la principale difficulté lors de la conception d'un kit promotionnel ?

Le rendre mémorable et créer quelque chose que le destinataire voudra conserver et ne pas jeter à la poubelle.

Qu'est-ce qui vous plait le plus dans la conception d'un kit promotionnel ?

Probablement le défi de créer quelque chose de nouveau et d'intéressant. Ce qui me plait dans mon métier de designer graphique ce sont les projets variés sur lesquels je travaille. Je peux travailler sur

¿Cómo debería ser el kit promocional perfecto?

Primero y por encima de todo debería ser atractivo y llamativo. Hay tantos elementos de publicidad, *marketing* y promociones en el mercado que necesitas encontrar un medio para destacar entre la multitud. Así que, sea supersimple o llamativo y chillón, tiene que captar la atención de algún modo. Yo soy de la opinión de que las mejores promociones tienen algún concepto detrás. La idea más simple o un elemento de diseño pueden hacer un kit inolvidable.

¿Cuál es la principal dificultad cuando se diseña un kit promocional?

Hacer que sea inolvidable y conseguir que la persona que lo recibe quiera quedárselo, y no que vaya directo a la papelera.

¿Con qué disfrutas más cuando diseñas un kit promocional?

Posiblemente, con el reto de crear algo nuevo e interesante. Una de las cosas que me gusta de ser diseñador gráfico es la variedad de proyectos en los que trabajo. Puedo estar trabajando en los

Creative director and founder of Stereotype Design
New York, USA
www.stereotype-design.com
mike@stereotype-design.com
Project on page 52

Directeur créatif et fondateur de Stereotype Design
New York, États-Unis
www.stereotype-design.com
mike@stereotype-design.com
Project sur la page 52

Director creativo y fundador de Stereotype Design
Nueva York (Estados Unidos)
www.stereotype-design.com
mike@stereotype-design.com
Proyecto en la página 52

ing a promotional campaign for Pepsi. An album will have a long shelf life but a promotional kit is usually considered expendable. So I like to consider it in the same way as designing a CD or book: how can I get someone to really love this kit and not only use it, but keep it as well?

How do you check or test the effectiveness of your work and designs, and more specifically your press kits? Do you receive any kind of feedback from the client or the consumer?
I always receive feedback from the client. That's just the nature and process of design. I've been fortunate to work with clients that truly respect design and realize its importance and power. Because of this, a project will sometimes turn into a true collaboration where their input and ideas make the final product that much better. I rarely get feedback from the consumer outside of my client hiring me again which is always a good sign.

What's your working method when designing a promotional kit? Is there a particular path you follow?
The first thing I'll do is to have a meet-

des albums de Morphine et Katy Perry, tout en concevant une campagne promotionnelle pour Pepsi. Un album a une longue durée de vie mais un kit promotionnel n'est pas considéré de la même manière. J'aime donc l'envisager les considérer de la même façon que lorsque je conçois un CD ou un livre : comment réussir que quelqu'un apprécie vraiment ce kit, l'utilise et veuille le conserver ?

Comment vérifiez-vous l'efficacité de votre travail et de vos designs et, plus précisément, de vos kits de presse ? Recevez-vous un feedback de la part du client ou du consommateur ?
Je reçois toujours un feedback du client, c'est dans la nature et le processus du design. J'ai eu la chance de travailler avec des clients qui respectent réellement le design et sont conscients de son importance et de son pouvoir. De ce fait, un projet deviendra parfois une véritable collaboration où leur contribution et leurs idées rendront le produit final bien meilleur. J'obtiens rarement un feedback de la part du consommateur, hormis le fait que le client m'engage de nouveau, ce qui est toujours bon signe.

álbumes de Morphine y Katy Perry y, al mismo tiempo, diseñando una campaña promocional para Pepsi. Un álbum tiene una vida bastante larga, pero no se le suele conceder la misma importancia a un kit promocional, por lo que intento pensar igual que cuando diseño un CD o un libro: ¿cómo puedo conseguir que a alguien le guste este kit como para que lo use y además lo guarde?

¿Cómo compruebas o mides la efectividad de un trabajo o un diseño y, especialmente, de un kit de prensa? ¿Recibes feedback de los clientes o los consumidores?
Siempre tengo feedback de los clientes; está en la naturaleza y en el proceso del diseño. He tenido la suerte de trabajar con clientes que respetan de verdad el diseño y que son conscientes de su importancia y su poder. Por ello, a veces un proyecto se transforma en un auténtico trabajo de grupo en el que sus aportaciones e ideas perfeccionan el producto final. Sin embargo, nunca he tenido feedback de un consumidor, aparte del cliente que vuelve a contratarme, lo que siempre es buena señal.

ing or discussion with the client so I really understand what they're trying to do and say, what exactly it is they need to communicate to their audience and consumer. After that I'll come up with a few rough ideas and once a client has chosen a direction, I'll flesh out the rest of the piece. I don't necessarily follow a path or routine as each project and assignment can vary so much. If there is one constant, it would probably just be my approach of always trying to create a quality and useful piece.

What are your favorite materials for a promotional kit? Why?
I wish I had the chance to use a variety of interesting materials more often, but usually a budget will restrict me to paper and ink. But one fun promo that comes to mind was something I did for MTV where I silk screened fluorescent ink on fabric to create a massive T-shirt tag.

Do you need to "like" the product you're helping to promote to do a good job with it? Be sincere.
Honestly it does help if you like or use the product yourself. It's always exciting

Quelle est votre méthode de travail lors de la conception d'un kit promotionnel ? Suivez-vous un processus particulier ?
Premièrement, je rencontre le client ou je discute avec lui, afin de comprendre vraiment ce qu'il essaye de transmettre, de savoir ce dont il a besoin de communiquer à son public et au consommateur. Ensuite, je lui propose quelques idées générales et, une fois que le client choisit une direction, je développe le reste. Je ne suis pas forcément un processus ou une routine car chaque projet ou mission est unique. Si une chose ne change pas, c'est vraisemblablement mon approche, qui consiste à toujours essayer de créer un élément de qualité et utile.

Quels sont vos matériaux favoris pour un kit promotionnel ? Pourquoi ?
J'aimerais avoir la possibilité d'utiliser plus souvent de divers matériaux intéressants mais, en général, le budget me limite au papier et à l'encre. Cependant, je me souviens d'une promo amusante est une que j'ai faite pour MTV où j'ai appliqué avec de l'encre fluorescente sur du tissu pour créer une gigantesque marque de un tee-shirt.

¿Qué método de trabajo sigues cuando diseñas un kit promocional? ¿Te basas en algunas pautas en concreto?
Lo primero que hago es reunirme o hablar con mi cliente para entender totalmente lo que trata de transmitir, lo que necesita comunicar exactamente a su mercado y a sus clientes. Después le presento algunas ideas y, cuando se decanta por alguna dirección, doy cuerpo al kit. No tengo ningún patrón ni rutina en concreto. Cada proyecto es un mundo. Si tuviera que señalar un elemento omnipresente, sería mi enfoque de intentar crear siempre una promoción de calidad y útil.

¿Cuáles son tus materiales favoritos para un kit promocional? ¿Por qué?
Me gustaría poder utilizar con mucha más frecuencia materiales diferentes, pero a menudo el presupuesto me limita al uso de papel y tinta. Me viene ahora a la cabeza una promoción que hice para MTV en la que teñí tela con tinta fluorescente para crear una enorme etiqueta de camiseta.

¿Necesitas que te guste el producto que estás promocionando para hacer una buena promoción? Sé sincero.

to get a new project from someone or something you love or have been a fan of for a while. And there's less research or background information to learn. But that doesn't mean you necessarily have to. I've worked on tons of projects where I'm unfamiliar with the product, but I think that can add to the challenge, and in some cases can actually help because you come at it from a neutral place.

What's the difference between designing a promotional kit and designing any other kind of work?
I think it's important to create something that doesn't feel like a sales pitch. A customer doesn't want to feel like something is being forced on them and because there's so much advertising out there that does just that, people can be fairly cynical of a promotional kit or campaign, and rightfully so. I always want to create something that will not only serve its intended purpose, but will also be used and hopefully even kept by the recipient. So if I design, say, a poster promotion, my first goal is to clearly communicate its message, but I'm also hoping the person who receives it will like it so much that

Pour faire un bon travail, devez-vous « aimer » le produit dont vous assurez en partie la promotion ? Répondez sincèrement.
Honnêtement, cela aide si vous aimez ou utilisez vous-même le produit. Il est toujours passionnant d'obtenir un nouveau projet de quelqu'un ou quelque chose que vous aimez ou dont vous avez été fan pendant un temps. Cela réduit le travail de recherche, mais n'implique pas que vous en êtes dispensé. J'ai travaillé sur des tonnes de projets dont le produit ne m'était pas familier mais je pense que cela peut être un « plus » pour le défi et parfois aider, car vous avez un regard neutre.

Quelle différence y-a-t-il entre la conception d'un kit promotionnel et celle d'un autre genre de travail ?
Je pense qu'il est important de créer quelque chose qui n'ait pas l'air d'un simple objet en vente. Un client ne veut pas se sentir forcé par quelque chose et, étant donné qu'il y a tellement de publicité qui fait cela partout, les gens remplazar peuvent être por: sont plutôt cyniques concernant un kit ou une cam-

Sinceramente, ayuda que te guste o que uses tú mismo el producto. Es estimulante hacer un proyecto para alguien o algo que te gusta o de lo que has sido admirador durante un tiempo. Y así no hace falta documentarse tanto. Pero eso no significa que no tengas que hacerlo. He trabajando en miles de proyectos en los que no sabía nada del producto, y creo que eso aumenta el reto, y en algunos casos incluso puede ayudar, ya que partes de una posición neutra.

¿Cuál es la diferencia entre diseñar un kit promocional y diseñar otro tipo de trabajo?
Creo que es importante crear algo que no parezca un simple argumento de venta. El consumidor no quiere sentirse forzado, y como hay tanta publicidad que lo hace, la gente se vuelve bastante cínica respecto a los kits promocionales o a las campañas, y con todo el derecho del mundo. Me gusta crear cosas cuyo objetivo no sea exclusivamente la promoción, sino que puedan utilizarse también y que el destinatario incluso quiera guardarlas. Por lo tanto, si estoy diseñando, por ejemplo, un póster para una promoción, el primer

they hang it up on their wall at the office, or even frame it for home. That's the ultimate compliment!

How will promotional kit design evolve along the upcoming years? How will new technologies and the fast evolution of the net affect it?
The internet has definitely change promo kits. Most magazine media kits are now just PDFs that you can download from the web and in a lot of ways that makes the most sense. Unfortunately, almost all of the creativity is eliminated when something like that gets stripped down to a letter sized Acrobat file. Not that there isn't creativity in online promotion. I remember a fun promo for *Snakes on a Planet* that was fun, ahead of its time, and almost assuredly better than the movie itself. So I definitely see a lot of promotional campaigns going in that direction. At the same time, I've been hearing print is dead for almost 20 years now and if that was true, I would have been out of work a long time ago.

What's the best promotional work you've ever seen, and what product

pagne de promotion, ce qui est compréhensible. J'aime créer quelque chose qui ne serve pas qu'à la vente mais qui soit utile et que le destinataire ait envie de le garder. Si je conçois un poster, mon objectif premier est de transmettre son message mais j'espère aussi qu'il plaira tellement à la personne qui le recevra qu'elle voudra l'accrocher au mur de son bureau, ou même l'encadrer chez elle. C'est le plus beau compliment !

Comment la conception de kits promotionnels va-t-elle évoluer dans les années qui viennent ? Comment les nouvelles technologies et l'évolution rapide du réseau vont-ils l'affecter ?
Internet a sans aucun doute modifié les kits promotionnels. La plupart des kits média des magazines sont maintenant des PFD que vous pouvez télécharger sur Internet et, dans la plupart des cas, c'est la meilleure idée. Malheureusement, presque toute la créativité disparaît lorsque le projet est en fichier Acrobat au format A4. Cela ne veut pas dire qu'il n'y a pas de créativité dans la promotion en ligne. Je me souviens d'une promotion amusante pour *Des serpents dans l'avion*

objetivo es comunicar el mensaje, pero también espero que a la persona que lo reciba le guste tanto que lo cuelgue en la pared de su oficina o que lo enmarque y lo ponga en su casa. ¡Eso sería el mejor halago del mundo!

¿Cómo evolucionará el diseño de los kits promocionales en los próximos años? ¿Cómo influirán las nuevas tecnologías y la rápida evolución de la Red?
Sin duda, Internet ha cambiado los kits promocionales. La mayoría de los kits promocionales de revistas están en formato PDF que puedes descargarte y, en muchos casos, es la opción más acertada. Desgraciadamente, casi toda la creatividad queda deslucida cuando un diseño se reduce a un archivo Acrobat en tamaño DIN A4. Con esto no quiero decir que no haya creatividad en las promociones *on-line*. Me estoy acordando ahora de una promoción divertida para la película *Serpientes en el avión*, muy adelantada para aquellos años, y que sin duda era mejor que la propia película, así estoy convencido de que muchas campañas promocionales van a ir por ese camino. Al mismo tiempo, hace veinte años

was it related to? Why do you like it? Did you buy the product or did you hire the service just because of its promotional work?

The first thing that always comes to my mind when thinking of great promotional design is Charles S. Anderson's work for French Paper. His rich, energetic, layered, retro-themed designs have become so recognizably French – and that says it all right there. They're perfectly designed for French's main consumer: graphic designers who are drawn to his use of typography, color, design elements, and found art to create not only a great promotion but a valued reference. I still have an embossed metal lunchbox promo piece containing beautifully designed swatch books of their specialty papers.

qui était, en avance sur son temps et sûrement meilleure que le film. Je suis convaincue qu'un grand nombre de campagnes promotionnelles continueront dans cette direction. Cela fait vingt ans que l'on nous dit que l'imprimerie est morte, si c'était le cas, je n'aurais plus de travail depuis longtemps.

Quel est le meilleur travail promotionnel que vous ayez vu et de quel produit s'agit-il ? Pourquoi vous a-t-il ? Avez-vous acheté le produit ou loué le service juste pour son travail promotionnel ?

Ce qui me vient à l'esprit en premier lorsque je pense à un fantastique design promotionnel, c'est le travail de Charles S. Anderson pour le French Paper. Ses designs riches, énergiques, superposés et aux thèmes rétro sont devenus tellement reconnaissables de French, ce qui implique que la promo a fonctionné. Ils sont conçus pour les principaux clients de French, des designers graphiques qui sont attirés par son utilisation de la typographie, la couleur, les éléments de design et ont trouvé de l'art pour créer non seulement une excellente promotion mais une référence précieuse. J'ai encore une boîte à sandwich en métal contenant des livres illustrant leurs papiers spéciaux.

que dicen que la imprenta está muerta. Si eso fuera cierto, haría mucho tiempo que me habría quedado sin trabajo.

¿Cuál es el mejor trabajo de promoción que has visto? ¿Qué promocionaba? ¿Por qué te gustó? ¿Compraste el producto o contrataste el servicio sólo por el trabajo promocional?

El que viene siempre primero a la cabeza cuando pienso en la mejor promoción es el trabajo de Charles S. Anderson para French Paper. Sus diseños, ricos, enérgicos, por capas y de temática *retro*, son inconfundiblemente French, lo que quiere decir que la promoción ha funcionado. Están diseñados a la perfección para los clientes principales de French: diseñadores gráficos que se siente atraídos por su uso de la tipografía, el color, elementos de diseño y consideran que arte es crear no sólo una buena promoción, sino una referencia de valor. Todavía guardo una fiambrera de metal en relieve de una promoción que tenía dentro un libro de muestras de sus especialidades en papeles.

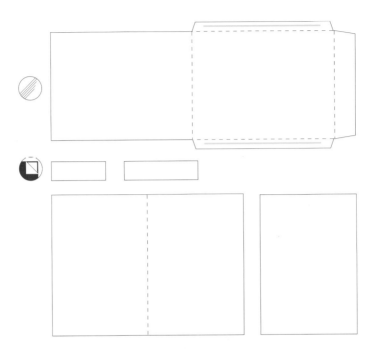

Self-Promotional

The main elements of the self-promotional press kit designed for StudioNOW are a series of stickers with words symbolizing the graphic design (timing, love, loud, greatest) and several greeting cards and envelopes that together communicate different messages related to the studio's work or with the design in general. These elements are placed in a paper bag that later is handed out to potential customers. Customers can combine these elements as they like, creating their own artistic display.

Les principaux éléments du kit de presse auto-promotionnel conçu pour StudioNOW sont une série d'autocollants avec des mots faisant référence au design graphique (*timing*, *love*, *loud*, *greatest*) ainsi que plusieurs cartes de vœux et enveloppes qui, selon leur combinaison, transmettent différents messages en rapport avec le travail du studio et le design en général. Ces éléments sont glissés dans un sac en papier qui sera ensuite offert aux clients potentiels. Ceux-ci pourront alors combiner les différents éléments à leur guise et créer ainsi leur propre manifeste artistique.

Los elementos principales del kit de prensa autopromocional diseñado para StudioNOW son una serie de pegatinas con palabras que hacen referencia al diseño gráfico (*timing*, *love*, *loud*, *greatest*…) y varias tarjetas de felicitación y sobres que, combinados, transmiten diferentes mensajes relacionados con el trabajo del estudio o con el diseño en general. Dichos elementos se introducen en una bolsa de papel que posteriormente se regala a los clientes potenciales, quienes pueden combinarlos como deseen para crear su propio manifiesto artístico.

BANK
Berlin, Germany_Berlin, Allemagne_Berlín (Alemania)
www.bankassociates.de ı tellme@bankassociates.de

MILANO INCONTRA BERLINO

ADIDAS ORIGINALS F/W 07/08

StudioNOW is a young and international creative production company.

StudioNOW is committed, authentic and innovative.

We are based in Berlin.

What do we do?

What counts?

How do we work?

Who are our clients?

MTV DESIGNERAMA ON STAGE 2005

DIESEL TEST PATROL F/W 05/06

MTV DESIGNERAMA ON STAGE 2006

StudioNOW is a young and international creative production company.

StudioNOW is committed, authentic and innovative.

We are based in Berlin.

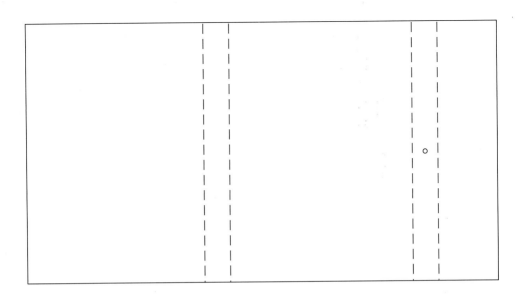

Makoto Yamaguchi

The self-promotional press kit designed by Makoto Yamaguchi, director of the design studio Makoto Yamaguchi Design in Tokyo, initially stands out for its extreme minimalism. The kit, completely black in a DIN A4 format, closes with an elastic fastener also in black. The kit includes reproductions of some of the most noteworthy work by Makoto Yamaguchi from 2000 to 2008. Its goal, in the words of the designer, is "to spread the word on our work, its quality and philosophy".

Le kit de presse auto-promotionnel conçu par Makoto Yamaguchi, directeur du studio de design Makoto Yamaguchi Design à Tokyo, se distingue à première vue par son extrême minimalisme. Le kit, entièrement noir et au format approximatif A4, se ferme à l'aide d'un élastique, noir lui-aussi. Il comporte des reproductions de certains des travaux les plus remarquables de Makoto Yamaguchi réalisés entre 2000 et 2008. Son objectif est, pour reprendre les mots du designer lui-même, de « faire connaître notre travail, sa qualité et sa philosophie ».

El kit de prensa autopromocional diseñado por Makoto Yamaguchi, director del estudio tokiota Makoto Yamaguchi Design, destaca a primera vista por su minimalismo extremo. El kit, completamente negro y del tamaño aproximado de un DIN A4, se cierra con una goma del mismo color. El dosier incluye reproducciones de algunos de los trabajos más destacados del creativo japonés realizados durante el periodo comprendido entre los años 2000 y 2008. Su objetivo, en palabras del propio diseñador, es «dar a conocer nuestro trabajo, su calidad y su filosofía».

Makoto Yamaguchi
Tokyo, Japan_Tokyo, Japon_Tokio (Japón)
www.ymgci.net ı mail@ymgci.net

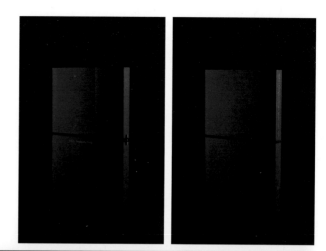

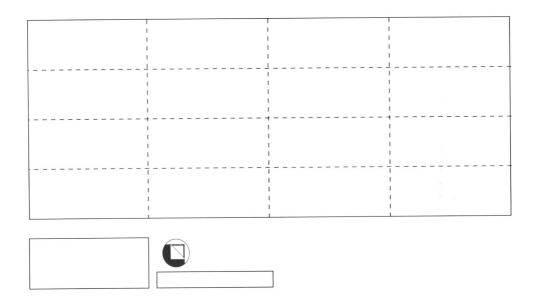

The Foreign Policy 2009 calendar

The Foreign Policy 2009 calendar was designed and produced to raise awareness and promote the work of the agency Foreign Policy Design Group. Its design was inspired by the name of the agency and several related concepts: politics, maps, world leaders, and so on. All of which were included in the promotional calendar, which consists of three elements: the calendar itself, the business card and the label that closes it. The map-calendar, when folded out, measures 50 × 20 inches.

Le calendrier Foreign Policy 2009 a été conçu et produit pour présenter et promouvoir le travail de l'agence Foreign Policy Design Group. Son design s'inspire du nom de l'agence (politique étrangère, en français) et de divers concepts associés : la politique, les cartes politiques, les chefs d'État de tous les pays, etc. Tout cela a été inclus dans le calendrier promotionnel qui se compose de trois éléments : le calendrier, l'étiquette qui le ferme et la carte de visite de l'agence. La carte-calendrier dépliée mesure 125 × 50 centimètres.

El calendario de Foreign Policy 2009 fue diseñado y producido para dar a conocer y promocionar el trabajo de la agencia Foreign Policy Design Group. Su diseño se inspiró en el nombre de la agencia («política exterior», en español) y en varios conceptos asociados: la política, los mapas, los líderes de todos los países del mundo… Todas estas ideas se incluyeron en el calendario promocional, que se compone de tres elementos: el calendario en sí, la tarjeta de presentación y la etiqueta que lo cierra. El mapa-calendario mide desplegado 125 × 50 centímetros.

Foreign Policy Design Group
Singapore _Singapour _Singapur (República de Singapur)
www.foreignpolicydesign.com ı affairs@foreignpolicyltd.com

161

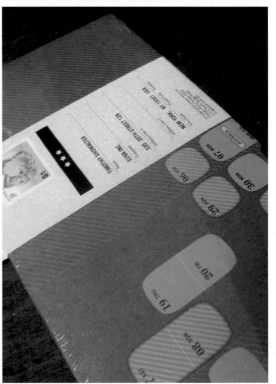

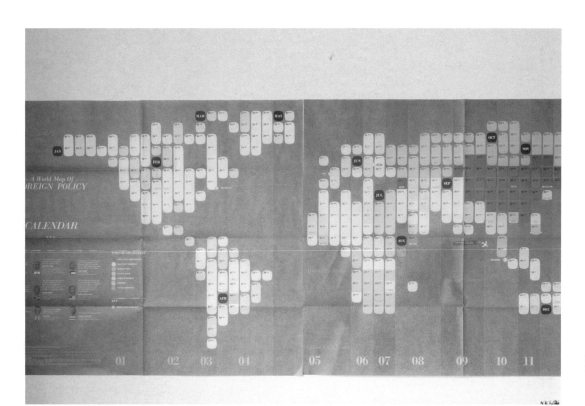

163

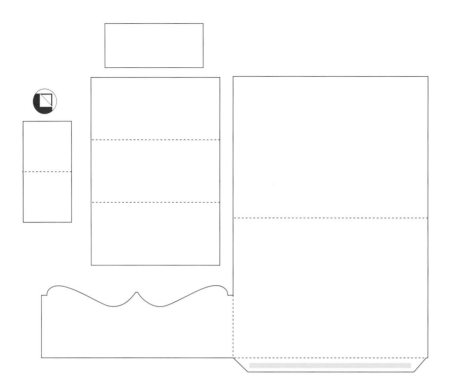

Harmonie Intérieure

Harmonie Intérieure is an online store created by Frédérique and Fabien Barral in which they sell their designs. To solve the common problem of limited budgets, they have used their extensive contacts book, which contains several printing houses. Instead of printing hundreds of promotional brochures for their shop, Frédérique and Fabien Barral have printed black folders that they have then cut with a specific outline, folded and sealed with a sticker. Inside there is a promotional brochure about their work, printed on a white background.

Harmonie Intérieure est une boutique en ligne créée par Frédérique et Fabien Barral pour vendre leurs designs. Pour résoudre le problème habituel du budget insuffisant, ils ont fait appel à leur agenda bien rempli de contacts, dans lequel figurent plusieurs imprimeurs. Au lieu d'imprimer des centaines de catalogues promotionnels de leur boutique, Frédérique et Fabien Barral ont simplement imprimé des chemises noires, qu'ils ont ensuite découpées selon un modèle spécifique, pliées en deux et fermées avec un autocollant. À l'intérieur, ils ont glissé une brochure d'information promotionnelle de leur travail, imprimée sur fond blanc.

Harmonie Intérieure es una tienda *online* creada por Frédérique y Fabien Barral en la que venden sus diseños. Para solucionar el habitual problema de los presupuestos escasos, han recurrido a su amplia agenda de contactos, en la que figuran varios impresores. En vez de imprimir centenares de catálogos promocionales de su tienda, Frédérique y Fabien han impreso únicamente carpetas de color negro que luego han cortado con un patrón específico, doblado y cerrado con una pegatina. En su interior han introducido un folleto informativo promocional sobre su trabajo, impreso sobre fondo blanco.

Fabien Barral
Auvergne, France_Auvergne, France_Auvergne (Francia)
www.fabienbarral.com ı ecrire@fabienbarral.com

Harmonie intérieure

Decorative Workshop

www.harmonie-interieure.com

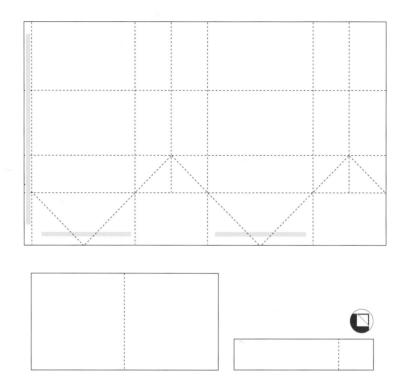

More Yellow

The traditional advertising agencies have "grown-up", in the words of the designer Fabien Barral and Jordan Mauriello, from More Yellow. And it is here, in the field of innovation, creating new marketing tactics, new advertising strategies, where this agency stands out. To promote its services, the creative team of More Yellow designed a series of promotional items inspired by the aesthetics of the fast food world, including a brochure, a new website and various stationery items that were sent to potential clients to show work of the studio.

Selon les designers Fabien Barral et Jordan Mauriello, de More Yellow, les agences de publicité traditionnelles ont « vieilli ». Et c'est là, dans le domaine de l'innovation, de la création de nouvelles tactiques de marketing, de nouvelles stratégies publicitaires, que l'agence se distingue. Afin de promouvoir leurs services, les créateurs de More Yellow ont conçu une série d'éléments promotionnels inspirés du monde des fast-foods : une brochure d'information, une nouvelle page Web et divers articles de bureau ont été envoyés aux clients potentiels pour leur présenter le travail du studio.

Las agencias de publicidad tradicionales han «envejecido», en palabras de los diseñadores Fabien Barral y Jordan Mauriello, de More Yellow. Y es ahí, en el terreno de la innovación, de la creación de nuevas tácticas de marketing, de nuevas estrategias publicitarias, donde la agencia destaca. Para promocionar sus servicios, los creativos de More Yellow diseñaron una serie de objetos promocionales inspirados en la estética del mundo de la comida rápida, entre ellos un folleto informativo, una nueva página web y varios elementos de papelería, que fueron enviados a potenciales clientes para mostrar el trabajo del estudio.

Fabien Barral, Jordan Mauriello
Mission Viejo, USA_Mission Viejo, États-Unis_Mission Viejo (Estados Unidos)
www.moreyellow.com ı ecrire@fabienbarral.com

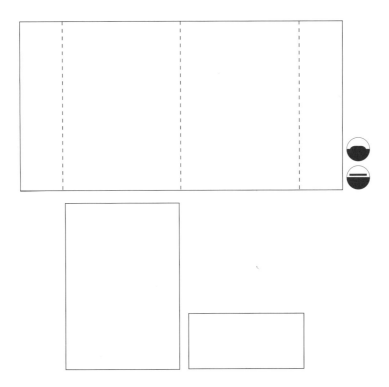

This Is Studio Portfolio

The promotional portfolio by This Is Studio is probably the most important design of all those that it has created in its history. Given that the portfolio represents the studio, it must be as perfect as possible. The result is a simple product, comfortable to hold and discreet and let's the work of the studio stand out. It is sent to potential customers, can be used during business meetings and functions as a project file. Individual projects are printed on DIN A4 paper. The cover is a double page with a pink interior and weighs 10 oz.. The promotional kit is completed with a DVD and business cards.

Le portfolio promotionnel de This Is Studio est probablement le design le plus important de tous ceux que ce studio a réalisé tout au long de son histoire. Il représente le studio et se doit donc d'être aussi parfait que possible. Le portfolio est simple, agréable au toucher et discret ; il est conçu de façon à laisser la vedette aux travaux du studio. Il est envoyé aux clients potentiels, est utilisé pour les réunions de travail et fait office d'archives des projets. La couverture est une feuille double de 280 grammes, rose à l'intérieur. Chaque projet est imprimé individuellement sur une feuille au format A4. Un DVD et des cartes de visite viennent compléter le kit promotionnel.

El portafolio promocional de This Is Studio es, posiblemente, el trabajo más importante de todos cuantos ha realizado este estudio de diseño a lo largo de su historia. Dado que representa al estudio, debe ser lo más perfecto posible. El resultado es un portafolio sencillo, agradable al tacto y discreto, pues cede el protagonismo a los trabajos. Se envía a posibles clientes, es usado durante las reuniones de trabajo y funciona como archivo de proyectos. La portada es una doble página de interior rosado y gramaje de 280 gramos, y los proyectos individuales se imprimen en papel DIN A4. El kit promocional se completa con un DVD y tarjetas de visita.

This Is Studio
London, UK_Londres, Royaume-Uni _Londres (Reino Unido)
www.thisisstudio.com ı info@thisisstudio.com

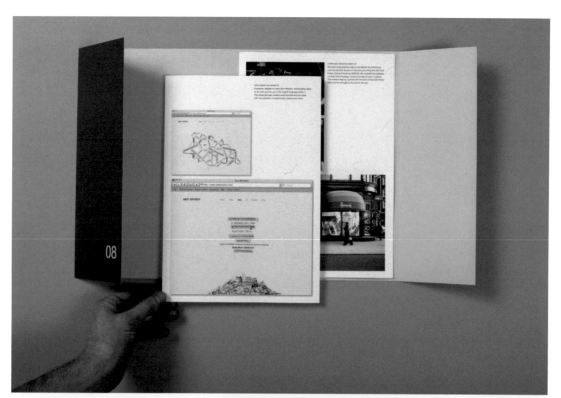

Press kits for fashion and beauty brands are usually the most carefully presented from a graphic design point of view because apart from the standard use, the actual kit needs to become an object of desire, as does the product or service that it is promoting. The fashion and beauty market is a highly competitive market in which innovation is the order of the day and where standing out from the rest often is a virtually impossible task. Fashion and beauty press kits are those that most use unconventional printing techniques and those that tend to opt for unconventional materials such as vinyl, tissue paper or simply different thicknesses and qualities of paper. Fashion and beauty press kits also tend to be aimed at a predominantly female audience, which lets you view graphic solutions designed specifically for women.

Les kits de presse des marques de mode et de beauté sont en général les plus soignés en matière de design graphique, puisque à leur fonction habituelle s'ajoute la nécessité d'en faire des objets de désir à part entière, au même titre que le produit ou service dont ils font la promotion. De plus, la mode et la beauté représentent un marché hautement compétitif où les nouveautés sont à l'ordre du jour et où faire la différence devient très souvent une tâche quasiment impossible. Pour cette raison, les kits de presse de mode et de beauté sont ceux pour lesquels on a le plus souvent recours aux techniques d'impression non conventionnelles, de même que l'on opte en général pour des matériaux non conventionnels, comme le vinyle, le papier de soie ou, simplement, des papiers de différentes épaisseurs, textures et qualités. Un autre point intéressant concernant ces kits de presse est qu'ils sont en général destinés à un public majoritairement féminin, ce qui permet d'opter pour des solutions graphiques pensées exclusivement pour les femmes.

Los kits de prensa de las marcas de moda y belleza suelen ser los más cuidados desde el punto de vista de su diseño gráfico, pues a su función habitual debe sumar la necesidad de convertirse en un objeto de deseo por sí mismos, junto con el producto o el servicio que promocionan. Los mercados de la moda y la belleza son, además, altamente competitivos, las novedades están a la orden del día, y destacar se convierte en no pocas ocasiones en una tarea casi imposible. Los kits de estos sectores son por ello los que más uso hacen de las técnicas de impresión no convencionales y aquellos en los que se suele optar por materiales alternativos, como el vinilo, el papel de seda o papeles de diferentes grosores, texturas y calidades. Otro punto interesante de estos kits de prensa es que suelen estar destinados a un público mayoritariamente femenino, lo que permite ver soluciones gráficas pensadas a propósito para ellas.

Fashion and beauty

Mode et beauté

Moda y belleza

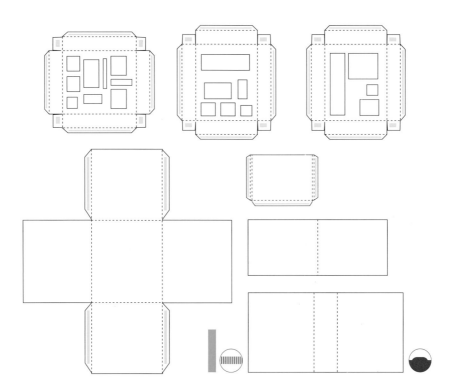

Beauty Bank

Faced with the challenge of presenting a new collection of beauty brands by Beauty Bank into the global market, the BorsaWallace designers opted to divide the brands into segments, with the aim of enhancing their individual image. The three promotional portfolios are presented in a single box, but are differentiated by color. The matte black is associated with the brand Flirt, pale blue represents the classic American Beauty collection, while pure white is the color chosen for hypo-allergenic Good Skin products. Each of the portfolios includes a sample of products, and an interior pocket to hold the commercial information. All three portfolios have a magnetic closure.

Les designers de BorsaWallace ont relevé le défi de présenter une nouvelle collection de produits de beauté de Beauty Bank sur le marché mondial en choisissant de segmenter les marques afin de renforcer leur image personnelle. Les trois portfolios promotionnels sont présentés dans la même boîte mais se différencient par leur couleur. Le noir mat est associé à la marque Flirt, le bleu pâle représente la collection de style classique American Beauty, et le blanc pur fait référence aux produits hypoallergéniques de Good Skin. Chacun des portfolios comporte un échantillon des produits de la marque, ainsi qu'une poche intérieure avec les dossiers contenant les informations, et dispose d'une fermeture magnétique.

Enfrentados al reto de presentar una nueva colección de marcas de belleza de Beauty Bank en el mercado global, los diseñadores de BorsaWallace optaron por la segmentación de dichas marcas con el objetivo de reforzar su imagen individual. Los tres muestrarios promocionales se presentan en una caja única, pero se diferencian por su color. El negro mate se asocia a la marca Flirt, el azul pálido representa la colección de estilo clásico American Beauty, mientras que el blanco puro es el color escogido para los productos hipoalergénicos de Good Skin. Cada portafolio, que cuenta con un cierre magnético, contiene una muestra de los productos de la marca, y en un bolsillo interior están los dosieres con información comercial.

Frank Borsa, Jeffrey M. Wallace/BorsaWallace
New York, USA_New York, États-Unis_Nueva York (Estados Unidos)
www.borsawallace.com ɪ info@borsawallace.com

179

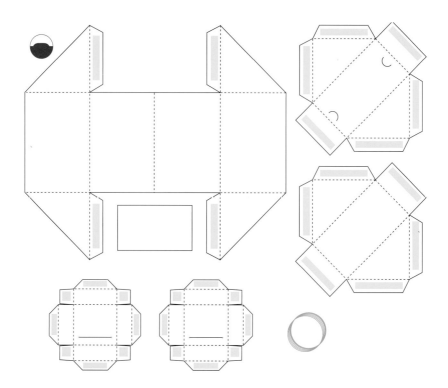

Pantene Texturize

How do you invite the press and media to "play" with, and report on, the new Pantene Texture beauty products collection? With a press kit that, when opened, "launches" by surprise a slinky, the traditional child's toy made from a coiled wire capable of descending stairs. Inside the box, you can find a press kit on the product that leads reporters to a micro-website with tips and techniques used by some of the best stylists and experts from the world of fashion and beauty.

Comment inviter la presse et les médias à « jouer » avec la nouvelle collection de produits de beauté Pantene Texturize et à en informer le grand public ? Grâce au kit de presse, qui, en s'ouvrant, « lance » par surprise un *slinky*, ce jouet traditionnel pour enfant, en forme de ressort, qui est capable de descendre des escaliers une fois son mouvement amorcé. À l'intérieur de la boîte, on trouve également un dossier de presse sur le produit qui renvoie les journalistes à une micro-page Web offrant des conseils et des techniques utilisées par certains des meilleurs stylistes et experts du monde de la mode et de la beauté.

¿Cómo invitar a la prensa y los medios de comunicación a jugar y a informar sobre la nueva colección de productos de belleza Pantene Texturize? Con un kit de prensa que, al abrirse, «lanza» por sorpresa un *slinky*, el tradicional juguete para niños que consiste en un alambre enrollado capaz de bajar escaleras con un leve impulso. En el interior de la caja se puede encontrar también un dosier de prensa sobre el producto, que conduce a los periodistas a una micropágina web con consejos y técnicas utilizadas por algunos de los mejores estilistas y expertos del mundo de la moda y la belleza.

Jason Davis, Jeannine Kennedy/BorsaWallace
New York, USA_New York, États-Unis_Nueva York (Estados Unidos)
www.borsawallace.com ı info@borsawallace.com

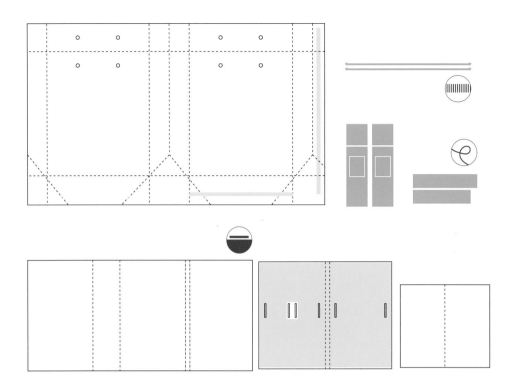

Sebastian Professional

For the relaunch of the Sebastian Professional beauty brand, the Borsa-Wallace studio has used the phrase "What's next" as a starting point to design all of the promotional items. The Sebastian Professional press kit is flexible enough to hold a sample of products of different sizes with a stretchy rubber band that holds them in place. A second important design element is the use of contrast, as demonstrated by the choice of a strict color palette based almost exclusively in black and white, and the combination of matte and shiny textures in a single element.

Pour le design de tous les éléments promotionnels visant à relancer la marque de beauté Sebastian Professional, le studio BorsaWallace a pris la phrase « What's next » (et après ?) comme point de départ. Le kit de presse de Sebastian Professional est suffisamment modulable pour contenir un échantillon de produits de différentes tailles, grâce à la souplesse de l'élastique qui les retient. L'utilisation des contrastes est un autre élément du design qui ressort particulièrement, comme le montrent le choix d'une palette de couleurs stricte, exclusivement à base de noir et de blanc, et le mélange de textures mates et brillantes pour un même élément.

Para el relanzamiento de la marca de belleza Sebastian Professional, el estudio BorsaWallace ha partido de la frase *What's next* («¿qué será lo próximo?») para el diseño de todos los elementos promocionales. El kit de prensa de Sebastian Professional es lo suficientemente flexible como para albergar una muestra de productos de distintos tamaños de la marca gracias a la goma elástica que los sujeta. Un segundo elemento destacado del diseño es el uso de contrastes, como demuestra la elección de una estricta paleta de colores, basada casi exclusivamente en el blanco y el negro, y la combinación de texturas mates y brillantes en un mismo elemento.

Cecilia Molina, Tae Eun Kim, Cristina Ortega/BorsaWallace
New York, USA_New York, États-Unis_Nueva York (Estados Unidos)
www.borsawallace.com ı info@borsawallace.com

Marcello

After the victory of Nicolas Sarkozy in the French elections, the country, in the words of designer Cléo Charuet, entered a bling-bling phase for all that is flamboyant and conspicuous. Hence, the idea arose for using these three promotional posters for Cartier International. Initially, the posters seem to be a large format magazine. As they are unfolded, the posters grow in size. The almost life-size bags are printed on the non-glossy side, while the other side is a bright golden color, on which the Cartier logo has been printed.

Après la victoire de Nicolas Sarkozy aux élections présidentielles, et pour reprendre les mots de la designer Cléo Charuet, la France est entrée dans une phase *bling-bling*, un style très tape-à-l'œil et ostentatoire. C'est de là qu'est née l'idée de réaliser ces trois affiches promotionnelles pour Cartier International. À première vue, elles ressemblent à un magazine grand format. Et à mesure qu'elles se déplient, les affiches sont de plus en plus grandes. Les sacs sont montrés presque en taille réelle sur la face mate du papier alors que l'autre face est entièrement dorée, avec le logo Cartier imprimé dessus.

Tras la victoria de Nicolas Sarkozy en las elecciones francesas, el país, en palabras del diseñador Cléo Charuet, entró en una fase de *bling bling*, de ostentación y de gusto por lo llamativo. De ahí surgió la idea de la realización de estos tres carteles promocionales para Cartier International. Los carteles parecen a primera vista una revista de gran formato. A medida que se despliegan, los pósteres son cada vez más y más grandes. Los bolsos impresos en él se muestran casi a tamaño natural en la cara no satinada del papel, mientras que en la cara opuesta, de color dorado brillante, se ha impreso el logotipo de Cartier.

Cléo Charuet/Cleoburo
Paris, France_Paris, France_París (Francia)
cleoburo.com ı info@cleoburo.com

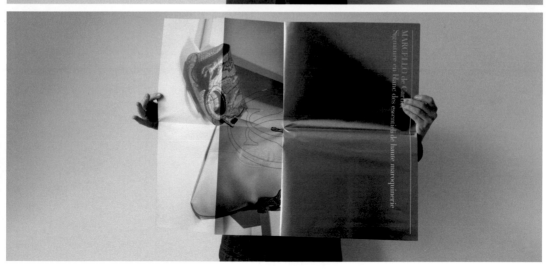

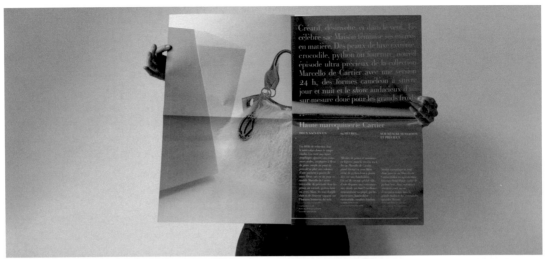

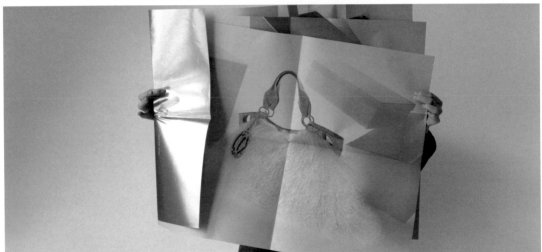

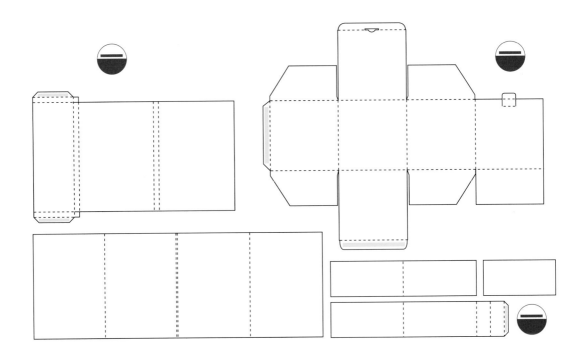

L'Oréal Série Expert

This is the promotional and sales kit designed by Ryan Crouchman for the high quality product line L'Oreal Série Expert. The bright stripes of various colors that can be seen in the images reflect the diverse palette of products in the range, while they also add a playful element to the design, based almost entirely on white to convey a sense of purity and accuracy. Photographs of various models along with the stripes are virtually the only source of color in the design.

Ce kit promotionnel et de ventes a été réalisé par Ryan Crouchman pour la gamme de produits de haute qualité Série Expert de la marque de beauté L'Oréal. Les bandes brillantes de plusieurs couleurs que l'on peut voir sur l'image reflètent le vaste éventail de couleurs proposé par les produits de la gamme, tout en ajoutant un aspect ludique au design qui est presque entièrement conçu à partir de la couleur blanche pour transmettre une impression de pureté et de précision. Les photos des différents mannequins sont presque les seuls éléments en couleurs présents dans le design, hormis les bandes brillantes.

Éste es el kit promocional y de ventas realizado por Ryan Crouchman para la línea de productos de alta calidad Série Expert de la marca de belleza L'Oréal. Las franjas brillantes de varios colores que pueden verse en las imágenes reflejan la variada paleta de colores de los productos de la gama y al mismo tiempo que añaden un punto divertido al diseño, basado casi por completo en el color blanco para transmitir una sensación de pureza y precisión. Las fotografías de varias modelos son prácticamente el único motivo de color presente en el diseño, aparte de las mencionadas franjas.

Ryan Crouchman
Montreal, Canada_Montréal, Canada_Montreal (Canadá)
www.ryancrouchman.com ı ryan@ryancrouchman.com

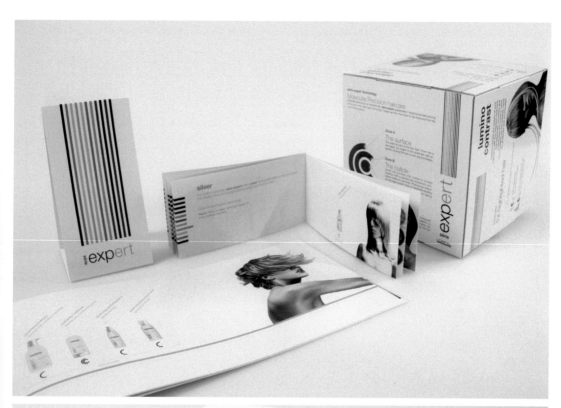

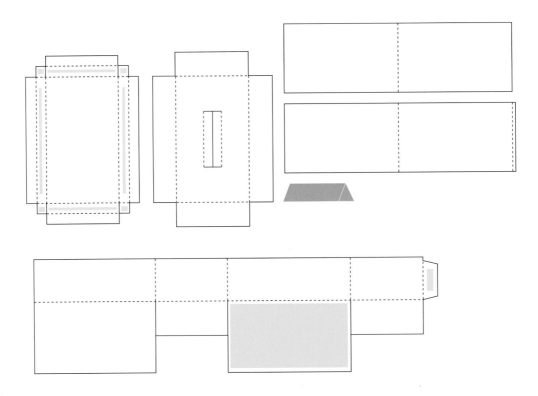

L'Oréal promotional gift and L'Oréal lookbook

The prism that can be seen on the right is one of the promotional gifts given to customers who visit any of the L'Oréal stores. The prism symbolizes and reflects L'Oréal's vast knowledge of the science of color throughout its history as one of the leading brands in the beauty industry. The following pages feature images designed by Ryan Crouchman for L'Oréal. The design of the promotional book was based on two of the elements L'Oréal is most interested in: color and structure.

Le prisme ci-contre est l'un des cadeaux promotionnels offerts à tout client passant la porte d'un établissement L'Oréal. Il symbolise et reflète l'expertise que L'Oréal a acquise, au cours de son histoire, dans la science de la couleur et qui en fait aujourd'hui l'une des marques leader du secteur de la beauté. Dans les pages suivantes, vous pourrez retrouver des images du *lookbook* conçu par Ryan Crouchman pour L'Oréal. Le design du livre promotionnel s'est inspiré de deux des éléments les plus importants pour L'Oréal : la couleur et la structure.

El prisma que puede verse a la derecha es uno de los regalos promocionales que se entrega a los clientes que acuden a alguno de los locales L'Oréal. El prisma simboliza el amplio conocimiento de la ciencia del color atesorado por L'Oréal a lo largo de su historia como una de las marcas punteras en el sector de la belleza. En las páginas siguientes pueden verse imágenes del *lookbook* diseñado por Ryan Crouchman para L'Oréal. El diseño del libro promocional se basó en dos de los elementos en los que L'Oréal pone un mayor interés: el color y la estructura.

Ryan Crouchman
Montreal, Canada_Montréal, Canada_Montreal (Canadá)
www.ryancrouchman.com ı ryan@ryancrouchman.com

195

Jeffrey M. Wallace

How should the perfect promotional kit be?
The perfect promotional kit should instantly communicate the product story or theme.

What's (or what should be) its objective?
Our main objective is, and has always been, to put something in front of the recipient that is intriguing enough to get them to open it. Once you've passed that hurdle, it's much easier to walk them through the rest of the story.

What's the main difficulty when designing a promotional kit?
The main difficulty is capturing a product's point of difference with a clear and simple message. If the recipient has to read too much or think too hard about what's in front of them, it's not an effective promotional delivery.

And what's the easiest thing about it?
No two projects are the same so it's always difficult to arrive at a solution. However, a good product with a great

Comment devrait être le kit promotionnel parfait ?
Le kit promotionnel parfait devrait communiquer instantanément l'histoire ou le thème du produit.

Quel est (ou quel devrait être) son objectif ?
Notre principal objectif est, et a toujours été, de mettre quelque chose devant le destinataire qui l'intrigue assez pour qu'il l'ouvre. Une fois cet obstacle franchi, le reste est nettement plus simple.

Quelle est la principale difficulté lors de la conception d'un kit promotionnel ?
La principale difficulté est de saisir l'aspect différent d'un produit avec un message clair et simple. Si le destinataire doit trop lire ou trop penser sur ce qui se trouve devant lui, ce n'est pas un travail promotionnel efficace.

Et qu'est-ce qui est le plus facile ?
Il n'y a pas deux projets pareilles et il est toujours difficile d'arriver à une solution. Cependant, un bon produit avec un aspect différent rend le processus plus facile.

¿Cómo debería ser el kit promocional perfecto?
El kit promocional perfecto debería comunicar al instante la historia del producto o el tema.

¿Cuál es (o cuál debería ser) su objetivo?
Nuestro objetivo es, y siempre ha sido, poner delante del receptor algo que lo intrigue lo suficiente como para querer abrirlo. Una vez que has franqueado ese obstáculo, el resto es mucho más sencillo.

¿Cuál es la principal dificultad cuando se diseña un kit promocional?
La principal dificultad es plasmar el rasgo distintivo del producto en un mensaje claro y simple. Si el receptor tiene que leer mucho o pensar demasiado sobre lo que tiene enfrente, la promoción no es efectiva.

¿Y qué parte del proceso de diseño es la más fácil?
No hay dos proyectos iguales, por lo que siempre es complicado alcanzar una solución. No obstante, un buen producto, con personalidad, facilita el proceso.

Principal of BorsaWallace
New York, USA
www.borsawallace.com
swipeology.blogspot.com
jwallace@borsawallace.com
Projects on pages 30, 38, 44, 46, 178, 180 and 182

Directeur de BorsaWallace
New York, États-Unis
www.borsawallace.com
swipeology.blogspot.com
jwallace@borsawallace.com
Projets sur les pages 30, 38, 44, 46, 178, 180 et 182

Director de BorsaWallace
Nueva York (Estados Unidos)
www.borsawallace.com
swipeology.blogspot.com
jwallace@borsawallace.com
Proyectos en las páginas 30, 38, 44, 46, 178, 180 y 182

point of difference really makes the process easier.

What do you most enjoy about designing a promotional kit?
Conceptualizing the kit and refining the idea is the best part of the design process. It's amazing how many different ideas can be born out of a single word or solid angle.

In your opinion, what kind of clients/ brands should make use of promotional or press kits?
The promotional kit is just one part of the mix in a marketing or public relations plan. Any product or brand that has a clear story to tell (and needs a boost in exposure) should make use of promotional press kits. The promotional or press kit is designed to be experiential. Any product that you want your audience to sample could make use of this type of vehicle.

How do you check or test the effectiveness of your work and designs, and more specifically your press kits? Do you receive any kind of feedback from the client or the consumer?

Qu'est-ce qui vous plait le plus dans la conception d'un kit promotionnel ?
La conceptualisation du kit et le perfectionnement de l'idée sont les meilleures phases du design. Il est étonnant de voir combien d'idées différentes peuvent provenir d'un seul mot ou d'un angle solide.

À votre avis, quel genre de clients/ marques devraient utiliser les kits promotionnels ou de presse ?
Le kit promotionnel est une partie d'un tout dans un projet de marketing ou de relations publiques. Tout produit ou marque qui a une histoire claire à raconter (et a besoin d'un coup de pouce pour sa diffusion) devrait utiliser des kits promotionnels ou de presse. Ils sont conçus pour être expérimentaux. Tout produit que vous souhaitez que votre public échantillonne pourrait utiliser ce type de support.

Comment vérifiez-vous l'efficacité de votre travail et de vos designs et, plus précisément, de vos kits de presse ? Recevez-vous un feedback de la part du client ou du consommateur ?
Étant donné que la plupart de notre travail s'adresse à la presse, il est facile de voir le

¿Con qué disfrutas más cuando diseñas un kit promocional?
Para mí, la mejor parte del diseño es el momento de buscar el concepto del kit y refinar la idea. Es impresionante la variedad de ideas que pueden surgir de una sola palabra o un punto de vista sólido.

Para ti, ¿qué tipo de clientes/marcas deberían utilizar kits promocionales o carpetas de prensa?
El kit promocional es una parte de un conjunto en un plan de *marketing* o de relaciones públicas. Cualquier producto o marca que tenga una historia clara que contar (y que necesite un empujón en su difusión) debería utilizar kits promocionales. Los kits promocionales o de prensa se diseñan para ser experimentales. Cualquier producto que quieras que pruebe tu público objetivo puede utilizar este tipo de medio.

¿Cómo compruebas o mides la efectividad de un trabajo o un diseño y, especialmente, de un kit de prensa? ¿Recibes *feedback* de los clientes o los consumidores?
Como la mayoría de nuestros trabajos

Since the majority of our work has been for press initiatives, it's easy to see the success of the delivery. If the work makes it into national magazines, broadcast shows or blogs... our work has been effective. On a broader level, what we create is just one component of an overall campaign that uses various disciplines to promote a product or brand, so effectiveness is ultimately measured by consumer behavior and how well a product performs.

What are your favorite materials for a promotional kit? Why?
Our use of materials changes often and depends on the product that we're promoting. Whether it's metal, leather and lacquer for Sebastian or lenticulars, lucite dowels and color-tinted acetates for Olay ProX, we are always seeking out materials that will help communicate the product story and align with the brand's image.

Do you need to "like" the product you're helping to promote to do a good job with it? Be sincere.
It's not necessary to "like" the product

succès de la promotion. Si le travail arrive dans des magazines nationaux, des spectacles diffusés ou des blogs... notre travail a été efficace. À un niveau plus large, ce que nous créons est juste un composant d'une campagne globale, qui utilise plusieurs disciplines pour promouvoir un produit ou une marque, et son efficacité se mesure selon le comportement des consommateurs et le rendement d'un produit.

Quels sont vos matériaux favoris pour un kit promotionnel ? Pourquoi ?
Nous changeons souvent de matériaux : tout dépend du produit dont nous faisons la promotion. Aussi bien le métal, le cuir et la laque de Sebastian que des lenticulaires, des chevilles en lucite et des acétates de couleur pour Olay ProX, nous sommes toujours à la recherche de matériaux qui nous aideront à communiquer l'histoire du produit et s'aligneront sur l'image de la marque.

Pour faire un bon travail, devez-vous « aimer » le produit dont vous assurez en partie la promotion ? Répondez sincèrement.
Il n'est pas nécessaire d' « aimer » le pro-

los hemos realizado para la prensa, es fácil ver el éxito de la promoción. Si el trabajo llega a tiendas de todo el país, programas, *blogs*... nuestro trabajo ha sido efectivo. En un nivel más amplio, lo que creamos es tan sólo un componente de una campaña general que se sirve de varias disciplinas para promocionar un producto o una marca, por lo que la efectividad se mide por el comportamiento del cliente y por el rendimiento del producto.

¿Cuáles son tus materiales favoritos para un kit promocional? ¿Por qué?
Solemos cambiar bastante de materiales: todo depende del producto que estemos promocionando. Ya sea metal, cuero, laca para Sebastian o imágenes tridimensionales, pasadores de Lucite o acetatos teñidos para Olay ProX, siempre estamos buscando materiales que nos ayuden a comunicar la historia del producto y asociarlos con la imagen de la marca.

¿Necesitas que te guste el producto que estás promocionando para hacer una buena promoción? Sé sincero.
No es necesario que nos «guste» el pro-

that we're promoting, but it is necessary to understand the product and its point of difference in the marketplace. When we're hired to work on a product, we really take the time to learn and understand that product category. We spend endless hours researching the brand and its competition so that we are able to elevate the new product's point of difference.

What's the difference between designing a promotional kit and designing any other kind of work?
The big difference between the design of a promotional kit and other work is the team behind the work. Strong conceptual thinking, sourcing and tight project management skills all come into play with each kit we produce.

What's the best promotional work you've ever seen, and what product was it related to? Why do you like it? Did you buy the product or did you hire the service just because of its promotional work?
Anything designed by Apple. They have way of communicating simply, clearly and effectively that we should all aspire to.

duit dont nous faisons la promotion, mais il est nécessaire de comprendre le produit et saisir sa différence par rapport aux auyres produits du marché. Lorsque promouvoir un produit, nous prenons le temps d'apprendre et de comprendre la catégorie du produit. Nous passons des heures à faire des recherches sur la marque et sa concurrence afin de pouvoir mettre en avant l'aspect différent du nouveau produit.

Quelle différence y-a-t-il entre la conception d'un kit promotionnel et celle d'un autre genre de travail ?
La grande différence entre le design d'un kit promotionnel et celui d'un autre travail réside dans l'équipe de travail. Tous les kits que nous réalisons requièrent une bonne conception, une gestion des ressources et savoir tirer profit de notre potentiel.

Quel est le meilleur travail promotionnel que vous ayez vu et de quel produit s'agit-il ? Pourquoi vous a-t-il ? Avez-vous acheté le produit ou loué le service juste pour son travail promotionnel ?
Tout ce qui est conçu par Apple. Il ont une manière de communiquer simple,

ducto que estamos promocionando, pero hace falta entenderlo y entender también sus diferencias respecto al resto de productos del mercado. Cuando nos encargan la promoción de un producto, nos tomamos un tiempo para conocer y entender la categoría del producto. Pasamos horas y horas documentándonos sobre la marca y su competencia para poder resaltar las peculiaridades del nuevo producto.

¿Cuál es la diferencia entre diseñar un kit promocional y diseñar otro tipo de trabajo?
La mayor diferencia entre diseñar un kit promocional y otro trabajo es el equipo que se encuentra detrás del trabajo: todos y cada uno de los kits que diseñamos requieren un profundo pensamiento conceptual, gestionar los recursos y explotar todo nuestro potencial.

¿Cuál es el mejor trabajo de promoción que has visto? ¿Qué promocionaba? ¿Por qué te gustó? ¿Compraste el producto o contrataste el servicio sólo por el trabajo promocional?
Cualquier producto diseñado por Apple.

What weight and importance do you give to the briefing of the client, when it doesn't fit your ideas? How do you match these two opposite views?
As mentioned before, it's the team partnership that helps to create solid ideas. Without a clear briefing from the client, the work can be extremely difficult so it's often our job to lead the thinking and give the client guidance to achieve their objective.

Name the items, personal objects and tools you absolutely could not work without.
My iPhone, my Nikon D80 camera, my red Caran d'Ache mechanical pencil, L'auteur grid pads (by Vernacular Press), black Pilot Razor Point II, my Schaedler precision rule, my orange Erik Magnussen carafe of water and, of course, daylight.

Describe your average working day.
Up at 5 am. Run or hit the gym. At the office by 9 am. Meetings, design, meetings, design review, meetings. Home by 7 pm. Cook dinner. Catch up on *Mad Men*, *Weeds* or *Top Chef*. In bed by 10:30 pm. And start again the next day.

claire et efficace, à laquelle nous devrions tous aspirer.

Quelle importance donnez-vous au briefing du client lorsqu'il ne partage pas vos idées ? Comment conciliez-vous les points de vue différents ?
Comme j'ai déjà mentionné, c'est le travail en équipe qui permet d'obtenir des idées fortes. Sans un briefing clair du client, le travail peut être extrêmement difficile et c'est donc souvent notre rôle d'orienter et de guider le client pour atteindre son objectif.

Quels sont les éléments, les objets personnels et les outils dont vous ne pourriez absolument pas vous passer pour travailler ?
Mon iPhone, mon appareil photo Nikon D80, mon porte-mine rouge Caran d'Ache, des blocs quadrillés L'auteur (de Vernacular Press), un Pilot Razor Point II noir, ma règle de précision Schaedler, ma carafe d'eau orange Erik Magnussen et, bien sûr, la lumière du jour.

Décrivez-nous votre journée de travail.
Je me lève à 5h. Je cours ou je fais de la

Su forma de comunicar es sencilla, clara y efectiva, que es a lo que nosotros deberíamos aspirar también.

¿Qué peso y qué importancia das al *briefing* del cliente cuando no piensa lo mismo que tú? ¿Cómo consigues encontrar un punto medio para dos puntos de vista diferentes?
Tal y como comenté antes, las ideas sólidas se consiguen trabajando en equipo. Sin unas instrucciones claras del cliente, el trabajo puede ser extremadamente complicado, por lo que, a veces, nuestra labor también es orientar las propuestas y guiar al cliente para que alcance su objetivo.

Nombra las cosas, los objetos personales y las herramientas sin las que te sería imposible trabajar.
Mi iPhone, mi cámara Nikon D80, mi portaminas rojo Caran d'Ache, blocs con cuadrículas de L'auteur (de Vernacular Press), un Pilot Razor Point II negro, mi regla de precisión Schaedler, mi jarra de agua naranja Erik Magnussen y, por supuesto, la luz del día.

Describe the perfect client.
The perfect client is smart and has a clear idea of their objectives.

gym. Je suis au bureau à 9h. Réunions, design, réunions, revue de design, réunions. Je rentre chez moi à 19h. Je prépare le dîner. Je regarde *Mad Men, Weeds* ou *Top Chef*. Je me couche à 22h30. Et je recommence le lendemain.

Décrivez le client parfait.
Le client parfait est intelligent et a une idée claire de ses objectifs.

Describe un día de trabajo normal.
Me levanto a las cinco de la madrugada. Voy a correr o al gimnasio. En la oficina a las nueve. Reuniones, diseños, reuniones, revisiones de diseños, reuniones. En casa a las siete. Preparo la cena. Veo *Mad Men*, *Weeds* o *Top Chef*. En la cama a las diez y media. Y vuelta a empezar al día siguiente.

Describe al cliente perfecto.
El cliente perfecto es inteligente y tiene una idea clara de sus objetivos.

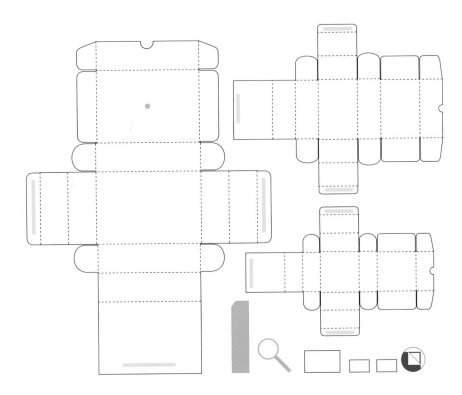

Rexona Invisible Ice: The Invisible Game

The Invisible Game by Rexona Invisible Ice tries to set itself apart from the conventional press kit which only seeks to publicize a new product. So, it offers the recipient a challenge, inviting them to test in situ the effectiveness of the new white anti-stain formula. Along with the new deodorant Rexona Invisible Ice there is a black T-shirt and a magnifying glass to carry out the demanding quality test and to ensure that there is no trace of stains. The kit is inspired by Rexona Invisible Ice campaign starring the detective Stripes in San Francisco in the 1970s.

L'Invisible Game de Rexona Invisible Ice prétend s'éloigner du kit de presse conventionnel dont l'unique but est de faire connaître un nouveau produit. Pour cela, il lance un défi au destinataire du kit, en l'invitant à tester in situ l'efficacité de la nouvelle formule anti-traces blanches. Le nouveau déodorant Rexona Invisible Ice est accompagné d'un tee-shirt noir et d'une loupe permettant d'effectuer un minutieux test de qualité en vérifiant qu'aucun indice (traces blanches) n'a été laissé. Le kit s'inspire de la campagne de Rexona Invisible Ice où l'on retrouve le détective Stripes à San Francisco dans les années 1970.

El Invisible Game de Rexona Invisible Ice busca alejarse del convencional kit de prensa con el que sólo se busca dar a conocer un nuevo producto. Para ello, ofrece un reto al receptor del kit, invitándole a probar in situ la efectividad de la nueva fórmula antimanchas blancas. Con el nuevo desodorante Invisible Ice se adjunta una camiseta negra y una lupa con la que realizar un exigente test de calidad, comprobando así que no existen «pruebas del delito» (manchas). El kit se inspira en la campaña de Rexona Invisible Ice protagonizada por el detective Stripes en el San Francisco de los años setenta del siglo pasado.

Tinkle Consultants
Barcelona, Spain_Barcelone, Espagne_Barcelona (España)
www.tinkle.es ı infobcn@tinkle.es

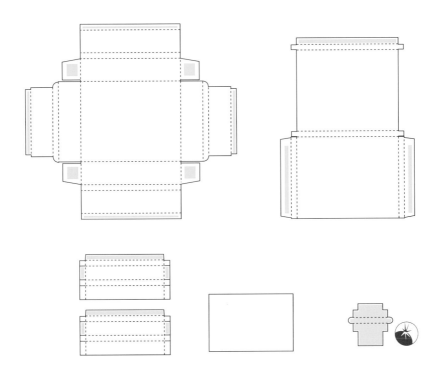

Decade Pittsburgh press kit

The purpose of this project was to create an object representing the spirit and philosophy of the clothing store Decade Pittsburgh (decadepittsburgh. com). The store has been made from recycled materials (the roof is made using old doors), it evokes the DIY spirit of rock'n'roll in the 60s and 70s. The Decade press kit has been produced with recycled pallets, old hinges, and has been hand painted. Each of the kits has been handmade and is associated with a rock'n'roll star whose picture appears on the T-shirt found inside the box.

Ce projet avait pour but de créer un objet représentant l'esprit et la philosophie de la boutique de vêtements Decade Pittsburgh (decadepittsburgh. com). Construite à partir de matériaux recyclés, comme les vieilles portes utilisées pour le toit, la boutique rappelle l'esprit DIY (do it yourself soit « faites-le vous-même ») du rock'n'roll des années 1960 et 1970. Le kit de presse de Decade a été réalisé à partir de palettes recyclées et d'anciennes charnières et a été peint à la main. Chacun de ces kits est associé à une star du rock'n'roll qui figure sur le tee-shirt se trouvant à l'intérieur de la boîte.

La finalidad de este proyecto era crear un objeto que representara el espíritu y la filosofía del establecimiento de ropa Decade Pittsburgh (decadepittsburgh.com). La tienda, construida con materiales reciclados –como se puede ver en el techo, para el que se utilizaron puertas viejas–, evoca el espíritu DIY (do it yourself, o «hazlo tú mismo») del rock de los años sesenta y setenta. El kit de prensa de Decade, elaborado a partir de palés reciclados y bisagras antiguas, se ha realizado y se ha pintado a mano. Cada uno se asocia a una estrella del rock, cuya imagen aparece en la camiseta que se encuentra en el interior de la caja.

Graphic Nutrition Collective
Pittsburgh, USA_Pittsburgh, États-Unis_Pittsburgh (Estados Unidos)
http://graphicnutritioncollective.tumblr.com ı libbym1@comcast.net

207

EXCLUSIVELY DECADE
GRAND OPENING WEEK

FRIDAY JUNE 22 – FRIDAY JUNE 29

COME IN MEET STEVE (DECADE'S OWNER) AND GET CLOTHED WITH 10% OFF YOUR PURCHASE DURING THE GRAND OPENING WEEK

FOR MORE INFORMATION VISIT DECADE AT
www.Myspace.com/decadepittsburgh

★ Decade carries a variety of clothing lines, such as Dim Mak, Flux, Jet, FREEGUMS, Monument, Bogus, Worn Free, Kasil Jeans, and Punkster.

STORE HOURS:
TUESDAY THRU SATURDAY
NOON-9 PM AND SUNDAY
ONE-6 PM

Decade is located at
1407 East Carson St. in the Southside

decade
pittsburgh

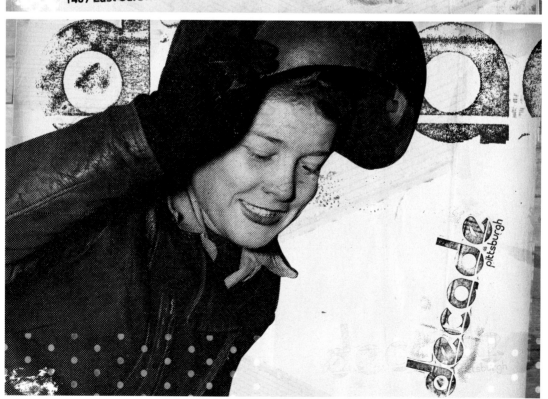

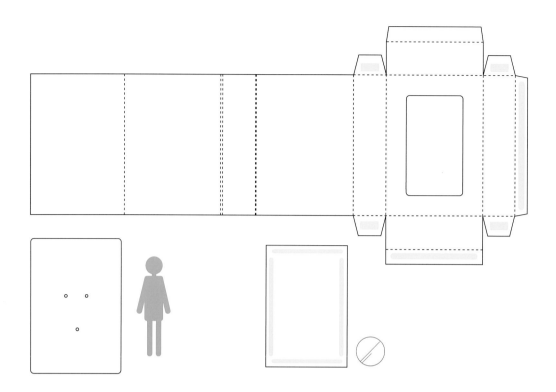

Industry spring campaign

The campaign designed by the studio Curse of the Multiples for the Industry fashion label plays with the idea of followers of fashion as "dolls" that can be dressed up. The inspiration came from the collection of figures known as toyz. First, the boxes for the figure were designed, later the models were photographed and finally the two images were combined. This press kit includes a brief description of the characters. The complete kit also includes the label's catalog and several more items of stationery, all designed from very simple elements.

La campagne conçue par le studio Curse of the Multiples pour la marque de mode Industry joue sur l'idée que les adeptes du monde de la mode sont comme des « poupées » à habiller. Cette idée trouve son inspiration dans les figurines de collection que l'on appelle « toyz ». Les boîtes pour les « figurines » ont d'abord été conçues, puis les mannequins ont été photographiés et les deux images ont ensuite été combinées. Le kit de presse comporte une petite description de chaque personnage. Le kit complet comprend également le catalogue de la marque et divers articles de bureau, tous conçus à partir d'éléments très simples.

La campaña diseñada por el estudio Curse of the Multiples para la marca de moda Industry representa a los seguidores del mundo de la moda como muñecos a los que vestir. La inspiración surgió de las figuras de coleccionismo conocidas como toyz. En primer lugar se diseñaron las cajas para la figura, posteriormente se fotografió a los modelos y, para acabar, se montaron las dos imágenes. En el kit de prensa se adjunta un breve texto relacionado con cada uno de los personajes. El kit completo incluye además el catálogo de la marca y material de papelería, todo diseñado a partir de elementos muy sencillos.

Curse of the Multiples
Montreal, Canada_Montréal, Canada_Montreal (Canadá)
www.curseofthemultiples.com ı info@curseofthemultiples.com

213

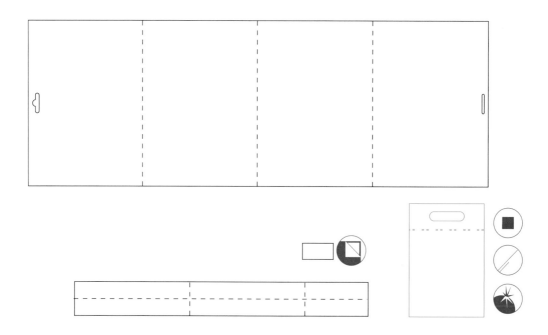

Visual Group promo kit

The photography agency, Client, asked the David Barath studio to design a promotional kit to be distributed during the Bread & Butter fashion trade show. The kit should be striking but simple, and be of the quality so that users do not throw it away immediately. It opted for an accordion-folded brochure, printed on both sides that is sealed by a strip of black paper that, when broken, makes the client feel like they are opening a gift. The silver envelope is guaranteed to capture the attention of the recipient. The brochure showcases the work of photographers from the agency.

L'agence de photographes Client a confié au studio de David Barath le design d'un kit promotionnel qui serait distribué pendant le salon de la mode Bread & Butter. Le kit devait être tape-à-l'œil tout en restant simple, et être d'une qualité suffisante pour ne pas finir directement à la poubelle. Le studio a opté pour une brochure pliée en forme d'accordéon, imprimée des deux côtés et fermée par un bandeau en papier noir donnant au client l'impression de déballer un cadeau. L'enveloppe argentée a pour objet de capter l'attention du destinataire. Le dépliant présente le travail des photographes de l'agence.

La agencia de fotógrafos Client encargó al estudio de David Barath el diseño de un kit promocional que iba a repartirse durante la feria de moda Bread & Butter. El kit debía ser llamativo pero sencillo, y tener la calidad suficiente para que los usuarios no lo tiraran a la basura tras recibirlo. Se optó por un folleto plegado en forma de acordeón, impreso por las dos caras y cerrado por una faja de papel negro que, al romperse, produce en el cliente la sensación de estar abriendo un regalo. El sobre plateado capta la atención del destinatario, y en el folleto se muestra el trabajo de los fotógrafos de la agencia.

David Barath Design
Budapest, Hungary_Budapest, Hongrie_Budapest (Hungría)
www.davidbarath.com ı david@davidbarath.com

VISUAL GROUP
CREATIVE+
PHOTO+
PRODUCTION
CONTACT
WWW.VISUALGROUP.HU
CAMPAIGN REFERENCES
Elle Dekor (HU), La Perla (ITA), Max Factor (ITA), Yellow Cab (HU), Revlon (ITA), Divina (ITA), Paolo Tonali (ITA), Retro Jeans (HU), Heineken (BG), Coca-Cola (HU), Fanta (HU, HR), Bomba Energy Drink (HU), E-On (HU), Knjaz Milos (SR)
EDITORIAL REFERENCES
Elle (HU, ITA, D, UK), Elle Dekor (HU), Vogue Gioiello (ITA), Flair (AUS, HU), Grazia (ITA), Marie Claire (HU, ITA), Glamour (HU, ITA, GER), JOY (HU, SR, HR, TR), Playboy (HU), AnyWay (AUS), H.O.M.E. (HU, AUS, GER, CZ), Cosmopolitan (HU, GER)
AGENCY REFERENCES
Ogilvy (HU), PUBLICIS (HU), McCann Erickson (HU), Young and Rubicam (HU), Laboratory (HU), ACG.Hey (HU), Well (HU), Sylva (HU).
Visual Group
ZOLTAN TOMBOR
LASZLO EMMER
PAPP & SCHNEIDER
NORBERT ZSOLYOMI
KRISTOF NEMETH
TAMAS DOBOS

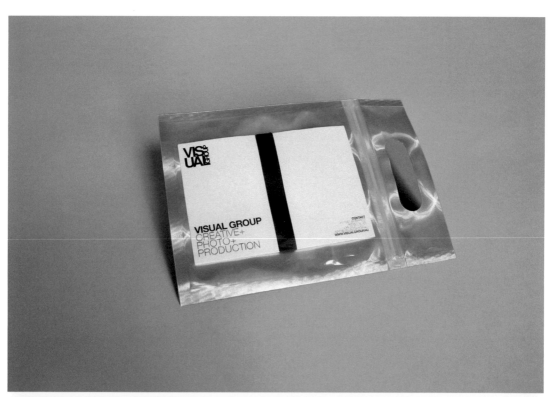

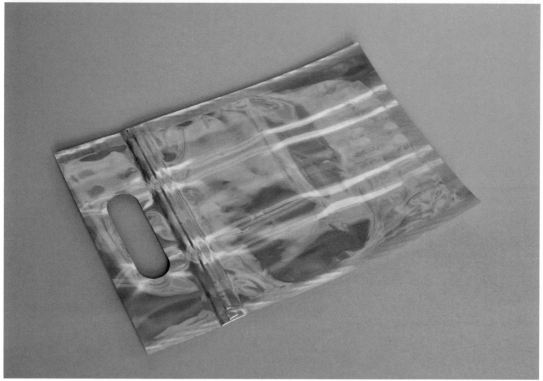

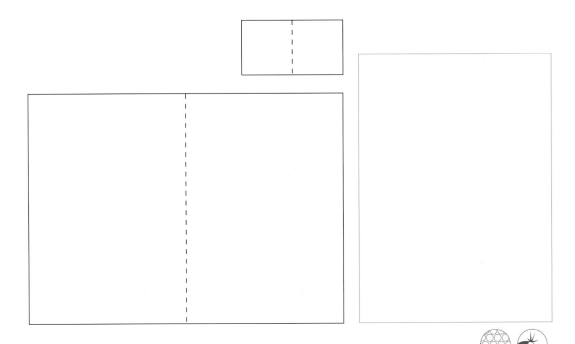

Make-up bag

Stuffandthings is a fashion accessory manufacturer in Hong Kong that entrusted Milkxhake to design a promotional kit with which to advertise and publicize some of the company's materials. To do this, Milkxhake invited five young new generation Chinese artists to take part in the project: each artist was given a bag made from one of these materials and six DIN A3 size samples of other materials to be used in the design of several masks. The result can be seen in these pages.

Stuffandthings est un fabriquant d'accessoires de mode de Hong Kong qui a confié à Milkxhake le design d'un kit promotionnel destiné à promouvoir et à faire connaître certains des matériaux de l'entreprise. Pour cela, Milkxhake a invité cinq jeunes issus de la nouvelle génération d'artistes chinois à prendre part au projet : chaque artiste s'est vu attribuer un sac fabriqué à partir de l'un des matériaux, ainsi que six échantillons taille A3 d'autres matériaux, qu'ils devraient utiliser pour le design de plusieurs masques. Vous pouvez voir ici le résultat obtenu.

Stuffandthings es un fabricante de accesorios de moda de Hong Kong que encargó a Milkxhake el diseño de un kit promocional con el que publicitar y dar a conocer algunos de los materiales de la compañía. Para ello, Milkxhake invitó a cinco jóvenes pertenecientes a la nueva generación de artistas chinos a tomar parte en el proyecto: a cada artista se le proporcionó una bolsa fabricada con uno de los materiales y seis muestras de tamaño DIN A3 de otros materiales para que los utilizaran en el diseño de varias caretas. El resultado es el que puede verse en estas páginas.

Milkxhake
Hong Kong, China_Hong Kong, Chine_Hong Kong (China)
www.milkxhake.org ı mix@milkxhake.org

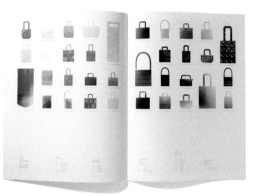

Art director and graphic designer at David Barath Design
Budapest, Hungary
www.davidbarath.com
david@davidbarath.com
Project on page 216

Directeur artistique et designer de David Barath Design
Budapest, Hongrie
www.davidbarath.com
david@davidbarath.com
Projet sur la page 216

Director artístico y diseñador gráfico de David Barath Design
Budapest (Hungría)
www.davidbarath.com
david@davidbarath.com
Proyecto en la página 216

How should the perfect promotional kit be?
Simple and direct.

What's (or what should be) its objective?
It has to raise attention of the future clients and provoke emotions. In case of Visual Group promotion kit clients had the feeling of receiving a gift, with the simple tool of wrapping.

What's the main difficulty when designing a promotional kit?
There is no difficulty. It is as difficult as designing anything else. It has to be beautiful and useful at the same time.

And what's the easiest thing about it?
I cannot answer this question. There is no such thing as something easy when designing. Every task is simple and difficult at the same time, but this is what I enjoy most in this job.

What do you most enjoy about designing a promotional kit?
I like to get inside the client's head. I like to invent things that the client will like,

Comment devrait être le kit promotionnel parfait ?
Simple et direct.

Quel est (ou quel devrait être) son objectif ?
Il doit attirer l'attention de futurs clients et provoquer des émotions. Dans le cas du kit promotionnel de Visual Group, les clients ont eu l'impression de recevoir un cadeau simplement parce qu'il était enveloppé.

Quelle est la principale difficulté lors de la conception d'un kit promotionnel ?
Il n'y a pas de difficulté. C'est aussi difficile que de concevoir autre chose. Il doit être beau et utile en même temps.

Et qu'est-ce qui est le plus facile ?
Je ne peux pas répondre à cette question car il n'y a rien de facile dans le design. Chaque tâche est simple et difficile en même temps mais c'est ce me plaît le plus dans ce métier.

Qu'est-ce qui vous plaît le plus dans la conception d'un kit promotionnel ?
J'aime penser en me mettant dans la

¿Cómo debería ser el kit promocional perfecto?
Simple y directo.

¿Cuál es (o cuál debería ser) su objetivo?
Tiene que llamar la atención de futuros clientes y levantar emociones. Por ejemplo, en el caso del kit promocional de Visual Group, los clientes tenían la impresión de haber recibido un regalo, simplemente porque estaba envuelto.

¿Cuál es la principal dificultad cuando se diseña un kit promocional?
No hay ninguna dificultad. Es tan difícil como diseñar cualquier otra cosa. Debe ser atractivo y útil al mismo tiempo.

¿Y qué parte del proceso de diseño es la más fácil?
No puedo a responder a esta pregunta, ya que no hay nada fácil en el diseño. Todas las tareas son simples y difíciles al mismo tiempo, y eso es lo que más me gusta de este trabajo.

¿Con qué disfrutas más cuando diseñas un kit promocional?
Creo que pensando con la cabeza del

David Barath

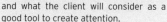

and what the client will consider as a good tool to create attention.

In your opinion, what kind of clients/brands should make use of promotional or press kits?
Probably, all companies should have promotional kits. Everyone needs to have an identity and marketing. Generally, my clients come from fashion and publishing business, but I think I could design a promotional kit for any client. It depends on the briefing and the needs.

How do you check or test the effectiveness of your work and designs, and more specifically your press kits? Do you receive any kind of feedback from the client or the consumer?
Clients I have designed promotional or press kits for always tell me how much journalists like them. They never forget to mention that journalists come to them after the presentation and say how beautiful their press kit is. It has happened with almost every press kit I have designed to date. In case of Visual Group, clients, as mentioned before, liked the idea of "gift wrapping" very much.

tête du client. J'aime inventer des choses que le client va aimer et qu'il va considérer comme un bon outil pour attirer l'attention.

À votre avis, quel genre de clients/marques devraient utiliser les kits promotionnels ou de presse ?
Toutes les sociétés devraient avoir des kits promotionnels. Tout le monde a besoin d'une identité et de marketing. En général, mes clients viennent du secteur de la mode et de l'édition mais je crois que je pourrais concevoir un kit promotionnel pour n'importe quel client. Cela dépend des indications et des besoins.

Comment vérifiez-vous l'efficacité de votre travail et de vos designs et, plus précisément, de vos kits de presse ? Recevez-vous un feedback de la part du client ou du consommateur ?
Les clients pour lesquels j'ai conçu des kits promotionnels ou de presse me disent toujours que les journalistes les apprécient énormément. Ils n'oublient jamais de mentionner que les journalistes viennent après la présentation et font des éloges concernant le kit de presse.

cliente. Me gusta inventar cosas que le gustarán al cliente y que el cliente considerará una buena herramienta para destacar.

Para ti, ¿qué tipo de clientes/marcas deberían utilizar kits promocionales o carpetas de prensa?
Posiblemente todas las empresas deberían tener kits promocionales. Todo el mundo necesita una identidad y *marketing*. La mayor parte de mis clientes provienen del sector de la moda y la edición, pero creo que podría diseñar un kit promocional para cualquier cliente; depende de sus indicaciones y las necesidades.

¿Cómo compruebas o mides la efectividad de un trabajo o un diseño y, especialmente, de un kit de prensa? ¿Recibes *feedback* de los clientes o los consumidores?
Todos los clientes para los que he diseñado kits promocionales o kits de prensa me dicen que les gustaron mucho a los periodistas. Nunca se les olvida hablarme sobre el periodista que se les acercó tras la presentación y les felicitó por el kit de prensa. Hasta ahora, me ha pasa-

What's your working method when designing a promotional kit? Is there a particular path you follow?
I analyse the client and the future target group, and consider all possible solutions that both will probably like.

What are your favorite materials for a promotional kit? Why?
There are no favorites, but I always like unusual materials, printing and manufacturing methods: like special papers, textiles added to paper, special solutions like embroidery, embossed printing, lacquering. Many clients cannot afford these special finishes, but you also can make wonders from a simple sheet of paper.

Do you need to ''like'' the product you're helping to promote to do a good job with it? Be sincere.
Of course it helps a lot. I have been lucky until now, because all the clients I have designed promotional kits for have been very receptive. The majority of my clients are involved in fashion, publishing and culture. and they are generally very sophisticated, sensitive and open-mind-

Cela s'est produit dans la plupart des cas jusqu'à présent, lorsque j'ai conçu un kit de presse. Dans le cas de Visual Group, des clients ont aimé l'idée de « l'emballage cadeau ».

Quelle est votre méthode de travail lors de la conception d'un kit promotionnel ? Suivez-vous un processus particulier ?
J'analyse le client et le future cible et envisage toutes les solutions possibles que les deux vont probablement aimer.

Quels sont vos matériaux favoris pour un kit promotionnel ? Pourquoi ?
Je n'ai pas de matériaux favoris mais j'aime les matériaux, les méthodes d'impression et de fabrication qui sortent du commun : des papiers spéciaux, des tissus ajoutés au papier, des solutions spéciales comme la broderie, l'impression gaufrée, la laque. De nombreux clients ne peuvent pas se permettre ces finitions spéciales mais vous pouvez aussi faire des merveilles à partir d'une simple feuille de papier.

Pour faire un bon travail, devez-vous « aimer » le produit dont vous assu-

do siempre que he diseñado un kit de prensa. En el caso de Visual Group que he mencionado antes, a los clientes les gustó mucho la idea de envolverlo como si fuera un regalo.

¿Qué método de trabajo sigues cuando diseñas un kit promocional? ¿Te basas en algunas pautas en concreto?
Analizo el cliente y el público al que va dirigida la promoción y estudio todas las opciones que puedan gustarles a ambos.

¿Cuáles son tus materiales favoritos para un kit promocional? ¿Por qué?
No tengo ninguno favorito, pero me gusta trabajar con materiales y métodos poco comunes, como papeles especiales, tejidos añadidos al papel y soluciones especiales, como bordados, impresiones en relieve o lacados. Muchos clientes no pueden permitirse estos acabados especiales, pero también puedes asombrarles con una simple hoja de papel.

¿Necesitas que te guste el producto que estás promocionando para hacer una buena promoción? Sé sincero.
Por supuesto, ayuda mucho. Hasta aho-

ed. They generally trust me and like my ideas, so it is easy to work with them.

How will promotional kit design evolve along the upcoming years? How will new technologies and the fast evolution of the net affect it?

As for the net, I am not really interested. I prefer print media, virtual world has no interest for me. I think the virtual world will never be able to substitute the material one, the one you can touch and feel. As for print media, I think quality will have more importance. The more special, the more personalized, the more demanding, the more sophisticated, the better. This means special solutions, special papers, special printing techniques, special ideas.

What's the best promotional work you've ever seen, and what product was it related to? Why do you like it? Did you buy the product or did you hire the service just because of its promotional work?

I remember a promotional kit of a Boss perfume, when working for a publishing house. It was a metal suitcase, with six

rez en partie la promotion ? Répondez sincèrement.

Bien sûr, ça aide beaucoup. J'ai eu de la chance jusqu'à présent car tous les clients pour qui j'ai conçu des kits promotionnels se sont montrés très réceptifs. La plupart de mes client proviennent du secteur de la mode, de l'édition et de la culture; ils sont généralement très sophistiqués, sensibles et ont l'esprit large. Ils me font généralement confiance et aiment mes idées, il est donc facile de travailler avec eux.

Comment la conception de kits promotionnels va-t-elle évoluer dans les années qui viennent ? Comment les nouvelles technologies et l'évolution rapide du réseau vont-ils l'affecter ?

Internet ne m'intéresse pas. Je préfère les médias imprimés, le monde virtuel n'a pas d'intérêt pour moi. Je pense que le monde virtuel ne pourra jamais remplacer le monde réel, celui que vous pouvez toucher et sentir. Comme pour le média imprimé, je pense que la qualité aura davantage d'importance. Plus c'est particulier, personnalisé, exigeant et sophistiqué, mieux c'est. Cela signifie

ra he tenido suerte, ya que todos los clientes para los que he diseñado kits promocionales se han mostrado muy receptivos. La mayoría de mis clientes provienen del sector de la moda, la publicidad y la cultura y, en general, estas personas son muy sofisticadas, sensibles y tienen una actitud abierta. Casi siempre confían en mí y les gustan mis ideas. Es fácil trabajar con ellas.

¿Cómo evolucionará el diseño de los kits promocionales en los próximos años? ¿Cómo influirán las nuevas tecnologías y la rápida evolución de la Red?

La Red no me interesa. Prefiero los medios impresos; no me interesa el mundo virtual. Creo que el mundo virtual nunca podrá reemplazar al material, el mundo en el que puedes tocar y sentir. Y, en lo referente a los medios impresos, creo que se valorará más la calidad. Cuanto más especial, más personalizado, más exigente y más sofisticado, mejor. Y esto requiere soluciones especiales, papeles especiales, técnicas de impresión especiales e ideas especiales.

metal balls in it, like a petanque kit (the game French used to play with), and one of them was the perfume bottle itself. Furniture design companies have always amazing promotional kits (folders, invitation cards, etc.). Recently, Established and Sons have had a wonderful example of this. Unfortunately, their products are still very expensive. Generally, the promotional kits I like, promote luxury goods.

des solutions spéciales, des papiers spéciaux, des techniques d'impression spéciales, des idées spéciales.

Quel est le meilleur travail promotionnel que vous ayez vu et de quel produit s'agit-il ? Avez-vous acheté le produit ou loué le service juste pour son travail promotionnel ?
Je me souviens d'un kit promotionnel pour un parfum Boss, lorsque je travaillais dans une maison d'édition. C'était une valise en métal avec six boules métalliques à l'intérieur, comme un jeu de pétanques, et l'une d'entre elles était la bouteille de parfum. Les marques de designers de meubles ont toujours des kits promotionnels surprenants (dossiers, cartons d'invitation, etc.). Established and Sons en ont donné récemment un merveilleux exemple, malheureusement lerus produits sont toujours très chers. Généralement, les kits promotionnels que j'aime sont ceux qui font la promotion de produits de luxe.

¿Cuál es el mejor trabajo de promoción que has visto? ¿Qué promocionaba? ¿Por qué te gustó? ¿Compraste el producto o contrataste el servicio sólo por el trabajo promocional?
Recuerdo un kit promocional del perfume Boss, cuando trabajaba en una editorial. Era un maletín de metal, con seis bolas metálicas dentro, como un juego de petanca, y una de las bolas era el frasco del perfume. Las empresas de diseño de muebles siempre tienen kits promocionales fantásticos (carpetas, tarjetas de invitación...). Hace poco Established and Sons lanzó uno. Desgraciadamente, sus productos siguen siendo muy caros. Por lo general, los kits que me gustan son los que promocionan productos de lujo.

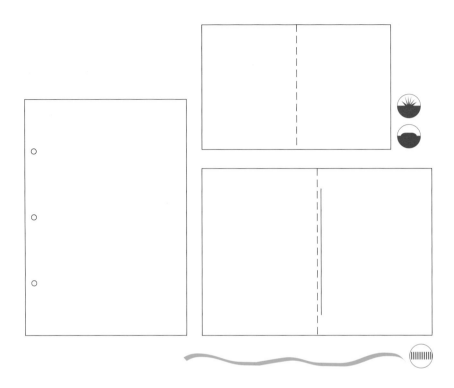

Sita Murt

The lookbooks and other promotional elements of the Spanish fashion label Sita Murt are based on its corporate typeface, Clarendon, which creates a clever play on the lettering by the simple variation and alternation of sizes, colors, materials and phrases. Using a very limited color palette (just white, black and electric blue used occasionally to highlight any important detail), the Sita Murt promotional elements capture the attention of the spectator with information about the brand. Playing with the font size breaks the uniformity of design.

Les *lookbooks* et autres éléments promotionnels de la marque de mode espagnole Sita Murt reposent sur sa typographie corporative, la Clarendon, en créant un jeu typographique très particulier par le simple fait de varier et d'alterner les tailles, les couleurs, les matériaux et les phrases. Avec une palette de couleurs très réduite (juste du blanc, du noir et quelques touches occasionnelles de bleu électrique usé pour certains détails significatifs), les éléments promotionnels de Sita Murt parviennent à centrer l'attention sur ce qui est important : les informations concernant la marque. Et en jouant sur la taille de la typographie, l'uniformité du design est brisée.

Los *lookbooks* y otros elementos promocionales de la marca de moda española Sita Murt se basan en su tipografía corporativa, la Clarendon, que crea un juego tipográfico muy peculiar mediante la simple variación y alternancia de tamaños, colores, materiales y frases. Haciendo uso de una paleta de colores muy reducida (blanco, negro y un azul eléctrico usado ocasionalmente para algún detalle significativo), los elementos promocionales de Sita Murt logran centrar la atención del espectador en la información sobre la marca. Jugando con el tamaño de la tipografía, se logra romper la uniformidad del diseño.

Mirja Jacobs/cla-se
Barcelona, Spain_Barcelone, Espagne_Barcelona (España)
www.cla-se.com ı info@cla-se.com

Our Lookbook Fall/ Winter 09/10
sita murt/

Our Lookbook Spring Summer '09
sita murt/

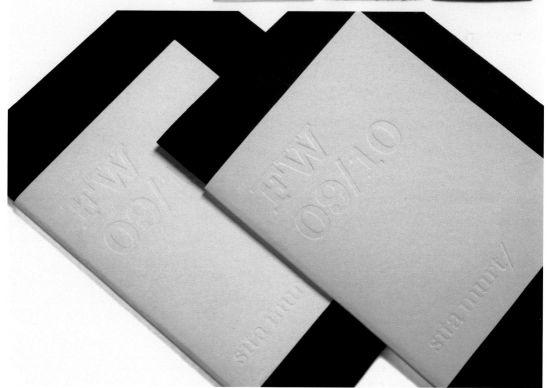

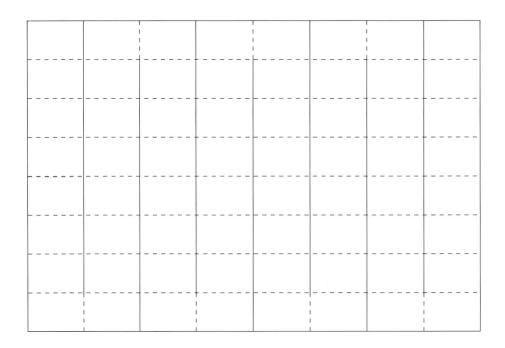

Lee Missy

Lee Jeans is a fashion brand specializing in the design and manufacture of denim and casual clothing for young people. In order to promote its products, the Design Ranch studio designed two fold-out accordion-shaped press kits for the brand that become giant posters showing several of the featured products of the season. The kit, partially inspired by the aesthetics and sensations associated with spas, was sent to designers, potential buyers, department stores and fashion boutiques.

Lee Jeans est une marque spécialisée dans la conception et la fabrication de jeans et de vêtements décontractés destinés à un public jeune. Dans le but de promouvoir ses produits, le studio Design Ranch a conçu pour la marque deux kits de presse en forme d'accordéons, pouvant se déplier pour devenir des posters géants et présenter les produits phares de la saison. Le kit, partiellement inspiré de l'esthétique et des sensations associées aux spas, a été envoyé à des stylistes, des acheteurs potentiels, des grands magasins et des boutiques de mode.

Lee Jeans es una marca de moda especializada en el diseño y la fabricación de vaqueros y ropa informal dirigida a un público joven. Con el objetivo de promocionar sus productos, el estudio Design Ranch diseñó dos kits de prensa para la marca en forma de acordeones desplegables que se convierten en gigantescos pósteres que muestran varios de los productos destacados de la temporada. El kit, parcialmente inspirado en la estética y las sensaciones asociadas con los *spas*, fue enviado a estilistas, compradores potenciales, grandes almacenes y tiendas de moda.

Design Ranch
Kansas City, USA_Kansas City, États-Unis_Kansas City (Estados Unidos)
www.design-ranch.com ı info@design-ranch.co

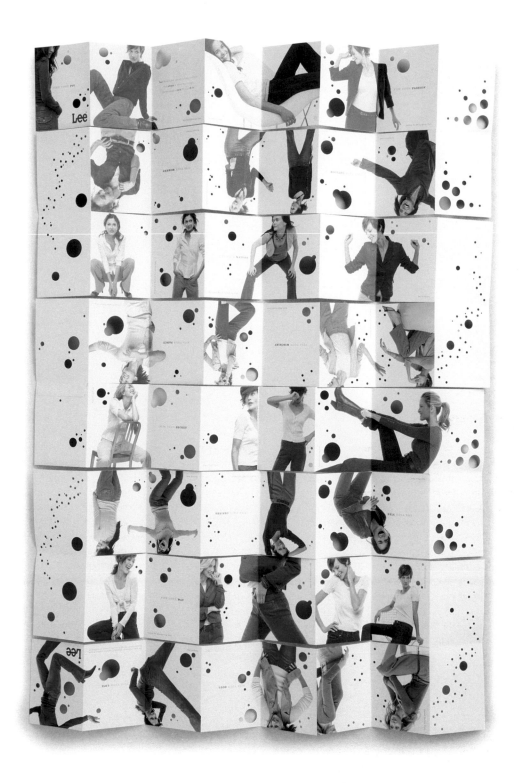

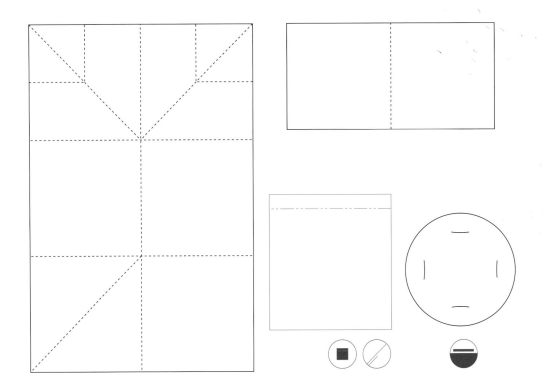

Hilfiger Denim

The Hilfiger Denim promotional kit that can be seen on these pages is presented in a square red vinyl bag. Once the bag is opened at the top, the contents of the kit is revealed: a fold-out three-dimensional press kit with images and information on the products and brand philosophy, and what looks like two seven-inch singles but are actually two CDs on a round plate the same size as a seven inch single. One of the CDs contains information about the brand, and the other is a collection of specially selected tunes.

Le kit promotionnel de la marque de mode Hilfiger Denim que vous pouvez voir ici est présenté dans une pochette carrée en vinyle rouge. La pochette s'ouvre par le haut pour dévoiler son contenu : un dossier de presse dépliant en 3D avec des images et des informations sur les produits et la philosophie de la marque, et ce qui ressemble à deux 45 tours mais qui sont en réalité des CD collés sur des ronds noirs de la même taille que les 45 tours. L'un des CD contient des informations relatives à la marque et l'autre est une compilation de thèmes musicaux sélectionnés pour l'occasion.

El kit promocional de la marca de moda Hilfiger Denim que puede verse en estas páginas se presenta en una bolsa cuadrada de vinilo rojo. Una vez que abrimos la bolsa por su parte superior, el kit revela su contenido: un dosier de prensa tridimensional desplegable con imágenes e información sobre los productos y la filosofía de la marca, y lo que parecen dos *singles* de siete pulgadas pero que no son más que dos CD sobre una lámina redonda del mismo tamaño que los mencionados siete pulgadas. Uno de los CD contiene información sobre la marca y el otro es un recopilatorio de temas musicales especialmente seleccionados.

Finally
Madrid, Spain_Madrid, Espagne_Madrid (España)
jferrin@finallypress.com

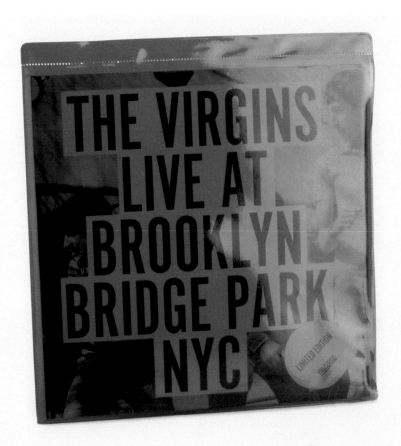

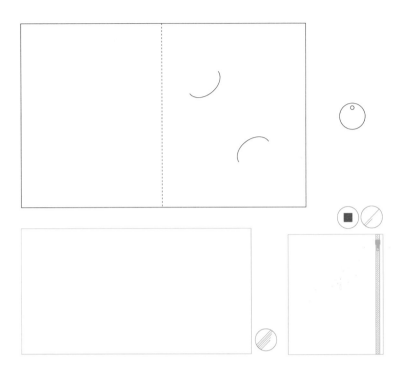

Adidas 2009

The Adidas lookbooks and promotional kits always have an added peculiar detail that makes them stand out. The example in these pages is presented in a plastic envelope closed by a zipper with a pin bearing the brand logo. Inside there is the usual lookbook, wrapped in tissue paper and the press CD, photographs and other material on the entire fall-winter 2009 collection of the brand and its top products.

Les *lookbooks* et kits promotionnels de la marque de sport Adidas présentent toujours une certaine singularité qui les rend différents. Celui que nous pouvons voir ici est présenté dans une enveloppe en plastique fermée par une fermeture Éclair à laquelle est accroché un pin's avec le logo de la marque. À l'intérieur se trouvent le *lookbook* habituel, enveloppé dans du papier de soie, et le CD de presse avec des informations, des photos et autres types de matériel sur la collection automne-hiver 2009 et ses produits phares.

Los *lookbooks* y kits promocionales de la marca de ropa deportiva Adidas siempre presentan algún detalle peculiar que los diferencia. El que podemos ver en estas páginas cuenta con la peculiaridad de que viene envuelto en un sobre de plástico cerrado por una cremallera de la que cuelga un pin con el logotipo de la marca. En su interior se encuentra el habitual *lookbook*, envuelto en papel de seda, y el CD de prensa con información, fotografías y otro tipo de material sobre la colección otoño-invierno de 2009 de la marca y sus productos más destacados.

Adidas
Herzogenaurach, Germany_Herzogenaurach, Allemagne_Herzogenaurach (Alemania)
www.adidas.com/es

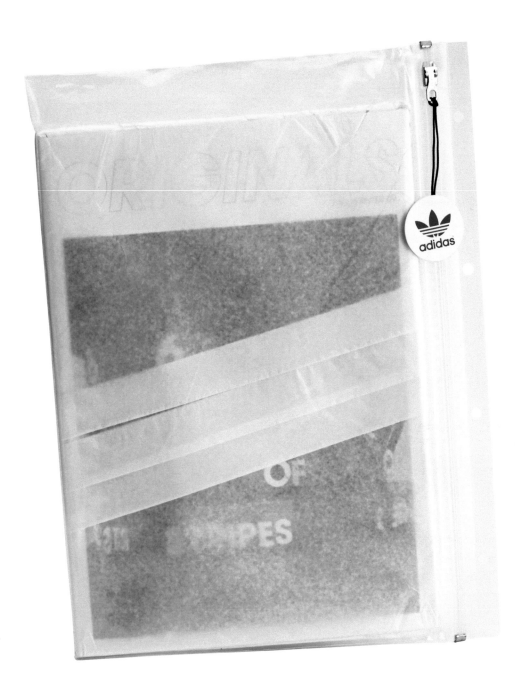

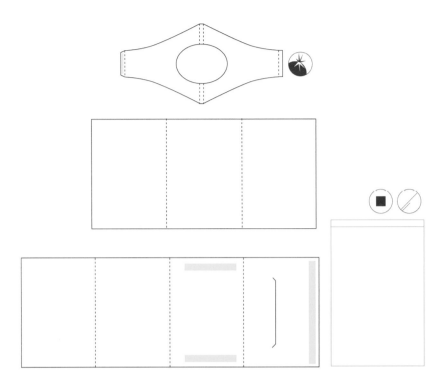

Adidas Men's Training

A glossy metallic plastic bag holds the Adidas Men's Training press kit for the fall-winter 2009 collection, consisting of two different elements. The first is a lookbook with traditional product images by the German brand. The second is a set of three information packs with sports-related titles: PowerWEB, and Tuned Compression and Seamless. The packs are held together by a metallic gray strip. The press kit also includes a CD with press material.

Dans une pochette en plastique brillant métallisé se trouve le kit de presse de la collection Adidas Men's Training automne-hiver 2009, composé de deux éléments. Le premier est un *lookbook* traditionnel avec des images des produits de la marque allemande. Le second est un ensemble de trois dossiers portant les titres suivants (en rapport avec le sport) : PowerWEB, Tuned Compression et Seamless. Les dossiers sont reliés grâce à un bandeau gris métallisé. Le kit de presse comporte également un CD avec du matériel de presse.

En el interior de una bolsa de plástico metalizado brillante puede encontrarse el kit de prensa de la colección Adidas Men's Training de otoño-invierno de 2009, formado por dos elementos. El primero de ellos es un *lookbook* tradicional con imágenes de los productos de la marca alemana. El segundo es un conjunto de tres dosieres con los títulos de sus tres tecnologías para ropa deportiva: PowerWEB, Tuned Compression y Seamless. Los dosieres se mantienen unidos gracias a una faja de color gris metalizado. El kit incluye además un CD con material de prensa.

Adidas
Herzogenaurach, Germany_Herzogenaurach, Allemagne_Herzogenaurach (Alemania)
www.adidas.com/es

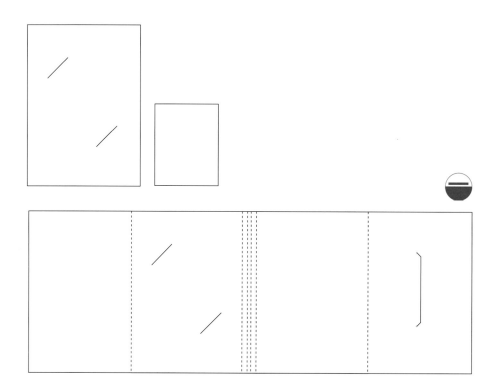

Adidas Women Me Myself

The press kit of the Adidas Women Me Myself collection for fall-winter 2009 included, along with the standard press CD with all relevant information about the brand and its recent products, photos of the same models that can be seen in the lookbook. These photos can be used separately or in the kit itself by fitting them into the small slots in the pages. The fold-out cover of the press, kit printed on a clear gray cardboard, adds an original detail and differentiates it from other similar press kits.

Le kit de presse de la collection Adidas Women Me Myself correspondant à la saison automne-hiver 2009 comporte, en plus du CD de presse habituel avec toutes les informations sur la marque et ses derniers produits, de petites cartes avec les photos des mannequins que l'on peut retrouver dans le *lookbook*. Ces cartes peuvent être séparées du kit ou bien y être intégrées grâce aux petites fentes qui se trouvent sur les pages. La couverture dépliante du kit de presse, imprimée sur un carton gris clair, ajoute une touche d'originalité et le différencie des autres kits de presse du même genre.

El kit de prensa de la colección Adidas Women Me Myself correspondiente a la temporada otoño-invierno de 2009 incluye, junto con el ya habitual CD de prensa con toda la información útil sobre la marca y sus productos recientes, pequeñas láminas con fotografías de las mismas modelos que pueden verse en las páginas del *lookbook*. Dichas láminas pueden separarse del kit o incluirse en él introduciéndolas en las pequeñas ranuras de sus páginas. La portada desplegable del kit de prensa, impresa en cartón de color gris claro, añade un detalle original y lo diferencia de otros kits de prensa similares.

Adidas
Herzogenaurach, Germany_Herzogenaurach, Allemagne_Herzogenaurach (Alemania)
www.adidas.com/es

Partner of Grain Limited and creative director at Madomat
London, UK
www.graincreative.com
www.madomat.com
cg@graincreative.com
studio@madomat.com
Projects on pages 12, 16, 26 and 260

Associé de Grain Limited et directeur créatif de Madomat
Londres, Royaume-Uni
www.graincreative.com
www.madomat.com
cg@graincreative.com
studio@madomat.com
Projets sur les pages 12, 16, 26 et 260

Socio de Grain Limited y director creativo de Madomat
Londres (Reino Unido)
www.graincreative.com
www.madomat.com
cg@graincreative.com
studio@madomat.com
Proyectos en las páginas 12, 16, 26 y 260

How should the perfect promotional kit be?
CG: Surprising, engaging, functional.
MP: Eye-catching, thought-provoking, tactile, on time and on budget.

What's (or what should be) its objective?
CG: To present a product or service in the best possible light, to stage the product and create the best possible experience, which is layered to allow for the perfect moment of drama without seeing the mechanisms or extras behind it.
MP: Perhaps this is deceptively simple, but it should effectively promote the goods or service for which it has been created.

What's the main difficulty when designing a promotional kit?
CG: Timelines. They are always too short. Otherwise a lot more could be possible.
MP: To create a piece which will stand out from the others, and which won't end up in the rubbish bin. The objective is for the recipient to be entranced enough to keep it. Another challenge is the usual limit on time and/or budget.

Comment devrait être le kit promotionnel parfait ?
CG : Surprenant, engageant, fonctionnel.
MP : Accrocheur, stimulant, tactile, délivré à temps et conforme au budget.

Quel est (ou quel devrait être) son objectif ?
CG : Présenter un produit ou un service selon la meilleure perspective possible, mettre en scène le produit et créer la meilleure expérience possible, selon différents échelons afin d'offrir le meilleur moment de l'oeuvre sans que les mécanismes et tout ce qui se cache derrière ne puisse se voir.
MP : Cela peut sembler facile, mais il devrait promouvoir efficacement les biens ou le service pour lequel il a été créé.

Quelle est la principale difficulté lors de la conception d'un kit promotionnel ?
CG : Les délais. Ils sont toujours trop courts, sinon on pourrait en faire davantage.
MP : Créer un élément qui se distinguera des autres et ne finira pas à la poubelle, l'objectif qu'il plaise suffisamment au destinatire pour qu'il le garde. Un autre défi est le temps imparti et/ou le budget.

¿Cómo debería ser el kit promocional perfecto?
CG: Sorprendente, comprometedor, funcional.
MP: Llamativo, que haga reflexionar, táctil, entregado a tiempo y dentro del presupuesto.

¿Cuál es (o cuál debería ser) su objetivo?
CG: Presentar un producto o servicio desde la mejor perspectiva posible, poner en escena el producto y crear la mejor experiencia posible, que se distribuya por capas para enseñar el momento perfecto de la obra sin mostrar los mecanismos o extras que hay detrás.
MP: Quizás es aparentemente simple, pero debería promocionar de forma efectiva los productos o el servicio para el que se ha creado.

¿Cuál es la principal dificultad cuando se diseña un kit promocional?
CG: Los plazos de entrega. Siempre son demasiado cortos. De no ser así, podríamos hacer mucho más.
MP: Crear un elemento que destaque entre los demás y que no acabe en el cubo

Christoph Geppert + Madelyn Postman

And what's the easiest thing about it?

CG: You have not got the usual problems of product liabilities due to the short lifespan of the kits.

MP: The brief, contents and objectives are generally set out clearly.

What do you most enjoy about designing a promotional kit?

CG: It feels like a little bit of stage design but the characters are products and services rather than people.

MP: The challenge of creating a beautiful and memorable piece which serves a very specific purpose. Whenever possible, we incorporate a secondary usage such as travel document holder or keepsake box in order to prolong the life of the object, minimizing waste whilst subtly reminding the recipient of the brand.

In your opinion, what kind of clients/ brands should make use of promotional or press kits?

CG: Any brand or client who speaks directly to their customers has the potential to benefit from such promotional kits. It can serve as a delivery mechanism for information, a service or for an actual

Et qu'est-ce qui est le plus facile ?

CG : Vous n'avez pas les problèmes habituels de responsabilité du produit du fait de la durée de vie courte des kits.

MP : Les indications, le contenu et les objectifs sont généralement définis clairement.

Qu'est-ce qui vous plaît le plus dans la conception d'un kit promotionnel ?

CG : Cela ressemble un peu à un décor de scène sauf que les personnages sont des produits et des services et non des personnes.

MP : Le défi de créer un élément beau et mémorable ayant un objectif précis. Lorsque cela est possible, nous prévoyons une utilisation secondaire comme un porte-documents de voyage ou une boîte souvenir afin de prolonger la durée de vie de l'objet, minimisant le gaspillage tout en rappelant subtilement la marque au destinataire.

À votre avis, quel genre de clients/ marques devraient utiliser les kits promotionnels ou de presse ?

CG : Toute marque ou tout client s'adressant directement à ses clients peut uti-

de la basura. El objetivo es que el destinatario quede lo suficientemente embelesado como para que se quede con eso. Otro reto es el límite habitual de tiempo y/o presupuesto.

¿Y qué parte del proceso de diseño es la más fácil?

CG: No tienes los problemas habituales de responsabilidad de los productos debido a la corta vida de los kits.

MP: Las instrucciones, los contenidos y los objetivos generalmente se determinan enseguida.

¿Con qué disfrutáis más cuando diseñáis un kit promocional?

CG: Se parece un poco al diseño de escenarios, pero los personajes son productos y servicios en vez de personas.

MP: El reto de crear un elemento bonito que no caiga en el olvido y que sirva para un propósito muy específico. Cuando es posible, incorporamos un uso secundario como, por ejemplo, una carpeta para documentos de viaje o una caja de recuerdos para prolongar así la vida del objeto, minimizando el gasto y recordando sutilmente la marca al destinatario.

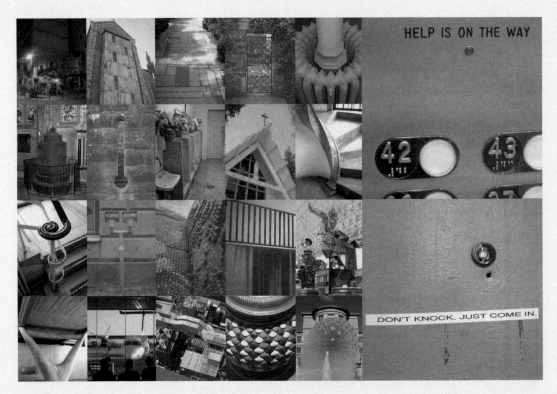

product. I guess that kits are more suitable for promoting products rather than services, since in the former case there is something to physically unwrap, which when well staged always has an element of Christmas.

MP: This is far-reaching. It can be any company offering a service or product which is trying to reach a specific audience.

How do you check or test the effectiveness of your work and designs, and more specifically your press kits? Do you receive any kind of feedback from the client or the consumer?

CG: The best feedback is the one when a client simply comes back to us for more work. Some of the relationships with our clients have lasted more than seven years. We rarely get detailed or specific feedback once we have delivered the kits. I guess it is the nature of promotions that once one is over, then they are forgotten. We have worked on some projects with LED feedback where we have used USB flash drives to delivery accompanying literature and with the permission of the recipient these USBs deliver feedback via the Internet.

liser de tels kits promotionnels. Il peut servir de mécanisme pour offrir des informations, un service ou un véritable produit. Je pense que les kits conviennent davantage à promouvoir des produits que des services, car dans le cas des produits, il y a quelque chose à déballer physiquement, ce qui rappelle toujours Noël lorsque c'est bien préparé.

MP : C'est primordial, il peut s'agir de n'importe quelle société proposant un service ou produit, qui essaye d'atteindre un public précis.

Comment vérifiez-vous l'efficacité de votre travail et de vos designs et, plus précisément, de vos kits de presse ? Recevez-vous un feedback de la part du client ou du consommateur ?

CG : Le meilleur feedback est lorsqu'un client revient pour nous donner plus de travail. Certaines relations avec nos clients ont duré plus de sept ans. Nous obtenons rarement un feedback détaillé ou précis une fois que nous avons livré les kits. Je crois que c'est la nature des promotions qui fait qu'une fois finies, elles sont oubliées. Nous avons travaillé sur quelques projets avec un feedback

Para vosotros, ¿qué tipo de clientes/ marcas deberían utilizar kits promocionales o carpetas de prensa?

CG: Cualquier marca o cliente que hable directamente con sus clientes puede aprovechar este tipo de kits promocionales. Puede servir como mecanismo de entrega de información, un servicio o un producto actual. Creo que los kits son adecuados para promocionar productos más que servicios, ya que en el caso de productos, hay algo que desenvolver físicamente, algo que cuando está bien arreglado siempre tiene un elemento navideño.

MP: Esto es transcendental. Puede ser cualquier empresa que ofrece un servicio o producto que intenta llegar a un público específico.

¿Cómo comprobáis o medís la efectividad de un trabajo o un diseño y, especialmente, de un kit de prensa? ¿Recibís *feedback* de los clientes o los consumidores?

CG: El mejor *feedback* es simplemente que un cliente vuelva a nosotros para darnos más trabajo. Algunas relaciones con clientes nuestros han durado más

MP: A field test for the effectiveness is when one of our acquaintances happens to receive a kit we've designed and they love it, without knowing that it's our own work! That's a great reward. It would be helpful, in fact, to have more feedback from the end consumer and from the client, but often we are already focussing on the next project. It's a reflection both of the pace of work and the pace of to-day's consumption.

What's your working method when designing a promotional kit? Is there a particular path you follow?
CG: No. Often there is a first idea from the briefing meeting, but sometimes this is the final one and sometimes not. We do a lot of visual research in areas totally unrelated to the products we are working on. We work on interiors as well, and sometimes the way a door mechanism works can give you ideas about how to create a custom-made box.
MP: We gather as much information as possible from the client, and from our own research, about the service or product and about the recipient of the kit. We also make sure that we understand the mindset and needs of the end user. Then, working within any contraints such as whether the kit will be posted or hand-delivered, we start designing. We usually offer the client two concepts, which are both feasible for timing and budget, and then develop the one that the client prefers.

What are your favorite materials for a promotional kit? Why?
CG: Any material that is unexpected. Surprise is still one of the most powerful agents. But there are the workhorses like paper and foam which often are the base of a lot of projects. Often a manufacturing method is more defining than the material itself.
MP: We like to vary materials for the kits, from paper and board, to wood, various types of USB flash drives, perspex, fabric, recycled plastic... the more unusual the better. As a studio we have a strong focus on being kind to the environment, so we try to put forward the most eco-friendly solution. We recently used a fabric made out of recycled PET water bottles for a press kit which was in the form of a bag.

Do you need to "like" the product you're helping to promote to do a good job with it? Be sincere.
CG: It helps but it is not necessary. The

technologique où nous avons utilisé des clés flash USB pour la livraison, accompagnées de documents, et avec l'autorisation du destinataire ces clés USB fournissaient le feedback par Internet.
MP : Un test sur le terrain concernant l'efficacité se produit lorsqu'une de nos connaissances reçoit un kit que nous avons conçu et qu'il lui plait, sans savoir que c'est notre propre travail ! C'est un excellent compliment ! En réalité, il serait utile d'avoir davantage de feedback de la part du consommateur final et du client, mais nous sommes souvent déjà concentrés sur le projet suivant. Cela reflète le rythme de travail et le rythme de la consommation de nos jours.

Quelle est votre méthode de travail lors de la conception d'un kit promotionnel ? Suivez-vous un processus particulier ?
CG : Non. Il y a souvent une première idée qui surgit de la réunion de briefing et c'est parfois l'idée finale et parfois non. Nous faisons de nombreuses recherches visuelles dans des secteurs qui n'ont rien à voir avec les produits sur lesquels nous travaillons. Nous travaillons sur des intérieurs et parfois la manière dont un mécanisme de porte fonctionne nous donne des idées sur la création d'une boîte sur mesure.
MP : Nous réunissons toutes les informations que possible fournies par le client et celles qui proviennent de nos propres recherches, concernant le service ou le produit et le destinataire du kit. Nous nous assurons aussi de bien comprendre la mentalité et les besoins de l'utilisateur final. Ensuite, nous travaillons avec des contraintes, comme le fait de savoir si le kit sera envoyé par la poste ou livré directement et nous commençons la conception. Nous proposons généralement deux concepts au client, faisables tous les deux au niveau du temps et du budget, puis nous développons celui que le client préfère.

Quels sont vos matériaux favoris pour un kit promotionnel ? Pourquoi ?
CG : Tout matériau inattendu. La surprise reste encore un des facteurs les plus puissants. Mais il y a encore des bêtes de somme comme le papier et la mousse qui sont souvent à la base de nombreux projets. Il arrive souvent qu'une méthode de fabrication en dise davantage que le matériau lui-même.
MP : Nous aimons varier les matériaux

de siete años. Raras veces recibimos *feedback* detallado o específico una vez que hemos entregado los kits. Creo que está dentro de la naturaleza de las promociones: cuando se acaban, se olvidan. Hemos trabajado en algunos proyectos con tecnología LED, en los que hemos utilizado dispositivos de memoria USB para entregar la documentación adjunta y, con el permiso del destinatario, estos USB proporcionan *feedback* vía Internet.
MP: Una buena prueba de campo de la efectividad tiene lugar cuando uno de nuestros conocidos recibe un kit que hemos diseñado y le encanta... ¡sin saber que hemos sido nosotros los que lo hemos creado! Es una gran recompensa. De hecho, sería de ayuda contar con más *feedback* del consumidor final y del cliente. Pero, muchas veces, cuando terminamos un proyecto, ya estamos con la mente puesta en otro. Es un reflejo tanto del ritmo de trabajo como del ritmo de consumo de hoy en día.

¿Qué método de trabajo seguís cuando diseñáis un kit promocional? ¿Os basáis en algunas pautas en concreto?
CG: No. A menudo surge una primera idea en la reunión de *briefing*: a veces es la idea final y otras veces la idea tarda más en aparecer. Hacemos una gran investigación visual en áreas totalmente opuestas sobre los productos en los que estamos trabajando. Trabajamos en interiores también, y a veces el modo en el que funciona el mecanismo de una puerta puede proporcionarte ideas sobre cómo crear una caja a medida.
MP: Reunimos toda la información posible proporcionada por el cliente y por nuestra propia investigación sobre el servicio o producto y sobre el destinatario del kit. También nos aseguramos de que entendemos la forma de pensar y las necesidades de usuario final. Entonces, trabajando con limitaciones, como que el kit se envíe por correo o se entregue en mano, comenzamos a diseñar. Normalmente, ofrecemos al cliente dos conceptos factibles en lo que a tiempo y presupuesto se refiere, y después desarrollamos el que el cliente prefiera.

¿Cuáles son vuestros materiales favoritos para un kit promocional? ¿Por qué?
CG: Cualquier material inesperado. La sorpresa sigue siendo uno de los agentes más poderosos. Pero existen elementos que tiran del carro, como el papel y la es-

very nature of design is that one understands many different products, services, scenarios and concepts. It is a lot about listening and observing and asking the right questions. Of course it adds another level if one is enthusiastic about the product. Though sometimes being more objective is better.

MP: More than liking a product, it is important to understand it, its users and its position within the market. If there is some kind of personal affinity with it, all the better.

How will promotional kit design evolve along the upcoming years? How will new technologies and the fast evolution of the net affect it?

CG: I think in many ways promotional kits will keep the place they own in the communication mix better than other mailing activities when it comes to presenting products. Nothing can replace the tangible aspect of actually holding it in your own hands. Also the chance to layer the experience is more powerful than in a new media context. As in the aforementioned project I think there are many ways of integrating new

pour les kits, du papier et du carton au bois, différents types de clés flash USB, du plexiglas, du tissu, du plastique recyclé, plus c'est inhabituel et mieux c'est. En tant que bureau, nous sommes très axés sur le respect de l'environnement et nous essayons de présenter la solution la plus écologique. Nous avons récemment utilisé un tissu fabriqué avec des bouteilles d'eau en PET recyclées pour un kit de presse en forme de sac.

Pour faire un bon travail, devez-vous « aimer » le produit dont vous assurez en partie la promotion ? Répondez sincèrement.

CG : Cela aide mais n'est pas nécessaire. La nature du design est que chacun comprend de nombreux produits, services, scénarios et concepts différents. Il s'agit d'écouter, d'observer et de poser les bonnes questions. Bien évidemment, si le produit vous plaît, cela ajoute une autre dimension, même si parfois il vaut mieux être plus objectif.

MP : Plus qu'aimer un produit, il est important de le comprendre, de comprendre ses utilisateurs et sa position sur le marché. S'il en plus existe une affinité

puma, que suelen ser la base de muchos proyectos. Con frecuencia, el método de fabricación define más que el material en sí.

MP: Nos gusta alternar materiales para los kits, desde papel y cartón hasta madera, diferentes tipos de dispositivos de memoria USB, plexiglás, tela, plástico reciclado... Cuanto más inusual, mejor. Como estudio, prestamos especial atención al respeto del medio ambiente, así que intentamos proponer la solución más ecológica. Recientemente hemos usado una tela hecha con botellas de agua de PET recicladas para un kit de prensa que tenía forma de bolsa.

¿Necesitáis que os guste el producto que estáis promocionando para hacer una buena promoción? Sed sinceros.

CG: Ayuda, pero no es necesario. La naturaleza propia del diseño reside en que uno entienda diferentes productos, servicios, perspectivas y conceptos. Es esencial escuchar y observar, y plantear las preguntas pertinentes. Naturalmente, adquiere otro carácter si te gusta el producto. Aunque a veces es mejor ser más objetivo.

technologies into promotional kits. Integrating USB keys or other electronic gadgets for direct feedback is certainly one. Another one is integrating video into presentations with small epaper screens with memory modules, which will become more widespread. Currently it is only used on a product design level but recently commercials have been integrated into magazines instead of printed ads.

MP: Over the past few years, we've seen a transition from the use of transparencies and slides to CDs and to the current prevalence of USB flash drives and online access to imagery. The inclusion (or absence) of these various objects hugely affects the kit design. Often we design the entire kit around the imagery medium, for example, to hold a CD or a USB drive. It's like the pearl inside of the oyster. Our most recent promotional kit, which was aimed at the press and at end consumers, included an updateable, programmed USB flash drive which relays data about the consumer's usage of the USB back to our client.

personnelle avec le produit, c'est encore mieux.

Comment la conception de kits promotionnels va-t-elle évoluer dans les années qui viennent ? Comment les nouvelles technologies et l'évolution rapide du réseau vont-ils l'affecter ?

CG : Je pense que les kits promotionnels vont conserver leur place dans le monde de la communication, mieux que les autres activités de mailing en termes de présentation de produits. Rien ne peut remplacer l'aspect tangible de « le » tenir vraiment dans vos mains. L'opportunité de superposer l'expérience est plus puissante dans un nouveau contexte de médias. Comme pour le projet précédemment mentionné, je pense qu'il y a de nombreuses manières d'intégrer des nouvelles technologies dans des kits promotionnels. L'incorporation de clés USB ou d'autres gadgets électroniques pour un feedback direct en est certainement une. Une autre intègre la vidéo dans des présentations avec de petits écrans de papier électronique, avec des modules de mémoire, qui vont être de plus en plus répandus. Cette technique est actuellement utilisée au niveau du design du produit mais récemment, des publicités vidéo ont été incorporées dans des magazines au lieu de publicités imprimées.

MP : Au cours des dernières années, nous avons vu une transition entre l'utilisation de transparents et diapositives et celle des CD, puis la prédominance actuelle des clés USB et de l'accès en ligne des images. L'inclusion (ou absence) de ces différents objets a une énorme influence sur le design du kit. Nous concevons souvent le kit entier autour du média de représentation, par exemple pour garder un CD ou une clé USB. C'est comme la perle dans l'huitre. Notre kit promotionnel le plus récent, qui était destiné à la presse puis aux consommateurs incluait une clé USB programmée qu'il était possible de mettre à jour, qui transmettait des données sur l'utilisation de la clé par le consommateur à notre client.

MP: Entender un producto, sus usuarios y su posición en el mercado es más importante que el hecho de que te guste. Si existe algún tipo de afinidad personal con él, mucho mejor.

¿Cómo evolucionará el diseño de los kits promocionales en los próximos años? ¿Cómo influirán las nuevas tecnologías y la rápida evolución de la Red?

CG: Creo que, en muchos aspectos, los kits promocionales mantendrán el lugar que ocupan en el conjunto de la comunicación mejor que otras actividades de mailing cuando se trata de presentar productos. Nada puede reemplazar la sensación tangible de cogerlo en tus propias manos. También la oportunidad de distribuir en fases la experiencia es más poderosa que en los nuevos medios de comunicación. Como en el proyecto anteriormente mencionado, creo que existen muchas maneras de integrar las nuevas tecnologías en los kits promocionales. Sin duda, uno de ellos consiste en integrar un dispositivo USB u otros aparatos electrónicos para conseguir un feedback directo. Otro consiste en insertar vídeos en las presentaciones con pequeñas pantallas de papel electrónico con módulos de memoria, que cada vez estarán más extendidas. Hasta hace poco, sólo se usaban en el diseño de producto, pero algunas han empezado a incluir anuncios en vídeo en lugar de publicidad impresa.

MP: Durante los últimos años, hemos vivido la transición del uso de las transparencias y las diapositivas a los CD y la prevalencia actual de los dispositivos de almacenamiento de USB y el acceso online a imágenes. La inclusión (o ausencia) de estos objetos repercute enormemente en el diseño del kit. A menudo diseñamos todo el kit en torno a la imaginería, por ejemplo, para guardar un CD o un dispositivo USB. Es como la perla dentro de la ostra. Nuestro kit promocional más reciente, que estaba dirigido a la prensa y a los consumidores finales, incluía un dispositivo de almacenamiento USB programado y con capacidad de actualización que transmite datos sobre el uso del consumidor del USB a nuestro cliente.

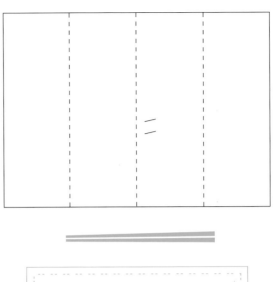

UniForm promotional items

UniForm is an urban clothing brand whose image has adorned T-shirts, bags, caps and badges since 1997. UniForm is an initiative by Form, the design studio created by Paul West and Paula Benson. Seven different collections were created for the label, each based on contemporary culture. The designs in these pages are some promotional elements of the seven collections. Asian Tuck n' Dibs, for example, is the son of the original Oriental collection Tuck n' Dibs, and its promotional kit includes a pair of chopsticks. The promotional designs have a slight retro and kitsch feel.

UniForm est une marque de vêtements urbains dont l'image orne tee-shirts, sacs, casquettes et pin's depuis 1997. Il s'agit d'une initiative de Form, le studio de design créé par Paul West et Paula Benson. Sept gammes différentes ont été créées pour la marque dont chacune tournait autour d'un thème en rapport avec la culture contemporaine. Les designs ici présentés sont des éléments promotionnels de certaines de ces sept gammes. Asian Tuck n' Dibs, par exemple, est la descendante orientale de la gamme originale Tuck n' Dibs, et son kit promotionnel comporte une paire de baguettes chinoises. Les designs promotionnels sont en général un brin kitsch et rétro.

Esta iniciativa de Form, el estudio de diseño creado por Paul West y Paula Benson, es una marca de ropa urbana cuya imagen adorna camisetas, bolsas, gorras y chapas desde 1997. Para la marca UniForm se crearon siete gamas diferentes, cada una basada en un tema relacionado con la cultura contemporánea. Los diseños de estas páginas son elementos promocionales de algunas de esas siete series. Asian Tuck n' Dibs, por ejemplo, es el hijo orientalizado de la gama original Tuck n' Dibs, y su kit incluye un par de palillos chinos. Los diseños promocionales tienen en general un aire un tanto *kitsch* y *retro*.

Paul West, Paula Benson, Claire Warner/Form
London, UK_Londres, Royaume-Uni_Londres (Reino Unido)
www.form.uk.com ı studio@form.uk.com

Asian Tuck n' Dibs — UniForm presents...

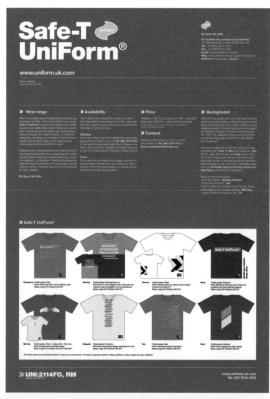

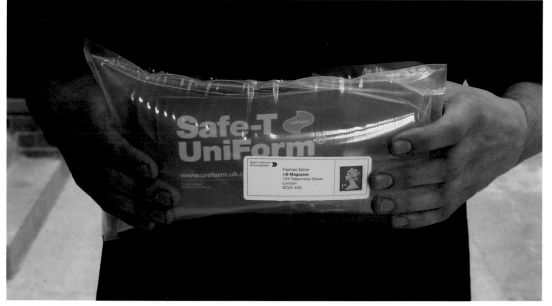

Black & White

This press kit was designed for Cartier with the aim of promoting a selection of fine jewelry pieces designed by the brand from the theme black and white. Inspired by the work of French surrealist photographer Gilbert Garcin, each piece of jewelry interacts with a small male figure. The word "black" is printed in several languages on the cover, and the word "white" on the back for which an ultra-light version of Archer typeface has been used. The book can be opened at either side and it measures 30 feet in total. It has been printed in 10 languages.

Ce kit de presse a été conçu pour Cartier dans le but de promouvoir une sélection de pièces de haute joaillerie créées par la marque sur le thème « noir et blanc ». Chaque pièce de joaillerie interagie avec un petit bonhomme, s'inspirant de l'œuvre du photographe français surréaliste Gilbert Garcin. Le mot « noir » a été imprimé en plusieurs langues sur la couverture, et le mot « blanc » (avec une version ultra-light de la typographie Archer), sur la quatrième de couverture. Le livre peut s'ouvrir des deux côtés et, une fois ouvert, il mesure 940 centimètres. Il a été imprimé en dix langues différentes.

Este kit de prensa fue creado para Cartier con el objetivo de promocionar una selección de las piezas de alta joyería diseñadas por la marca a partir del binomio blanco y negro. Inspiradas en la obra del fotógrafo surrealista francés Gilbert Garcin, cada pieza de joyería interactúa con un hombrecito. En la portada se ha impreso la palabra «negro» en varios idiomas y en la contraportada, la palabra «blanco», para la que se ha utilizado una versión *ultra light* de la tipografía Archer. El libro puede abrirse por sus dos lados y, extendido, mide 940 centímetros. Ha sido impreso en diez idiomas.

Cléo Charuet/Cleoburo
Paris, France_Paris, France_París (Francia)
cleoburo.com ı info@cleoburo.com

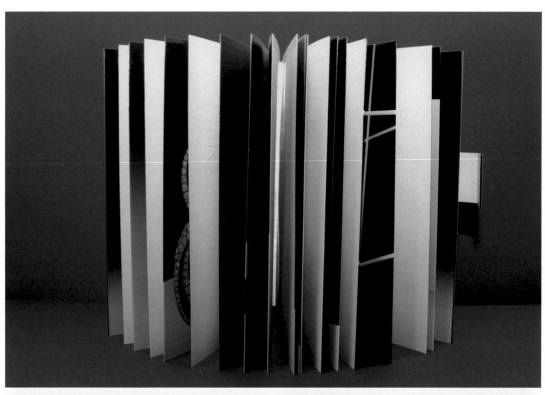

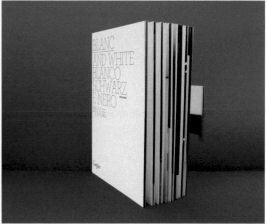

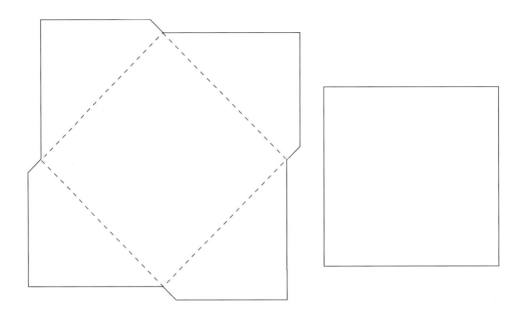

009 Textiles Swatch Mailer

Designed by Madomat for 009 Textiles, this press kit works both as a sample of materials and an information pack about the company and its products. For the cover, the image of one of the 009 Textiles designs has been used, and inside it includes information and expert opinions on the brand. The corners of the kit fold and fit into each other. The paper used is 7 oz Candido Chagall, printed in one-color offset with Pantone 282U. To save costs and minimize the environmental impact, the client card has been printed on the same sheet of paper as the press kits.

Conçu par Madomat pour 009 Textiles, ce kit de presse fonctionne à la fois comme un échantillon de matériaux et un dossier d'information sur l'entreprise et ses marchandises. L'enveloppe a été créée à partir de l'image de l'une des créations de 009 Textiles et contient des informations et des avis d'experts sur la marque. Les coins du kit se replient pour s'assembler les uns aux autres. Le papier utilisé est du Chagall Candido de 200 grammes, imprimé en offset monochrome avec du Pantone 282U. Pour limiter les coûts et minimiser l'impact sur l'environnement, la carte du client a été imprimée sur le même papier que les kits de presse.

Diseñado por Madomat para 009 Textiles, este kit de prensa funciona simultáneamente como muestra de materiales y dosier informativo sobre la empresa y sus productos. Para la cubierta se ha utilizado la imagen de uno de los diseños de 009 Textiles, y el interior incluye información y opiniones de expertos sobre la marca. Las esquinas del kit se pliegan y encajan las unas en las otras. El papel utilizado es Chagall Candido de 200 gramos, impreso en *offset* monocolor con Pantone 282U. Para ahorrar costes y minimizar el impacto ambiental se imprimió la tarjeta del cliente en la misma lámina de papel de los kits de prensa.

Madomat
London, UK_Londres, Royaume-Uni_Londres (Reino Unido)
www.madomat.com ɪ studio@madomat.com

Voted Best in Fabrics at the British Design
Awards 2007 (Elle Decoration Magazine), we at
009 embrace as design artists every possibility of
invention and inspiration. **All our work is lovingly
hand finished and we will adapt to customers'
specific wishes.** We design for curtains, cushions,
blinds, upholstery, wallpaper, backdrops, and
make up fabric for special occasions and clothes.
Our forte is exquisite individual detail in pattern,
colouring and illustrating a theme. Our credits
include Soho House, Bafta Club, Coco de Mer,
Rupert Sanderson and Hotels in India and France.
We are currently stocked at Liberty. "009 are a
name to know as well as to watch. Their ambition
is to make a commercial virtue out of being
design artists."–Vogue.com

009 Westbourne Studios 242 Acklam Road London W10 5JJ
Tel +44 (0)20 7575 3209 www.009textiles.co.uk design@009textiles.co.uk

Death Defying Acts

Prepared for DeAPlaneta, the press kit for *Death Defying Acts*, a movie about the famous escape artist Harry Houdini set in early twentieth-century Edinburgh, was to awaken the curiosity of the press. So the designers had the opportunity to play with the world of escapism. The press kit was carried out in two stages. First a key was sent with the phrase "Soon you'll discover the secrets of *Death Defying Acts*". After a few days, journalists received an airtight sealed water bag with a waterproof leaflet inside locked with a chain and padlock.

Au-delà de l'illusion (*Death Defying Acts*) nous plonge dans l'Édimbourg du début du siècle pour nous raconter l'histoire du célèbre prestidigitateur Harry Houdini. Élaboré pour DeAPlaneta, le kit de presse de ce film avait pour objectif d'éveiller la curiosité de la presse. Pour cela, les designers de Shackleton s'inspirèrent du monde de la prestidigitation. Ils ont donc élaboré un kit en deux étapes. La première consistait à envoyer une clé accompagnée de la phrase : « Bientôt vous découvrirez des secrets *Au-delà de l'illusion* ». Au bout de quelques jours, les journalistes ont reçu un sac rempli d'eau, fermé hermétiquement avec, à l'intérieur, une brochure imperméable fermée par une chaine et un cadenas.

Elaborado para DeAPlaneta, el kit de prensa de *El último gran mago (Death Defying Acts)*, una película sobre el famoso ilusionista Harry Houdini ambientada en el Edimburgo de principios del siglo XX, buscaba despertar la curiosidad de la prensa. Para ello, los creativos de Shackleton se inspiraron en el mundo del escapismo y llevaron a cabo una acción en dos fases: primero se envió sólo una llave con la frase «pronto descubrirás los secretos de *El último gran mago*» y, al cabo de unos días, los periodistas recibieron una bolsa de agua herméticamente sellada con un folleto impermeable en su interior cerrado con una cadena y un candado.

Shackleton 70mm
Madrid, Spain_Madrid, Espagne_Madrid (España)
www.shackleton70mm.com ı cranedo@shackleton70mm.com

Video game press kits are by far the most "playful" kits included in this book. First of all, they often have been created directly by communication agencies rather than by design agencies, so design fades into the backdrop in favor of the pure and hard "impact" on the customer. Secondly, it is common for agencies to probe curiosity by sending an odd object by mail without any other information (e.g. a bullet). After a few days, the recipient receives the full kit (i.e., the press kit for a war movie). Video game press kits also typically include a copy of the game, and several elements representing the world where it has been set, often with entertaining touches (specialist video game journalists tend to be younger than those specializing in other branches of cultural or entertainment journalism).

Les kits de presse de cinéma et de jeux vidéos sont, et de loin, les plus « ludiques » de tous ceux qui sont mentionnés dans ce livre. D'une part, ils sont en général réalisés directement par des agences de communication plus que par des agences de design, ce qui fait passer le design au second plan, au profit de « l'impact » pur et dur que le kit aura sur le client. D'autre part, il n'est pas rare que les agences piquent la curiosité du destinataire du kit en lui envoyant par courrier un objet singulier sans aucune information supplémentaire (une balle, par exemple). Au bout de quelques jours, le destinataire reçoit le kit complet (le dossier de presse d'un film de guerre, par exemple). En général, les kits de presse de jeux vidéo comportent également une copie du jeu ainsi que divers éléments en rapport avec l'univers qui l'entoure, très souvent avec des touches d'humour car les journalistes spécialisés dans les jeux vidéo sont généralement plus jeunes que ceux qui sont spécialisés dans d'autres domaines du journalisme culturel ou de loisir.

Los kits de cine y videojuegos son, con diferencia, los más «entretenidos» de todos los incluidos en este libro. En primer lugar, los suelen realizar directamente agencias de comunicación, más que agencias de diseño, con lo que la gráfica pasa a un segundo plano en beneficio del impacto puro y duro sobre el cliente. En segundo lugar, es habitual que las agencias despierten la curiosidad del receptor del kit enviándole por correo algún objeto peculiar sin información añadida de ningún tipo (por ejemplo, una bala). Al cabo de unos días, el destinatario recibe el kit completo (siguiendo con el ejemplo, el dosier de prensa de una película bélica). Los kits de videojuegos suelen incluir, además, una copia del juego y varios elementos que hacen referencia al mundo en el que se ha ambientado, frecuentemente con toques de humor, ya que los periodistas especializados en videojuegos suelen ser más jóvenes que los que se dedican a otras ramas del periodismo cultural o de ocio.

Movies and video games

Cinéma et jeux vidéo

Cine y videojuegos

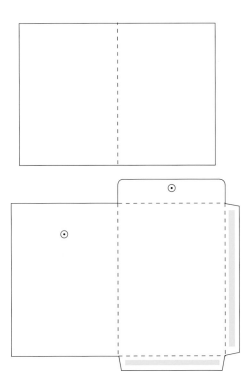

Michael Haneke: Now You Can Let Go

Conceived in 2007 as an additional promotional material for a presentation of the movies by the German-born Austrian director Michael Haneke, this press kit in the form of a set of eight-page booklets that include the analysis of the aforementioned Haneke movies and a biography of the director. The booklets are presented in a sealed envelope by a string. The reason that each of the brochures is delivered to recipients sealed is to prevent that the end of the movies are accidentally revealed.

Ce kit de presse a été conçu en 2007 comme matériel promotionnel supplémentaire pour une présentation des films de Michael Haneke, réalisateur autrichien né en Allemagne. Il se présente sous forme d'un ensemble de brochures, de huit pages chacune, comportant une analyse des films de Haneke et une biographie du réalisateur. Les brochures sont présentées dans une enveloppe fermée par une ficelle. Si chaque brochure est remise aux destinataires dans une enveloppe fermée, c'est pour éviter de leur révéler accidentellement la fin des films.

Concebido en 2007 como material promocional suplementario para una presentación de las películas del director austriaco nacido en Alemania Michael Haneke, este kit de prensa adopta la forma de un conjunto de folletos de ocho páginas en los que se recogen sinopsis de los filmes de Haneke, así como una biografía del director. Los folletos se presentan en un sobre cerrado por medio de un cordel. La razón de que cada folleto se entregue cerrado a los destinatarios es evitar revelarles por accidente el final de las películas.

Nikolay Saveliev
New York, USA_New York, États-Unis_Nueva York (Estados Unidos)
nikolaysaveliev.com, www.hugoandmarie.com ı nikolay@nikolaysaveliev.com

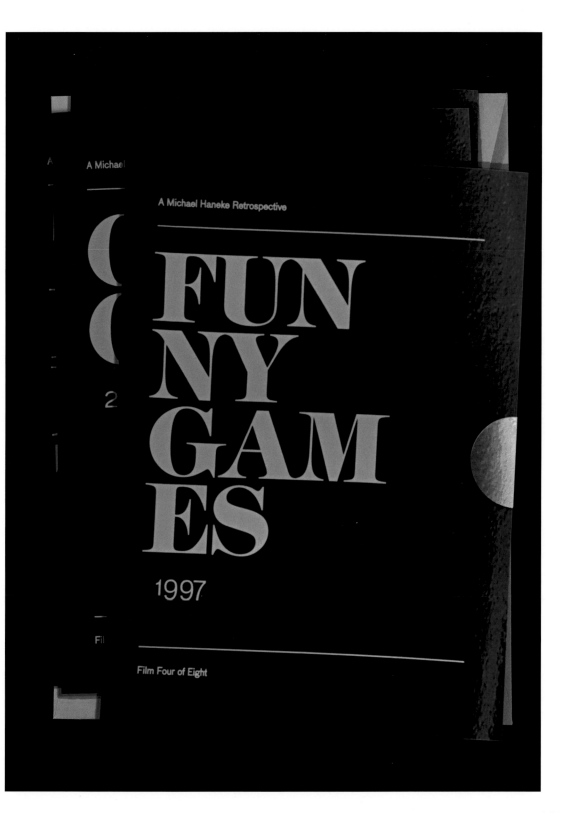

A Michael Haneke Retrospective

FUN NY GAM ES

1997

Film Four of Eight

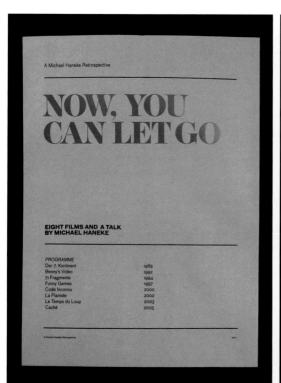

NOW, YOU CAN LET GO

**EIGHT FILMS AND A TALK
BY MICHAEL HANEKE**

PROGRAMME

Der 7. Kontinent	1989
Benny's Video	1992
71 Fragmente	1994
Funny Games	1997
Code Inconnu	2000
La Pianiste	2002
Le Temps du Loup	2003
Caché	2005

A Michael Haneke Retrospective

VOYE URI SM ?

Juliette Binoche	Anne Laurent
Daniel Auteuil	Georges Laurent
Lester Makedonsky	Pierrot Laurent
Maurice Bénichou	Majid
Walid Afkir	Majid's Son

WHO'S WATCHING

This week, a friend of mine suggested that Caché was Michael Haneke's attempt to "pay his dues" to the political left. She's oversimplifying things a bit, but her comments got me thinking. Where, exactly, to slot everybody's (ok, not everybody's) favorite Austrian provocateur in the movies-as-politics continuum? One critic, whom I respect very much likened *Code Unknown* (which is, in the interest of full disclosure, one of my very favorite films of the last decade) to the handiwork of a misanthropic Zeus, hurling accusatory thunderbolts without offering any hint as to how change might be properly catalysed.

I guess he's right: *Code Unknown*, for all its formal brilliance, is thin diagnosis without prescription. Of course, there's a famous saying, "Prescription before diagnosis is malpractice." That logic seems to be behind Haneke's recent shift—following the taboo-baiting placeholder of *The Piano Teacher*—toward a far more (I still thoroughly intellectualised) humanism in *Time of the Wolf* and *Caché*. More than *Code Unknown* and the chilly, condescending anti-thrillers (*Benny's Video*, *Funny Games*) that preceded it, these films suggest that behind Haneke's impeccably icy exteriors lies a hidden and beating heart.

Of course, Cachéis hardly warm and fuzzy. It initially scans as a veritable inventory of contempt for its bourgeois Parisian protagonists. Georges and Anne (Daniel Auteuil and Juliette Binoche) their name-dropping literati friends, and for Haneke's favorite target—Its televisorum—that are simply viceus in their depiction of middlebrow intellectual discourse. But there's even more luck in the shots showing Georges and Anne in their well-appointed home, boxed in by the signifiers of their cultural superiority. The composition of the frames is such that their crammed bookshelves and overstocked videotape library seem to be literally pinning them down.

Consider

The novels on their shelves, though, are the least of their problems. It's the unmarked cassettes being left on their notes for the film made it sound like an art-house flinge—scary videotapes portending doom!—and sure enough, *Caché* assumes the guise of a thriller in its early movements. Georges and Anne can't imagine who would want to take the time to

videotape the exterior of their home, or why. The sense of threat is heightened when the tapes start to be accompanied by black-and-white-and-not-all-over drawings of people with bleeding mouths and decapitated chickens. They're both perplexed, but Georges's heightened confusion—he's apoplectic, around the eyes—suggests that he's got an inkling of what's going on.

And thus does *Caché's* major theme emerge: the seductive lure and dangerous irresponsibility of suppression. What Georges is hiding isn't worth going into here—see the movie. What's important is the fact that on a conscious level, he's not even trying to do it. *Caché* suggests that wilful amnesia is a fine escape hatch for feelings of unpleasantness—unless, of course, something or someone resurfaces to remind you of what you're trying to forget. The tapes in *Caché* are precisely that kind of reminder, and while the narrative universe they inhabit is well-stocked with intrigue as in *Funny Games* and *Time of the Wolf*, Haneke proves himself a master of appropriating genre tropes even as he works to subvert them—the issue is not so much what the tapes reveal about Georges's past. It's what they say about his present state that's particularly disturbing.

Manohla Dargis of the New York Times has suggested that the tapes constitute "ontological evidence," and it's an apt observation. Critics who characterize Haneke's refusal in ever truly clarify who is sending Georges and Anne the tapes (or, even more crucially, what as churlish (as a colleague of mine did in his Toronto film festival coverage) merely reveal themselves as impressionable.

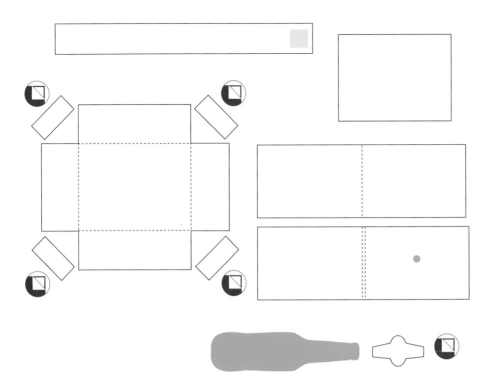

Gangs of New York

The press kit for *Gangs of New York*, the film by American director Martin Scorsese that tells the struggle of different clans during the birth of New York, is a wooden box, which has apparently aged over time. Inside, protected by straw, is the press pack about the film and three collector's items: three bottles of Guinness customized with pictures of Daniel Day-Lewis, Cameron Diaz and Leonardo DiCaprio. To promote the movie, Guinness was immediately thought of as a representative Irish product and its emigrant character.

Gangs of New York, du réalisateur américain Martin Scorsese, raconte les guerres de clans qui faisaient rage à New York à la naissance de la ville. Le kit de presse de ce film consiste en un coffret en bois donnant une impression d'ancienneté. À l'intérieur, et protégés par de la paille, on retrouve le dossier de presse du film et trois objets de collection : trois bouteilles de bière Guinness personnalisées avec des photos de Daniel Day-Lewis, Cameron Diaz et Leonardo DiCaprio. Pour la promotion du film, les designers ont immédiatement pensé à Guinness comme produit représentatif de l'Irlande et de son émigration.

El kit de prensa de la película *Gangs of New York*, del director estadounidense Martin Scorsese, que narra la lucha de los diferentes clanes durante el nacimiento de Nueva York, consiste en una caja de madera aparentemente envejecida por el paso del tiempo. En su interior, y protegidos con paja, se encuentran el dosier de prensa sobre la película y tres objetos de coleccionista: tres botellas de cerveza Guinness personalizadas con fotografías de Daniel Day-Lewis, Cameron Diaz y Leonardo DiCaprio. Para la promoción de la película se pensó inmediatamente en Guinness como un producto representativo de Irlanda y su carácter emigrante.

Jose Maisterra
Barcelona, Spain_Barcelone, Espagne_Barcelona (España)
www.josemaisterra.blogspot.com
josemaisterra@gmail.com

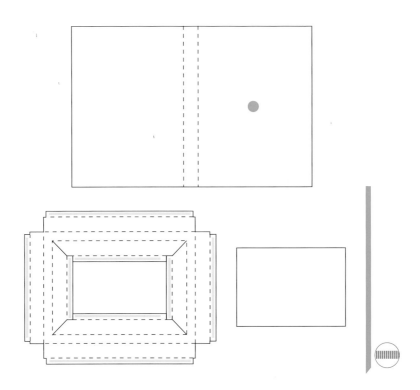

Camino

Camino, directed by Javier Fesser, premiered at the San Sebastian Film Festival in 2008. The press kit aimed to uniquely present and position the movie to the journalists covering the festival. To create the kit, designers were inspired by a scene from the movie which features some old letters. The letters were copied with information about the movie, and included a handwritten note from the director and photos from the movie. Subsequently, the kit was also used to accompany the movie when it was sent to members of the Spanish Film Academy.

Camino, un film réalisé par Javier Fesser, est sorti en 2008 à l'occasion du Festival du cinéma de Saint-Sébastien. Le kit de presse avait pour but de promouvoir le film et de le présenter d'une façon originale aux journalistes qui couvraient le festival. Pour l'élaboration de ce kit, les designers se sont inspirés d'une scène du film où apparaissent des lettres anciennes. Ils ont donc reproduit ces lettres en y inscrivant des informations sur le film et ont ajouté une note manuscrite du réalisateur ainsi que des photos du film. Plus tard, ce kit a été utilisé pour accompagner l'envoi de Camino à l'Academie espagnole du cinéma.

Camino, película dirigida por Javier Fesser, se estrenó en el Festival de Cine de San Sebastián en el año 2008. Con el kit de prensa se quería presentar la película de una manera distinta ante los periodistas que cubrían el festival. Para el desarrollo del kit, los creativos se inspiraron en una escena en la que aparecen unas cartas antiguas. Estas cartas se reprodujeron con información sobre el filme, y se añadieron una nota manuscrita del director y fotos de la película. Posteriormente, el kit se utilizó también para acompañar el envío de la cinta a los miembros de la Academia Española de Cine.

Shackleton 70mm
Madrid, Spain_Madrid, Espagne_Madrid (España)
www.shackleton70mm.com ı cranedo@shackleton70mm.com

Partners of BANK
Berlin, Germany
www.bankassociates.de
tellme@bankassociates.de
Project on page 154

Associés de BANK
Berlin, Allemagne
www.bankassociates.de
tellme@bankassociates.de
Projet sur la page 154

Socios de BANK
Berlín (Alemania)
www.bankassociates.de
tellme@bankassociates.de
Proyecto en la página 154

Sebastian Bissinger + Laure Boer

How should the perfect promotional kit be?
You should get a sensual impression of what the promoted thing is about.

What's (or what should be) its objective?
The press kit should be exciting and arouse interest.

What's the main difficulty when designing a promotional kit?
The challenge is to stay innovative. Like always.

And what's the easiest thing about it?
Don't know.

What do you most enjoy about designing a promotional kit?
To create a sensual impression of what the promoted thing is about.

How do you check or test the effectiveness of your work and designs, and more specifically your press kits? Do you receive any kind of feedback from the client or the consumer?
Yes, if you send something unexpected,

Comment devrait être le kit promotionnel parfait ?
Vous devriez obtenir une impression sensuelle de l'objet de la promotion.

Quel est (ou quel devrait être) son objectif ?
Le kit de presse devrait susciter des émotions et éveiller l'intérêt.

Quelle est la principale difficulté lors de la conception d'un kit promotionnel ?
Le défi consiste à être innovant. Comme toujours.

Et qu'est-ce qui est le plus facile ?
Je ne sais pas.

Qu'est-ce qui vous plaît le plus dans la conception d'un kit promotionnel ?
Créer une impression sensuelle de ce qui est l'objet de la promotion.

Comment vérifiez-vous l'efficacité de votre travail et de vos designs et, plus précisément, de vos kits de presse ? Recevez-vous un feedback de la part du client ou du consommateur ?
Oui, si vous envoyez quelque chose d'inat-

¿Cómo debería ser el kit promocional perfecto?
Lo promocionado debe darte una impresión atractiva.

¿Cuál es (o cuál debería ser) su objetivo?
El kit de prensa debería levantar emoción e interés.

¿Cuál es la principal dificultad cuando se diseña un kit promocional?
El reto es ser innovador. Como siempre.

¿Y qué parte del proceso de diseño es la más fácil?
No lo sé.

¿Con qué disfrutáis más cuando diseñáis un kit promocional?
Con la transmisión de una impresión sensual del material promocionado.

¿Cómo comprobáis o medís la efectividad de un trabajo o un diseño y, especialmente, de un kit de prensa? ¿Recibís *feedback* de los clientes o los consumidores?
Sí, si envías algo que sorprende, la gente

people react on it. Best if they call or email and you start to communicate. Also seeing website traffic going up is a success.

Do you need to "like" the product you're helping to promote to do a good job with it? Be sincere.
We find something interesting in every assignment as long as it is not a business we are really against. And in that case, we simply don't do it.

What's the difference between designing a promotional kit and designing any other kind of work?
It is nice to produce something which is almost a direct mailing adressed to a certain person. Not thousands of copies spread out everywhere, not an ad or an identity but an item, a real object.

How will promotional kit design evolve along the upcoming years? How will new technologies and the fast evolution of the net affect it?
People will always like to get "real" presents and to hold something in their hands. What is an MP3 compared to an original Blue Note pressing from 1963?

tendu, les gens réagissent. C'est mieux s'ils appellent ou envoient un e-mail, vous commencez à communiquer. Si vous voyez aussi une augmentation de la fréquentation du site Web, c'est un succès.

Pour faire un bon travail, devez-vous « aimer » le produit dont vous assurez en partie la promotion ? Répondez sincèrement.
Nous trouvons de l'intérêt à chaque mission tant qu'il ne s'agit pas d'un secteur que nous désapprouvons vraiment. Et, dans ce cas, nous n'acceptons pas le travail, tout simplement.

Quelle différence y-a-t-il entre la conception d'un kit promotionnel et celle d'un autre genre de travail ?
C'est agréable de produire quelque chose qui est quasiment du mailing direct adressé à une certaine personne. Pas des milliers de copies disséminées partout, pas une annonce ni une identité de marque mais un élément, un véritable objet.

Comment la conception de kits promotionnels va-t-elle évoluer dans les années qui viennent ? Comment les

reacciona. Lo mejor es cuando te llaman o te mandan un correo: así consigues abrir una vía de comunicación. Y también es todo un éxito ver cómo aumenta el tráfico de una página web.

¿Necesitáis que os guste el producto que estáis promocionando para hacer una buena promoción? Sed sinceros.
Siempre se encuentra algo interesante en todos los proyectos, salvo si es algo con lo que estás totalmente en contra. Y, en ese caso, simplemente, no lo hacemos.

¿Cuál es la diferencia entre diseñar un kit promocional y diseñar otro tipo de trabajo?
Es mejor crear algo que va a ser enviado casi exclusivamente a una persona que miles de copias repartidas a personas desconocidas, no un anuncio ni una identidad sino un elemento, un objeto real.

¿Cómo evolucionará el diseño de los kits promocionales en los próximos años? ¿Cómo influirán las nuevas tecnologías y la rápida evolución de la Red?
A la gente le gusta recibir regalos «de

What's the best promotional work you've ever seen, and what product was it related to? Why do you like it? Did you buy the product or did you hire the service just because of its promotional work?

"As a part of the creative collective Acne, the founding stones of Acne Jeans were laid in 1997 when one hundred pairs of jeans were designed and distributed to friends, family and clients. Soon, several stores and boutiques wanted to carry the characteristic jeans with bright-red stitching on raw denim."
Quote: www.scandinaviapresents.com

What weight and importance do you give to the briefing of the client, when it doesn't fit your ideas? How do you match these two opposite views?

The views are not opposite, both sides can enrich the process by developing a conciousness about their demands. When you think about something, many approaches are possible. The belief in delivering the "right" and finished solution to the client is not broadening any horizon – whether it is yours, the client's or the customer's – and it is also naive. What is marketing based on?

nouvelles technologies et l'évolution rapide du réseau vont-ils l'affecter ?
Les gens aiment recevoir de « véritables » cadeaux et tenir quelque chose en main. Qu'est-ce qu'un MP3 comparé à l'enregistrement de Blue Note de 1963 ?

Quel est le meilleur travail promotionnel que vous ayez vu et de quel produit s'agit-il ? Pourquoi vous a-t-il plu ? Avez-vous acheté le produit ou loué le service juste pour son travail promotionnel ?

« En tant que membre du collectif de création Acne, Acne Jeans a fait ses premiers pas en 1997 lorsque cent paires de jeans ont été conçues et distribuées aux amis, à la famille et à des clients. Peu de temps après, plusieurs magasins et boutiques ont voulu vendre les jeans caractéristiques avec des coutures au fil rouge vif ».
Citation : www.scandinaviapresents.com

Quelle importance donnez-vous au briefing du client lorsqu'il ne partage pas vos idées ? Comment conciliez-vous ces deux points de vue opposés ?

Les points de vue ne sont pas opposés,

verdad» y poder tocarlos con las manos. ¿Cómo puede compararse un MP3 con una grabación de Blue Note de 1963?

¿Cuál es el mejor trabajo de promoción que habéis visto? ¿Qué promocionaba? ¿Por qué os gustó? ¿Comprasteis el producto o contratasteis el servicio sólo por el trabajo promocional?

«Como parte del colectivo creativo de Acne, Acne Jeans dio sus primeros pasos en 1997 cuando diseñó y mandó una centena de pantalones vaqueros a amigos, familiares y clientes. Poco tiempo después, varias tiendas y boutiques querían tener los vaqueros típicos con puntadas de color rojo brillante.»
Cita: www.scandinaviapresents.com

¿Qué peso y qué importancia dais al briefing del cliente cuando no piensa lo mismo que vosotros? ¿Cómo conseguís encontrar un punto medio para dos puntos de vista diferentes?

Las ideas no son contrarias; ambos puntos de vista pueden enriquecer el proceso al conocer mejor lo que el cliente desea. Cuando tienes algo en mente, hay muchos enfoques posibles. La idea de

What's the promotional kit you would like to design and why?
Doesn't matter what as long as it is very expensive and intricate.

les deux parties peuvent enrichir le processus en prenant conscience de ce que le client souhaite. Lorsque vous avez quelque chose en tête, de nombreuses approches sont possibles. Si vous croyez que vous fournissez la « bonne » solution au client, vous n'élargissez pas les horizons : que ce soit votre idée, celle du client ou du consommateur, cela reste une attitude naïve. Sur quoi se fonde le marketing ?

Quel est le kit promotionnel que vous souhaiteriez concevoir et pourquoi ?
Peu importe tant qu'il est très cher et très compliqué.

ofrecer al cliente la solución «correcta» y definitiva reduce la amplitud de miras. Ya sea la idea tuya, del cliente o del consumidor, no deja de ser una actitud ingenua. ¿En qué se basa el *marketing*?

¿Qué kit promocional os gustaría diseñar y por qué?
Da igual, siempre y cuando sea muy caro y complicado.

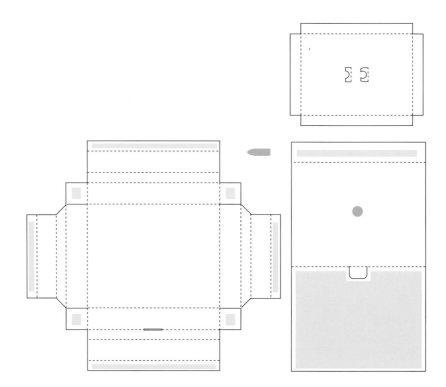

Bobby

The movie *Bobby* recounts the assassination of Robert Kennedy on June 5, 1968 at the Ambassador Hotel in Los Angeles. In the hotel, characters coexist representing the plurality of America at the time. Robert Kennedy was seen at the time as someone to channel a new perspective to the world, and represented a breath of fresh air that was supposed to revolutionize a troubled America in the 60s. The press kit for the film has only two elements: the press CD and a bullet, a metaphor for how such a small object can destroy the hopes of an entire nation.

Le film *Bobby* raconte l'assassinat de Robert Kennedy le 5 juin 1968 à l'Hôtel Ambassador de Los Angeles. Dans le film, les personnages qui cohabitent à l'hôtel représentent la pluralité qui régnait en Amérique à cette époque. Robert Kennedy était perçu en ce temps-là comme l'initiateur d'une nouvelle vision du monde et représentait une bouffée d'air frais qui était supposée révolutionner l'Amérique convulsive des années 1960. Le kit de presse du film ne comporte que deux éléments : le CD de presse et une balle, symbole de la façon dont une toute petite chose peut mettre fin aux espérances de toute une nation.

El filme *Bobby* narra el asesinato de Robert Kennedy el 5 de junio de 1968 en el Hotel Ambassador de Los Ángeles. En el hotel de la película conviven personajes que representan la pluralidad de los Estados Unidos de la época. Robert Kennedy era visto en su momento como el canalizador de un nuevo punto de vista sobre el mundo, y representaba una bocanada de aire fresco que supuestamente iba a revolucionar la convulsa América de los años sesenta. El kit de prensa de la película cuenta con sólo dos elementos: el CD de prensa y una bala, una metáfora de cómo algo muy pequeño puede acabar con las esperanzas de toda una nación.

Jose Maisterra
Barcelona, Spain_Barcelone, Espagne_Barcelona (España)
www.josemaisterra.blogspot.com ι josemaisterra@gmail.com

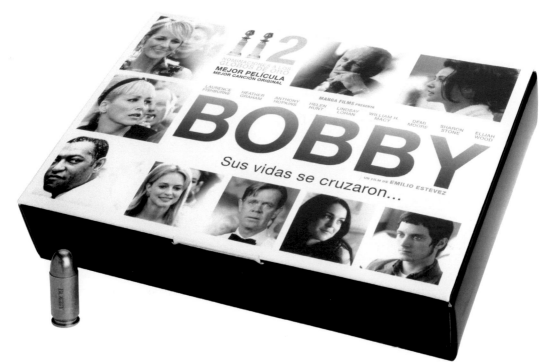

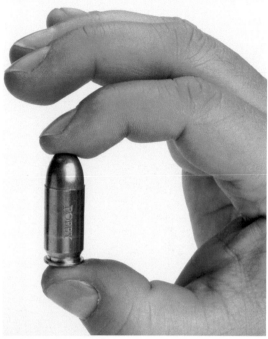

Ex

Ex is a crazy story about love and falling out of love, in which the relationships of the main characters with their former partners creates comical situations of jealousy, revenge and reconciliation. The movie press kit tries to ridicule that many people harbor a grudge against former partners. Hence, the voodoo doll to torture by stabbing pins in your ex "where it most hurts". Evidently, and with this type of press kit, the recipient soon comes to the conclusion that the movie is a crazy Italian comedy.

Ex est une comédie d'intrigue, d'amour et de haine farfelue, dans laquelle la relation des protagonistes avec leurs ex crée des situations comiques de jalousie, de vengeances et de réconciliations. Le kit de presse du film prétend tourner en dérision la rancœur que de nombreuses personnes nourrissent envers leurs ex. D'où la poupée vaudou, qui permet de torturer ses ex en leur plantant des aiguilles « là où ça fait mal ». Évidemment, avec un kit de presse comme celui-ci, le destinataire en arrivera rapidement à la conclusion que le film est une comédie à l'italienne un peu folle.

Ex es una loca comedia de enredo, de amor y desamor, en la que la relación de los protagonistas con sus ex parejas crea situaciones cómicas de celos, venganzas y reconciliaciones. Con el kit de prensa del filme se pretende ironizar sobre el rencor que muchas personas albergan contra sus ex; de ahí la inclusión de un muñeco de vudú con el que torturar al ex clavándole alfileres «donde más le duela». Evidentemente, y con un kit de prensa como éste, el destinatario no puede tardar en llegar a la conclusión de que la película es una chiflada comedia italiana.

Jose Maisterra
Barcelona, Spain_Barcelone, Espagne_Barcelona (España)
www.josemaisterra.blogspot.com
josemaisterra@gmail.com

en cines de julio

EX

Todos tenemos uno

www.ex-todostenemosuno.com

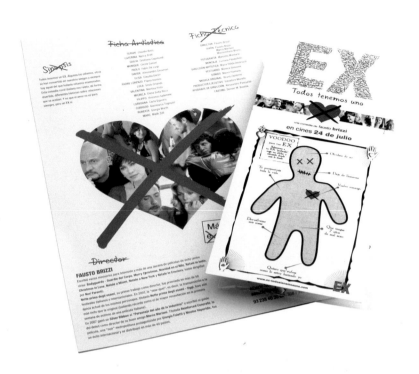

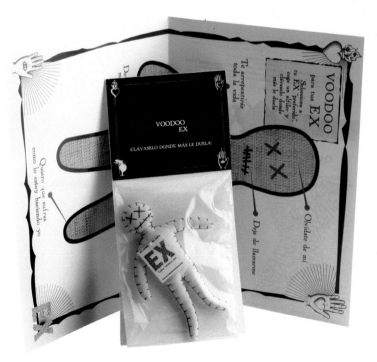

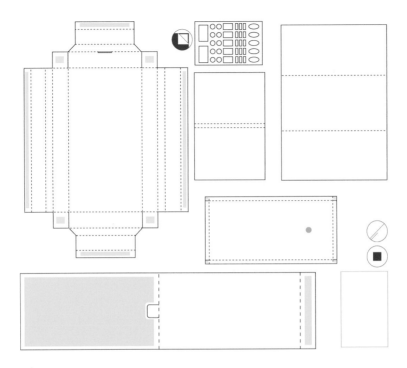

Halo Wars

The press kit for the famous real-time strategy Xbox 360 video game *Halo Wars*, a multi-million seller, is a rectangular box. The cover features images of the leading characters of the game on a blue background. The back cover features an image of their enemies on a red background. The box includes a copy of the game and the traditional press CD, as well as a plastic bag that contains a poster with a scene from the game and a sheet of stickers.

Le kit de presse du célèbre jeu de stratégie en temps réel *Halo Wars* (sur Xbox 360), vendu à des millions d'exemplaires, consiste en une boîte rectangulaire. Sur son couvercle, on peut voir les personnages principaux du jeu vidéo sur un fond bleu. Et au dos, on retrouve leurs ennemis sur un fond rouge. Ce coffret comporte un exemplaire du jeu et le CD traditionnel avec le matériel de presse, ainsi qu'une pochette en plastique dans laquelle se trouve un poster représentant une scène du jeu et des autocollants à coller dessus.

El kit de prensa del famoso videojuego de estrategia en tiempo real *Halo Wars* para Xbox 360, de ventas multimillonarias, consiste en una caja rectangular en cuya cubierta puede verse una imagen de los protagonistas del juego, identificados con el color azul. En la contracubierta aparece una imagen de sus enemigos sobre fondo rojo. En el interior de la caja, los destinatarios encuentran una copia del juego y el ya tradicional CD con el material de prensa, además de una bolsa de plástico en cuyo interior hay un póster con un escenario del videojuego y una lámina con pegatinas para enganchar en él.

Javier Ronco/Ronco Diseño & Creación
Madrid, Spain_Madrid, Espagne_Madrid (España)
www.roncodc.es
javier@roncodc.es

p in.

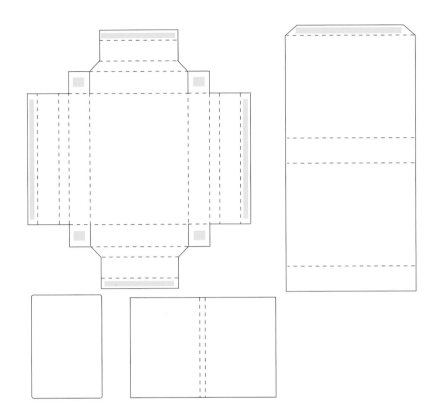

Ninja Blade

The very complete *Ninja Blade* for Xbox 360 (Microsoft) video game press kit is a cardboard box containing a T-shirt with the logo of the game, a copy of the game, the press DVD and information packs with humorous facts about the game and instructions on how to become a professional ninja. The kit also includes a 50% discount on a typical ninja-style activity, tandem jumping from a plane organized by Skydive Madrid that recipients may take advantage of if they wish.

Le kit de presse extrêmement complet du jeu vidéo *Ninja Blade* pour Xbox 360 (de Microsoft) consiste en une boîte en carton dans laquelle se trouvent un tee-shirt avec le logo du jeu, un exemplaire de celui-ci, le DVD contenant toutes les informations de presse et plusieurs documents avec des données sur le jeu et des instructions humoristiques pour devenir un ninja professionnel. Ce kit comporte également une remise de 50 % pour une activité « propre » aux ninjas, le saut en tandem d'un avion, organisé par Skydive Madrid, dont les destinataires pourront profiter s'ils le souhaitent.

El completísimo kit de prensa del videojuego *Ninja Blade* para Xbox 360 (de Microsoft) consiste en una caja de cartón en cuyo interior puede encontrarse una camiseta con el logotipo del videojuego, una copia de éste, el DVD con toda la información de prensa y varias láminas impresas con datos sobre el juego e instrucciones humorísticas para convertirse en un *ninja* profesional. El kit incluye además un descuento del 50% en una actividad «propia» de *ninjas*, un salto en tándem desde una avioneta, organizado por Skydive Madrid, que los destinatarios pueden aprovechar si lo desean.

Carlos Gugel/Entreplanta Comunicación
Madrid, Spain_Madrid, Espagne_Madrid (España)
www.entreplanta-comunicacion.com ɪ carlos@entreplanta-comunicacion.com

XBOX 360

NINJA BLADE

LA ACCIÓN NINJA
TE TRASLADA
AL FUTURO

PREPÁRATE
PARA VER LO
NUNCA VISTO

NINJA BLADE

CONOCE A KEN OGAWA, EL MAESTRO NINJA

La ciudad de Tokio ha sido invadida por criaturas mutantes y solo un héroe puede salvarla de su apocalíptico destino. Conviértete en el maestro ninja Ken Ogawa y adéntrate en un vibrante y espectacular juego de acción que te dejará sin aliento. ¡Acepta el reto!

GRÁFICOS IMPACTANTES
Déjate seducir por el impresionante grado de realismo que presenta Ninja Blade. ¡Vas a quedarte alucinado!

UNA MEZCLA EXPLOSIVA
Ninja Blade reúne en un mismo juego los vibrantes combates de *God of War* con la vistosidad y el descaro de la saga *Devil May Cry*.

DOSSIER PRENSA
NINJA BLADE

XBOX 360.

attack!

ESCENAS INTERACTIVAS
Tus reflejos se pondrán a prueba constantemente en unas secuencias interactivas de calidad cinemática.

EL PODER DE UN NINJA
Derrota a tus enemigos con las técnicas Ninja más salvajes y espectaculares que jamás hayas visto.

XBOX 360.

Ninja Blade

Tokio, siglo XXI, sólo tú puedes evitar la extinción del ser humano.

Un misterioso parásito ha desatado una oleada de destrucción, mutando a los humanos en criaturas salvajes y despiadadas. La enfermedad ha alcanzado la costa de Japón y el corazón de Tokio. Controla al neo-ninja Ken Ogawa y ábrete paso nadando, volando y combatiendo en un intenso juego de acción en el que tu objetivo es impedir la destrucción de la raza humana.

NINJA BLADE

- **Categoría:** Acción
- **Part Description:**
Ninja Blade-MS Xbox 360 Spanish PAL DVD Partial +
- **Part Number:** 5VA-00013
- **EAN:** 882224746083
- **Precio de Venta Estimado:** 64,99 € IVA incluido
- **Fecha de Lanzamiento:** 03 de Abril de 2009
- **Formato Caja:** DVD
- **Clasificación:** 16+
- **Links:**
http://www.xbox.com/es-ES/games/n/ninjablade/

Características

Habilidades neo-ninja especiales. Para derrotar a los monstruos mutados genéticamente, dispondrás de las habilidades especiales Ninja Visión y Todomé. Al activar Ninja Vision podrás detectar y analizar puntos débiles potenciales del enemigo, caminos secretos e información oculta dentro del entorno. Pero cuidado, porque al utilizar Ninja Vision eres más sensible al daño. Todomé es un ataque especial que asesta un golpe mortal que destruye el corazón del enemigo. El uso adecuado y calculado de visas tus habilidades será imprescindible para avanzar en el juego.

Arsenal de armas y herramientas Ninjutsu. Los poderes neo-ninja te proporcionan un amplio abanico de opciones. Los variados entornos te obligarán a plantear estrategias y a elegir con cuidado el grupo de armas y herramientas más adecuado para abrirte paso a lo largo de los distintos niveles. Podrás blandir dos espadas, lanzar garfios o granadas y muchas cosas más, así que escoge con cuidado. Ninjutsu es un poder especial que provoca una fuerte explosión eléctrica capaz de aturdir a los enemigos o protegerte de ataques. Sólo un verdadero maestro ninja puede desarrollar esta técnica.

Eventos interactivos en tiempo real. A lo largo del juego te encontrarás con eventos en tiempo real en los que te podrás interactuar directamente con las escenas cinemáticas. La rapidez de reflejos será crucial mientras interactúas con los botones del mando siguiendo con rapidez las indicaciones en pantalla para superar intensos combates.

Realismo moderno. Ninja Blade proporciona novedosos giros a la clásica saga ninja ofreciendo escenarios 3D inspirados en los rascacielos y edificios del Tokio moderno.

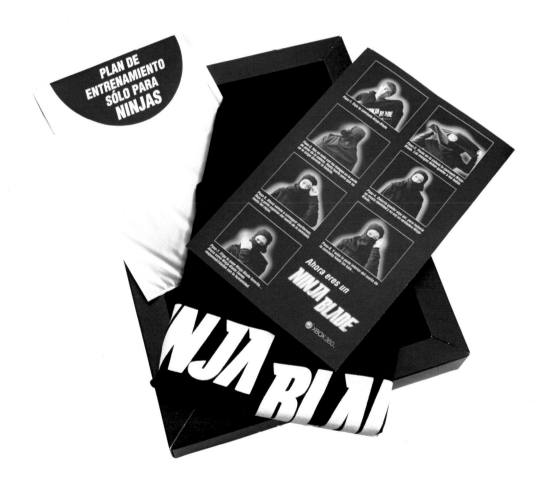

NINJA BLADE

CONOCE A KEN OGAWA, EL MAESTRO NINJA

La ciudad de Tokio ha sido invadida por criaturas mutantes y sólo un héroe puede salvarla de su apocalíptico destino. Conviértete en el maestro ninja Ken Ogawa y adéntrate en un vibrante y espectacular juego de acción que te dejará sin aliento. ¡Acepta el reto!

UNA MEZCLA EXPLOSIVA
Ninja Blade reúne en un mismo juego los vibrantes combates de **God of War** con la vistosidad y el descaro de la saga **Devil May Cry**.

DOSSIER PRENSA
NINJA BLADE

LA ACCIÓN NINJA
TE TRASLADA
AL FUTURO

¿Te atreves
a saltar como
Ken Ogawa?

Vive la experiencia
en tus propias carnes
y salta en caída libre
en Skydive Madrid...
¡APROVÉCHATE DE
NUESTRA IRRESISTIBLE
OFERTA PARA NINJAS!

PLAN DE
ENTRENAMIENTO
SÓLO PARA
NINJAS

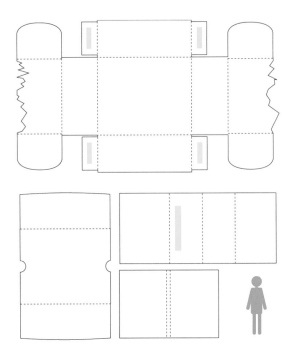

Alone in the Dark

The press kit of the video game *Alone in the Dark*, designed by the agency Weber Shandwick, is a black box with a crack down the middle. When the box is opened, the user discovers a cardboard sheet illustrating the main character of the game. Beneath there is a copy of the game, a DVD with press material, and a plastic figure of the hero intended to become collectors' items for fans. The kit was sent, as is usual with this type of items, to specialist press.

Le kit de presse du jeu vidéo *Alone in the Dark*, conçu par l'agence Weber Shandwick, consiste en un coffret noir avec une crevasse au milieu. En ouvrant la boîte, on trouve tout d'abord une feuille cartonnée avec l'image du personnage principal du jeu. En dessous, se trouvent un exemplaire du jeu, le DVD contenant le matériel de presse relatif à celui-ci, et une figurine du protagoniste qui deviendra un objet de collection pour les fans du jeu. Comme pour tous les kits de ce genre, il a été envoyé à la presse spécialisée.

El kit de prensa del videojuego *Alone in the Dark*, diseñado por la agencia Weber Shandwick, consiste en una caja de color negro en cuya tapa doble troquelada puede verse una grieta. Al abrir la caja, el usuario se topa con una lámina de cartón que muestra una imagen del protagonista del videojuego. Bajo esta lámina se encuentra una copia del juego, el DVD con el material de prensa y una figura de plástico del protagonista destinada a convertirse en objeto de coleccionismo entre los seguidores del videojuego. El kit se envió, como es habitual en este tipo de productos, a la prensa especializada.

Weber Shandwick
Madrid, Spain_Madrid, Espagne_Madrid (España)
www.webershandwick.es

Creative director and supervisor at Shackleton 70mm
Madrid, Spain
www.shackleton70mm.com
cranedo@shackleton70mm.com
jrueda@shackleton70mm.com
Projects on pages 264 and 274

Directeur créatif et chef de projet
de Shackleton 70mm
Madrid, Espagne
www.shackleton70mm.com
cranedo@shackleton70mm.com
jrueda@shackleton70mm.com
Projets sur les pages 264 et 274

Director creativo y supervisor de Shackleton 70mm
Madrid (España)
www.shackleton70mm.com
cranedo@shackleton70mm.com
jrueda@shackleton70mm.com
Proyectos en las páginas 264 y 274

Carlos Ranedo + Coke Rueda

Describe the perfect press kit.
One that you want to keep forever, or at least, that survives three or four cleanups or changes of offices.

What should its purpose be?
Draw attention to something that might have gone unnoticed.

What is the hardest thing about designing a press kit?
Being consistent with the movie or product you are promoting, and then you see it and say "hey, they we got it spot on".

And the easiest?
Once you have the idea, the rest comes naturally.

What do you most like about designing press kits?
Thinking about the reaction of the person who will receive it and knowing that they will like it.

What kind of customers should send out press kits?
The entertainment industry, especially the movie industry, as there are so many

Comment est le kit de presse parfait ?
C'est celui que vous voulez garder pour toujours ou, du moins, celui qui a survécu à trois ou quatre nettoyages de printemps ou changement de bureaux.

Quel devrait être son objectif ?
Attirer l'attention sur quelque chose qui aurait pu passer inaperçu.

Quelle est la principale difficulté lors de la conception d'un kit promotionnel ?
Conserver la cohérence avec le film ou le produit que vous montrez, pour que vous le voyiez et disiez « bravo, c'est tout à fait ça ! ».

Et qu'est-ce qui est le plus facile ?
Quand l'idée est là, le reste vient tout seul.

Qu'est-ce qui vous plaît le plus dans la conception d'un kit promotionnel ?
Penser à la réaction de la personne qui va le recevoir et savoir qu'il va lui plaire.

Quel type de clients devraient choisir d'envoyer des kits de presse ?
L'industrie du divertissement, plus particulièrement celle du cinéma, car de nom-

¿Cómo es el kit de prensa perfecto?
El que quieras guardar para siempre, o al menos, el que se libre de tres o cuatro limpiezas generales o cambios de despacho.

¿Cuál debería ser su objetivo?
Llamar la atención sobre algo que hubiera podido pasar desapercibido.

¿Cuál es la principal dificultad a la hora de diseñar un kit de prensa?
Mantener la coherencia con la película o el producto que estés mostrando, que lo veas y digas: «¡Qué bueno! Lo han clavado».

¿Y lo más fácil?
Cuando está la idea, su enriquecimiento viene solo.

¿Qué es lo que más os gusta de diseñar kits de prensa?
Pensar en la reacción de la persona que lo va a recibir y saber que le va a gustar.

¿Qué tipo de clientes deberían optar por el envío de kits de prensa?
La industria del entretenimiento, especialmente la del cine, pues muchos estre-

new releases that sometimes go unnoticed. The pressbook is a perfect way to reach the mind of the journalist.

Do you have any way to test and evaluate the effectiveness of a particular press kit?
We have had some greatly appreciated experiences. The explosion of blogs has made things easier to learn that some of our kits have been mentioned and photographed in the blogosphere, and on many occasions, in specialist magazines and even on television, as was the case for *Camino*.

What are your preferred materials for press kits?
All that is conventional, materials that are not typically used for pressbooks, but, for the characteristics that we are looking for, they fit perfectly into the concept and creation of the pressbook.

Do you need to like the product that you promote to design a good press kit?
Obviously, the ideal is that you are working with a movie or a director that fasci-

breuses sorties passent parfois inaperçues. Le pressbook est l'outil idéal pour atteindre l'esprit du journaliste.

Disposez-vous d'un moyen pour vérifier et évaluer l'efficacité d'un certain kit de presse ?
Nous avons eu quelques expériences très reconnues. Avec l'explosion des blogs, il a été facile de voir que quelques kits que nous avons faits étaient cités et photographiés dans la blogosphère. C'est souvent le cas dans des magazines spécialisés, et même à la télévision, comme cela a été le cas pour *Camino*.

Quels sont vos matériaux favoris pour les kits de presse ?
Tout ce qui n'est pas conventionnel, des matériaux qui ne s'utilisent pas en général pour faire des kits et qui, de par les caractéristiques que nous recherchons, correspondent parfaitement au concept et à la réalisation du pressbook.

Pour concevoir un bon kit de presse, devez-vous aimer le produit dont vous assurez la promotion ?
Il est évident que la motivation est opti-

nos pasan desapercibidos. El *pressbook* es una manera perfecta de llegar a la mente del periodista.

¿Tenéis alguna manera de comprobar y evaluar la efectividad de un determinado kit de prensa?
Hemos tenido algunas experiencias muy agradecidas. Con la explosión de los *blogs*, ha sido fácil ver que algunos de los envíos que hemos hecho aparecían citados y fotografiados en la «blogosfera». En muchas ocasiones, también en revistas especializadas e incluso en televisión, como en el caso de *Camino*.

¿Cuáles son vuestros materiales favoritos para los kits de prensa?
Todo lo que se salga de lo convencional, materiales que no se suelen utilizar para hacer envíos y que, por las características de lo que buscamos, encajan perfectamente en el concepto y la ejecución del *pressbook*.

¿Es necesario que te guste el producto que debes promocionar para diseñar un buen kit de prensa?
Obviamente, la motivación cuando tra-

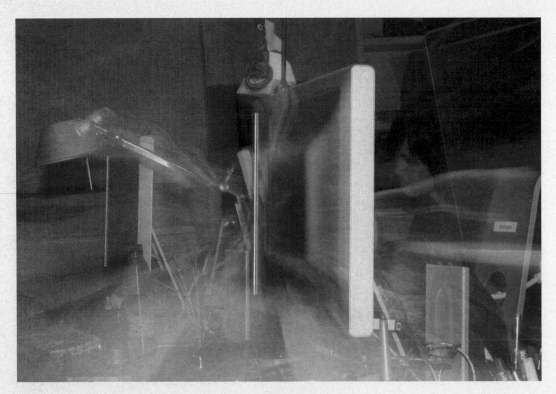

nates you, but I think we have done good work with projects that we did not feel specifically connected to.

What is the difference between designing a press kit and any other type of product?
A promotional pressbook or press kit should be something lasting that has a space on the table or shelf. With other types of communication work, permanence is much more difficult to achieve.

How will the design of press kits evolve in the next few years?
Clearly, as we have already used in some projects, the future lies in the integration of the internet, social networks, etc. Not only do you receive a pressbook (an actual card), but you enter another dimension that allows you to get closer to what you are living in fiction.

What is the best press kit you've ever seen?
One that stands out was the launch campaign for *The Dark Knight* in the United States. It was a cake with a note saying "call me" with a phone number written

male, lorsque vous travaillez sur un film ou un réalisateur qui vous fascine, mais je crois que nous avons fait du bon travail avec des projets avec lesquels nous ne identifions pas spécialement.

Quelle différence y-a-t-il entre la conception d'un kit promotionnel et celle d'un autre genre de travail ?
Quand nous pensons à un pressbook ou à un kit promotionnel, nous pensons à quelque chose de durable, qui se conservera sur la table ou l'étagère. Avec d'autres types de travail, cela est nettement plus difficile.

Comment la conception de kits de presse va-t-elle évoluer dans les années qui viennent ?
Il est clair, et nous l'avons déjà utilisé dans quelques projets, l'avenir repose sur l'intégration d'Internet, des réseaux sociaux, etc. Mis à part le fait de recevoir un pressbook - un document réel -, vous entrez dans une autre dimension qui vous permet d'accéder à ce qui se vit dans la fiction.

Quel est le meilleur kit de presse que vous ayez vu ?

bajas con una película o un director que te fascinan es máxima, pero creo que hemos hecho buenos trabajos con proyectos con los que no nos sentíamos especialmente identificados.

¿Cuál es la diferencia entre diseñar un kit de prensa y cualquier otro tipo de producto?
Cuando pensamos en un *pressbook* o un kit promocional, pensamos en algo perdurable, que se quede en la mesa o en la balda. Con otro tipo de trabajos de comunicación, la permanencia es mucho más difícil.

¿Cómo evolucionará el diseño de kits de prensa durante los próximos años?
Claramente, y ya lo hemos utilizado en algunos envíos, el futuro está en la integración de Internet, las redes sociales... No sólo recibes un *pressbook* -un documento real-, sino que entras en otra dimensión que te permite acercarte a lo que vives en la ficción.

¿Cuál es el mejor kit de prensa que habéis visto?
Recuerdo especialmente la campaña de

on it, and when you called, a mobile phone inside started ringing. Very powerful. Then the campaign continued with a newspaper, a letter with another phone in which the Joker told you to see the movie in downtown LA. Amazing.

How important is the client briefing? What if it does not fit in 100% with your ideas?
Normally, if the idea is good, it does not matter that it does not fit in perfectly with the briefing. Clients are sensitive to the quality of ideas, even when they go against their initial ideas.

Je me rappelle particulièrement de la campagne de lancement de *Le chevalier noir* aux États-Unis ; c'était un gâteau avec une note qui disait « appelez-moi » avec un numéro de portable inscrit. Lorsque vous appeliez, un téléphone portable sonnait à l'intérieur… Très convaincant ! La campagne continuait ensuite avec un journal, une lettre avec un autre téléphone où le Joker vous donnait rendez-vous pour voir le film au centre de Los Angeles. C'était incroyable.

Quelle importance donnez-vous au briefing du client lorsqu'il ne partage pas entièrement vos idées ?
Normalement, si l'idée est bonne, ce n'est pas grave si elle ne correspond pas parfaitement au briefing. Les clients sont sensibles à la qualité des idées, même quand elles vont à l'encontre de leurs idées de départ.

lanzamiento de *El caballero oscuro* en Estados Unidos: era una tarta con una nota que decía «llamame», con un número de móvil escrito, y, al llamar, sonaba un teléfono móvil en el interior… Muy contundente. La campaña seguía con un periódico, una carta con otro teléfono en el que Joker te citaba para ver la película en el centro de Los Ángeles. Increíble.

¿Qué importancia dais al *briefing* del cliente si éste no encaja al 100% con vuestras ideas?
Normalmente, si la idea es buena, no importa que no encaje perfectamente en el *briefing*. Los clientes son sensibles a la calidad de las ideas, aunque vayan contra sus planteamientos iniciales.

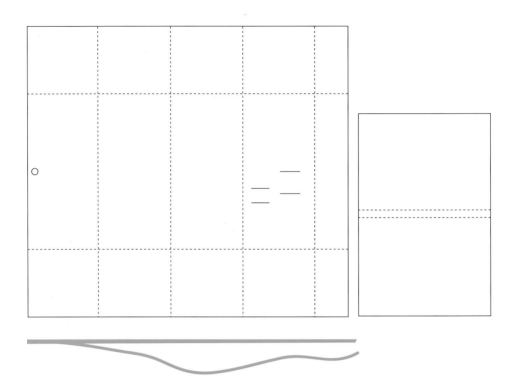

The Chronicles of Narnia: Prince Caspian

The press kit for the PC video game *The Chronicles of Narnia: Prince Caspian*, based on the movie, consists of a leather briefcase that is closed with a leather tie. Once opened, the portfolio displays its contents: a copy of the game and a small plastic dagger made from two pieces that must be fitted together: the blade of the sword and its handle, crowned with a lion's head representing one of the main characters from the series of movies based on the work of C. S. Lewis.

Le kit de presse du jeu vidéo pour PC *Le Monde de Narnia : le Prince Caspian*, adapté du film homonyme, consiste en un portfolio en cuir fermé par un cordon de la même matière. Une fois ouvert, le portfolio dévoile son contenu : un exemplaire du jeu vidéo et une petite dague démontable en plastique. Celle-ci se compose de deux pièces que le destinataire du kit devra assembler : la lame et le manche, décoré d'un buste de lion qui fait référence à l'un des personnages de la saga cinématographique fondée sur l'œuvre de C. S. Lewis.

El kit de prensa del videojuego para PC *Las crónicas de Narnia: el príncipe Caspian*, basado en la película homónima, consiste en un portafolios de piel cerrado con una cinta del mismo material. Una vez abierto, el portafolios muestra su contenido: una copia del videojuego y una pequeña daga desmontable de plástico formada por dos piezas que el receptor del kit debe encajar: la hoja de la espada y la empuñadura, rematada por la cabeza de un león, que hace referencia a uno de los personajes principales de la saga de películas basadas en la obra de C. S. Lewis.

Weber Shandwick
Madrid, Spain_Madrid, Espagne_Madrid (España)
www.webershandwick.es

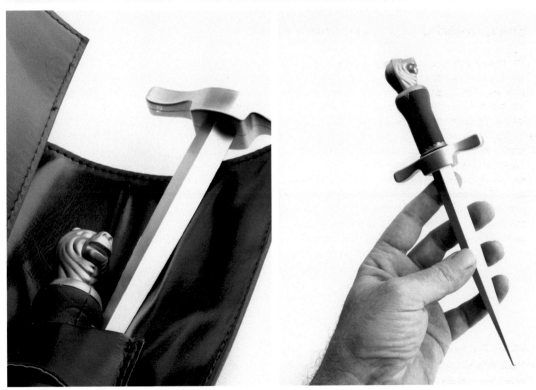

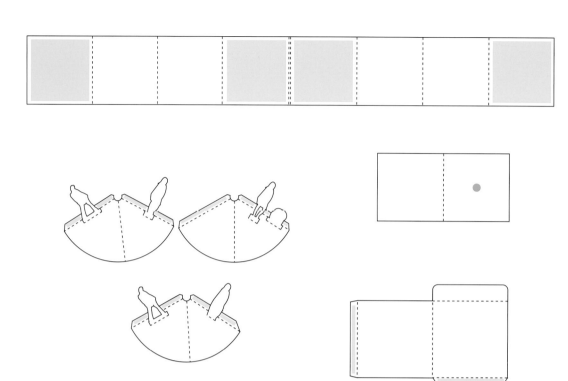

Tekken 6

Tekken is one of the most popular fighting video game series for gamers across the globe. To promote the launch of *Tekken 6*, the sixth installment of the series, the agency Weber Shandwick opted for a fold-out press kit that opens out completely to form a display in which cut-outs of the main characters of the game pop-out from a predominantly black and red background. Conceived as a collector's item, the press kit was sent to specialized media and includes a CD with all the information about the game, as well as press material.

Tekken est l'un des jeux vidéo de combat les plus populaires chez les adeptes du monde entier. Pour promouvoir la sortie de *Tekken 6*, le sixième volet de la saga, l'agence Weber Shandwick a opté pour un kit de presse dépliant qui, une fois ouvert, forme un *display* duquel ressortent certains des personnages principaux du jeu sur un fond à prédominance noire et rouge. Conçu comme un objet de collection, le kit de presse a été envoyé à la presse spécialisée et comporte un CD avec toutes les informations relatives au jeu, en plus du matériel de presse.

Tekken es una de las sagas de videojuegos de lucha más conocidas por los *gamers* de todo el planeta. Para la promoción del lanzamiento de la sexta entrega, la agencia Weber Shandwick optó por un kit de prensa desplegable que se abre por completo para formar un *display* en el que sobresalen las figuras recortadas de algunos de los protagonistas principales del juego sobre un fondo en el que predominan los colores negro y rojo. Concebido como objeto de coleccionista, el kit fue enviado a medios especializados e incluye un CD con toda la información sobre el juego, además de material de prensa.

Weber Shandwick
Madrid, Spain_Madrid, Espagne_Madrid (España)
www.webershandwick.es

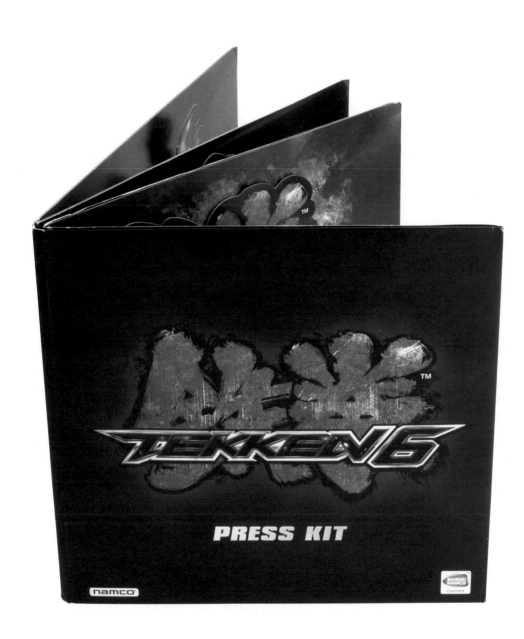

TEKKEN6

PRESS KIT

namco

310

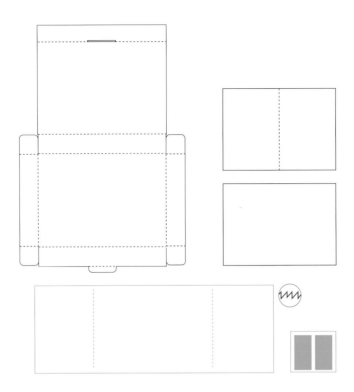

Gears of War 2

The team formed by Harold Vas, Guillermo Roda and Jorge Sánchez was responsible for the promotional kit for the second installment of the Xbox 360 video game *Gears of War*, one of the most famous and successful in recent years. For its launch, the specialist press received a box with the printed logo of the game which included, besides the usual CD with pictures of the game and press kit, a "cookbook" for battle, an unusual choice that adds an element of irony to the mythology of the game.

L'équipe formée par Harold Vas, Guillermo Roda et Jorge Sánchez s'est vu confier la réalisation du kit promotionnel du deuxième volet de *Gears of War*, l'un des jeux vidéo pour Xbox 360 les plus célèbres et les plus populaires de ces dernières années. À l'occasion de son lancement, la presse spécialisée a reçu un coffret orné du logo du jeu comportant, en plus du CD habituel avec des images du jeu et du dossier de presse, un « livre de recettes » pour la guerre, un élément peu ordinaire qui prétend ajouter une touche d'ironie à la mythologie du jeu.

El equipo formado por Harold Vas, Guillermo Roda y Jorge Sánchez fue el encargado de la realización del kit promocional de la segunda entrega del videojuego *Gears of War* para Xbox 360, uno de los títulos más famosos y de mayor éxito de los últimos años. Con ocasión de su lanzamiento, los medios de prensa especializados recibieron una caja impresa con el logotipo del juego, que incluía, además del habitual CD con imágenes del juego y el dosier de prensa, un supuesto libro de recetas gastronómicas para la batalla –a cual más llamativa–, un elemento que pretende añadir un detalle irónico a la mitología del juego.

Harold Vas/La Despensa
Madrid, Spain_Madrid, Espagne_Madrid (España)
www.ladespensa.es ı harold@ladespensa.es

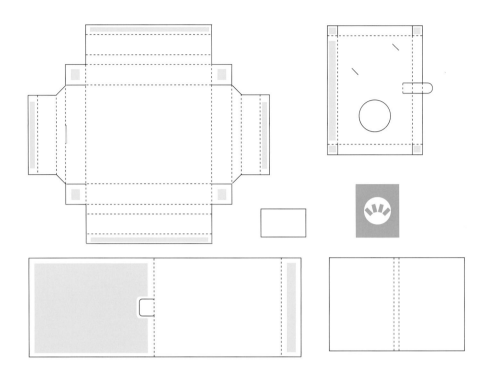

Forza Motorsport 3

To promote the launch of the racing simulator *Forza Motorsport 3* for Xbox 360, Javier Ronco from Ronco Diseño & Creación came up with a simple but imaginative and effective solution. Inside the press kit, which at first glance appears to include only a copy of the game, under a false base that can be raised by a tab there is also a box of aluminum valve caps, a direct nod to all motor sport fans and, especially, the followers of the *Forza Motorsport* game series.

Pour promouvoir le lancement du simulateur de courses *Forza Motorsport 3* (sur Xbox 360), Javier Ronco de Ronco Diseño & Creación a trouvé une solution simple mais originale. Le kit, qui à première vue ne semble contenir qu'un exemplaire du jeu, comporte également, sous un faux fond que l'on peut soulever grâce à une languette, une boîte de capuchons de valves en aluminium, un clin d'œil à tous les adeptes du monde du moteur, et plus particulièrement aux fans de la saga *Forza Motosport.*

Para promocionar el lanzamiento del simulador de carreras *Forza Motorsport 3* para Xbox 360, Javier Ronco, de Ronco Diseño y Creación, dio con una solución sencilla pero original y llamativa. En el interior del kit de prensa, que a primera vista parece incluir únicamente una copia del juego, el usuario puede encontrar además, bajo un fondo falso que puede levantarse por medio de una pestaña, una caja de tapones de aluminio para válvulas, un guiño directo a todos los aficionados del mundo del motor y, muy especialmente, a los seguidores de la saga de juegos *Forza Motosport.*

Javier Ronco/Ronco Diseño & Creación
Madrid, Spain_Madrid, Espagne_Madrid (España)
www.roncodc.es ı javier@roncodc.es

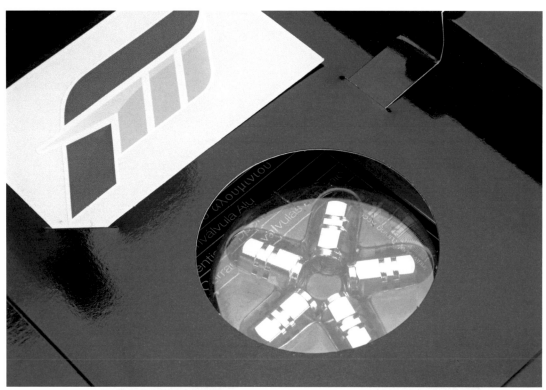

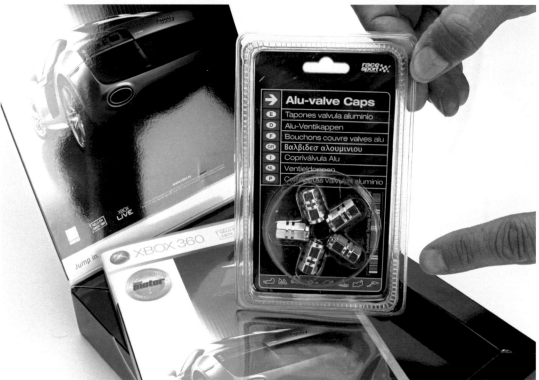

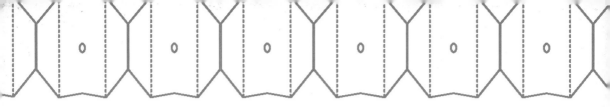

Press kits (and their corresponding supplements) included in this book do not exhaust all the possibilities available to the designer. For this reason, we have included in this chapter a few additional proposals to create press kits exclusive to this book. The proposals, some more basic or creative than others, are composed of different elements that make up the kit, and are accompanied by a pictorial representation of the final result. They have been designed for generic and non specific activities, and, as far as possible, for all types of content, and can be applied to any area depending on the messages' communication needs.

Les kits de presse (et les développements correspondants) cités dans ce livre n'épuisent pas toutes les possibilités qui sont à la portée du designer. C'est pour cette raison que nous avons inclus dans ce chapitre plusieurs propositions supplémentaires pour réaliser des kits de presse, expressément créées pour ce livre. Ces propositions, certaines plus basiques et les d'autres plus créatives, se composent des différents éléments formant le kit et sont accompagnées d'une illustration du résultat final. Elles ont été conçues pour des actions génériques et non spécifiques et, dans la mesure du possible, pour tout type de contenu. Elles peuvent donc s'appliquer à tout type de secteurs en fonction du message qui veut être transmis.

Los kits de prensa (y los correspondientes desarrollos) que el lector ha encontrado en las páginas de este libro no agotan todas las posibilidades al alcance de un diseñador. Por ello en este capítulo se han incluido varias propuestas adicionales para la realización de kits de prensa, creadas expresamente para este título. Estas propuestas, algunas más básicas y otras más creativas, se componen de los diferentes elementos que forman el kit y se acompañan de una representación ilustrada del resultado final. Han sido pensadas para acciones genéricas y no específicas, y, en la medida de lo posible, para todo tipo de contenido, por lo que son aplicables a cualquier área, en función de las necesidades de comunicación del mensaje.

Additional proposals

Propositions supplémentaires

Propuestas adicionales

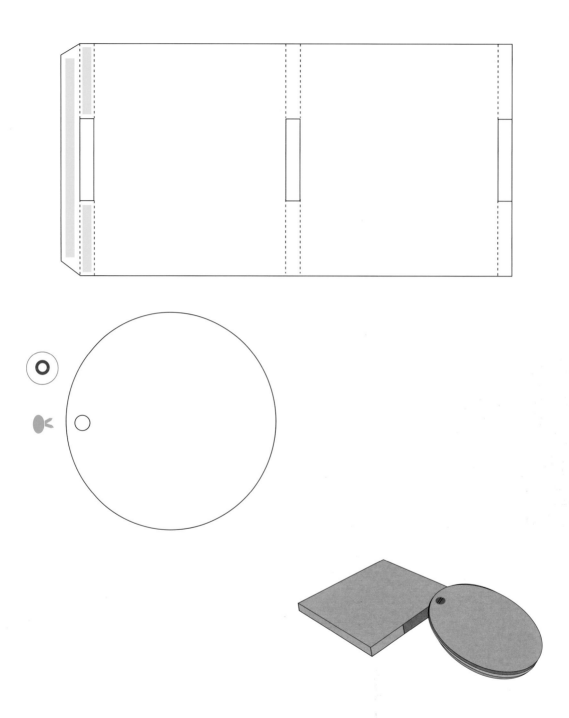

Kit consisting of circular card and cover

Kit composé d'un échantillon circulaire et d'un étui

Kit compuesto por muestrario circular y funda

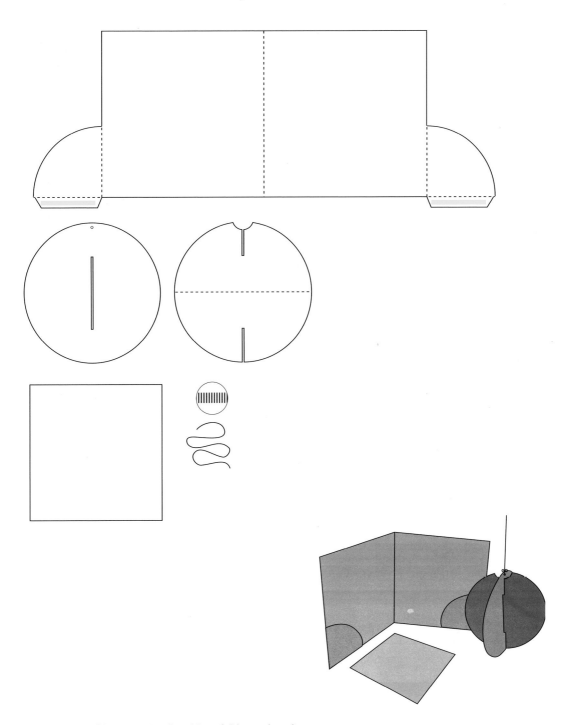

Kit consisting of hanging circular object, folder and card

Kit composé d'un objet volumétrique circulaire à accrocher, d'un dossier et d'une carte

Kit compuesto por volumétrico circular para colgar, carpeta y tarjeta

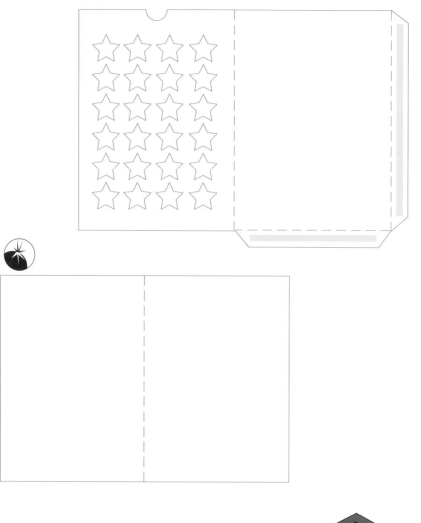

Kit consisting of die cut folder and brochure

Kit composé d'un dossier ajouré et d'une brochure

Kit compuesto por carpeta troquelada y díptico

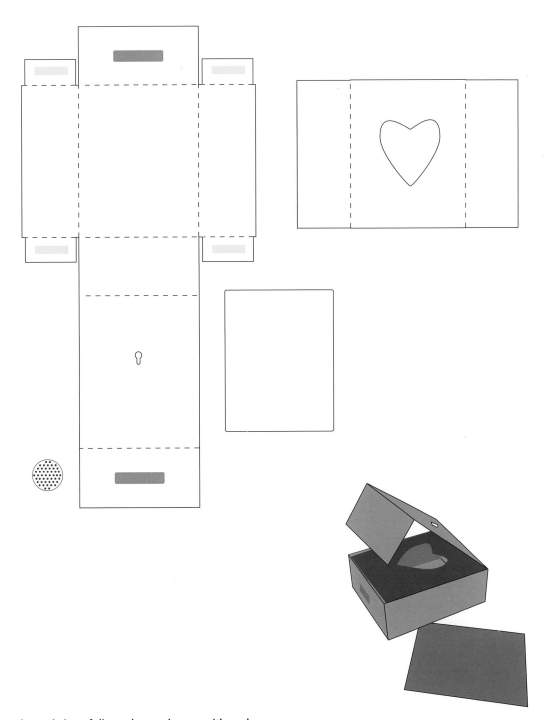

Kit consisting of die cut box and cover with card

Kit composé d'une boîte ajourée, d'un étui ajouré et d'une carte

Kit compuesto por caja troquelada, funda troquelada y tarjeta

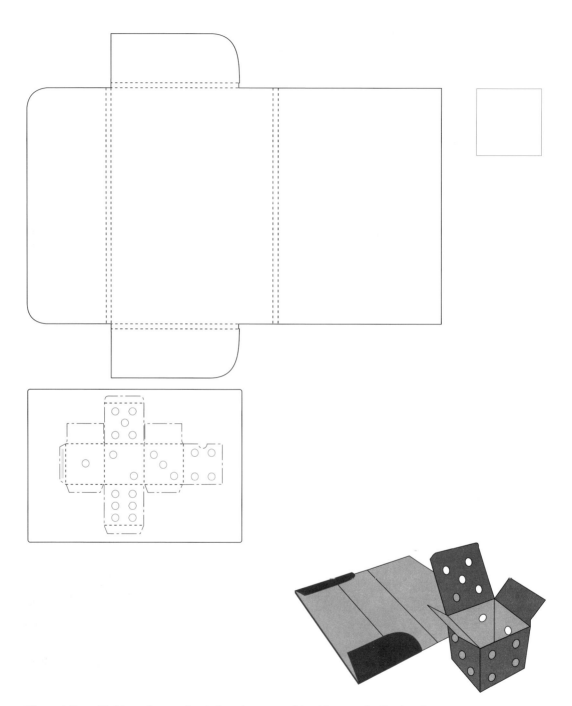

Kit consisting of folder, micro-perforated cards to assemble objects and adhesive closure

Kit composé d'un dossier, de fiches microperforées pour assembler des objets volumétriques et d'une fermeture par adhésif

Kit compuesto por carpeta, fichas microperforadas para montar volumétricos y cierre adhesivo

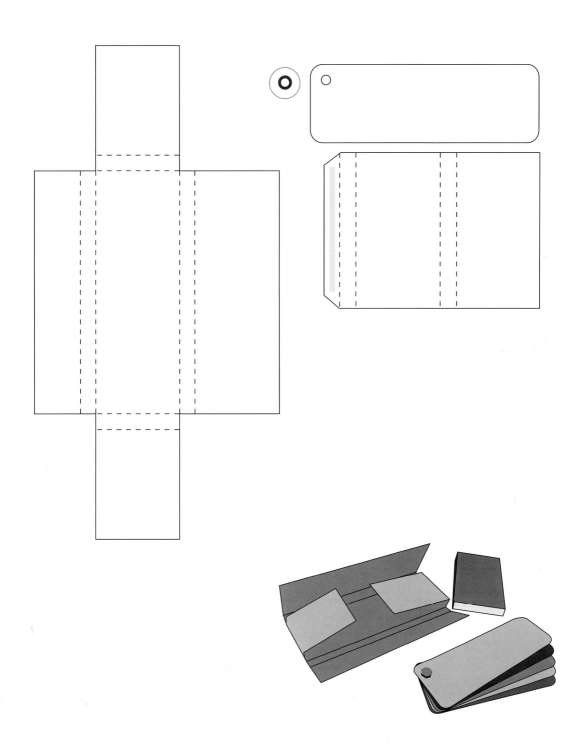

Kit consisting of rectangular chart, fold-out box and sleeve cover

Kit composé d'un échantillonnage rectangulaire, d'une boîte dépliable et d'une fermeture de type étui

Kit compuesto por muestrario rectangular, caja desplegable y cierre tipo faja

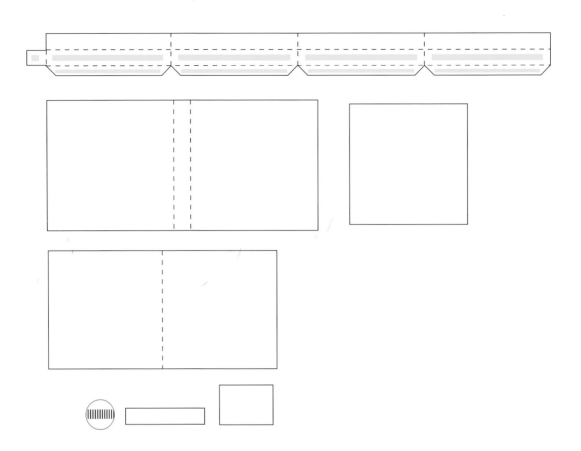

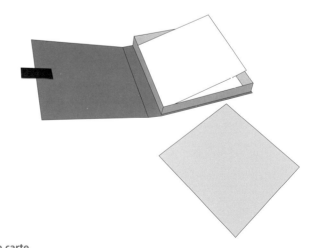

Kit consisting of box, stationery and card

Kit composé d'une boîte, d'un carton et d'une carte

Kit compuesto por caja, tarjetón y tarjeta

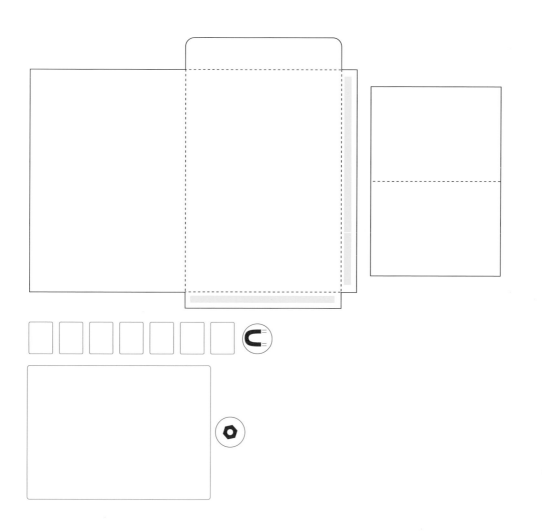

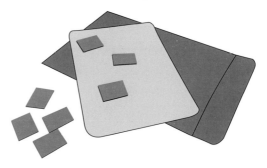

Kit consisting of envelope, metallic sheet, magnets and brochure

Kit composé d'une enveloppe, d'une feuille métallique, d'aimants et d'une brochure

Kit compuesto por sobre, lámina metálica, imanes y díptico

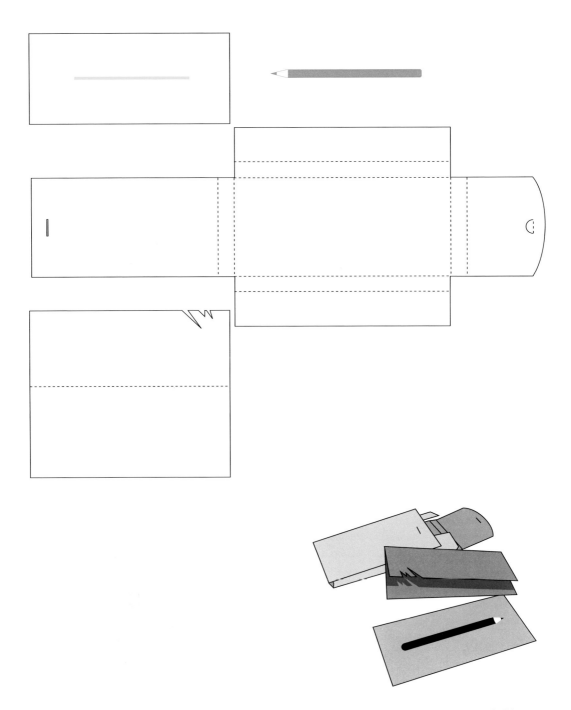

Kit consisting of fold-out box with tab closure, die cut brochure and complementary stationery holder
Kit composé d'une boîte dépliable avec languette de fermeture, d'une brochure ajourée et d'un carton pour écrire
Kit compuesto por caja desplegable cierre pestaña, díptico troquelado y tarjetón soporte obsequio escritura

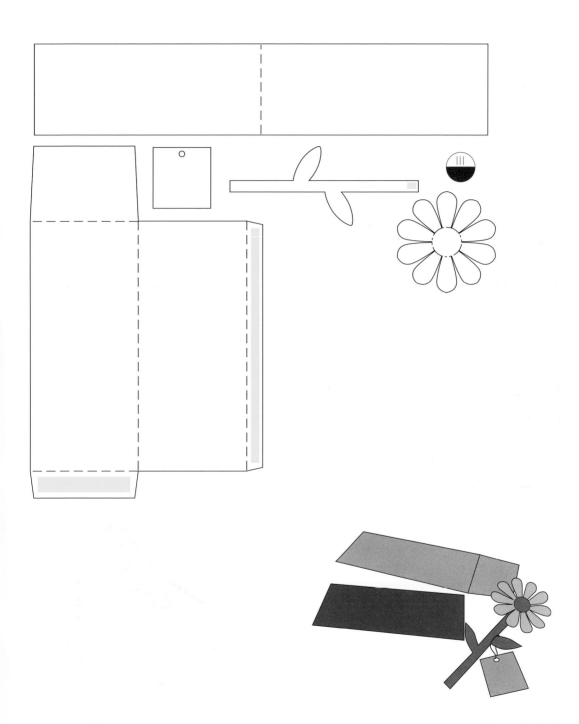

Kit consisting of envelope, brochure, perforated stationery and flower

Kit composé d'une enveloppe, d'une brochure, d'une carte perforée et d'une fleur

Kit compuesto por sobre, tarjetón díptico, tarjeta perforada y flor

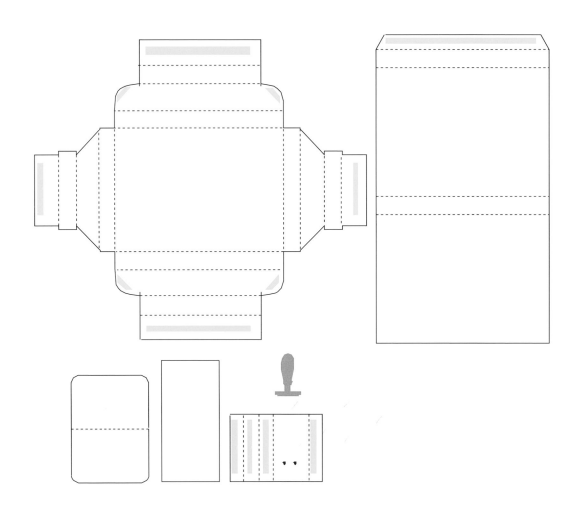

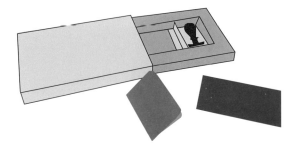

Kit consisting of passport-size booklet, stationery, stamp holder and box with sleeve cover

Kit composé d'un livret format passeport, d'une carte, d'un support pour timbre et d'une boîte avec fermeture type étui

Kit compuesto por libreta formato pasaporte, tarjetón, soporte para sello y caja con cierre tipo faja

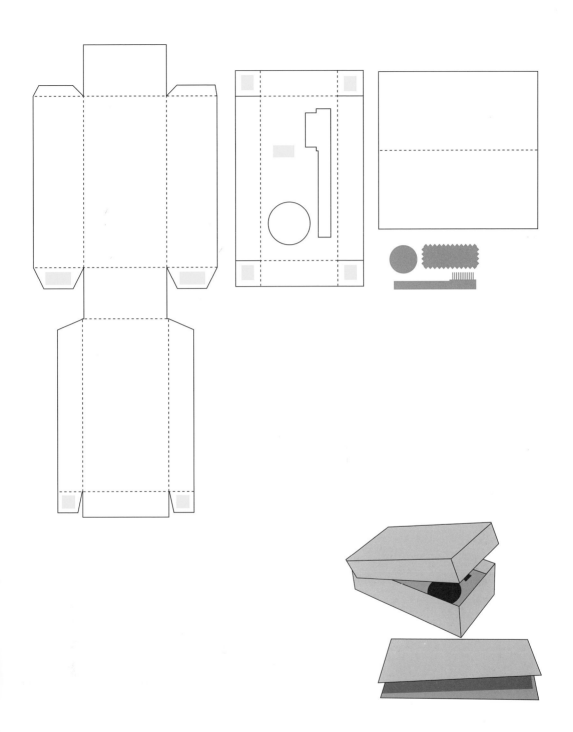

Kit consisting of box with lift up lid, gift and stationery holder

Kit composé d'une boîte avec couvercle basculant, support pour cadeau et carte

Kit compuesto por caja con tapa basculante, soporte para obsequio y tarjetón

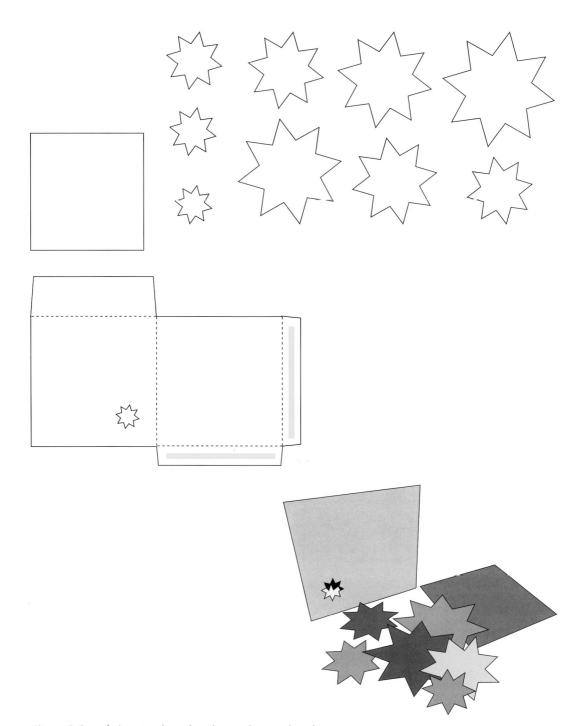

Kit consisting of nine star-shaped cards, envelope and card

Kit composé de neuf cartes en forme d'étoile, d'une enveloppe et d'une carte

Kit compuesto por nueve tarjetas con forma de estrella, sobre y tarjeta

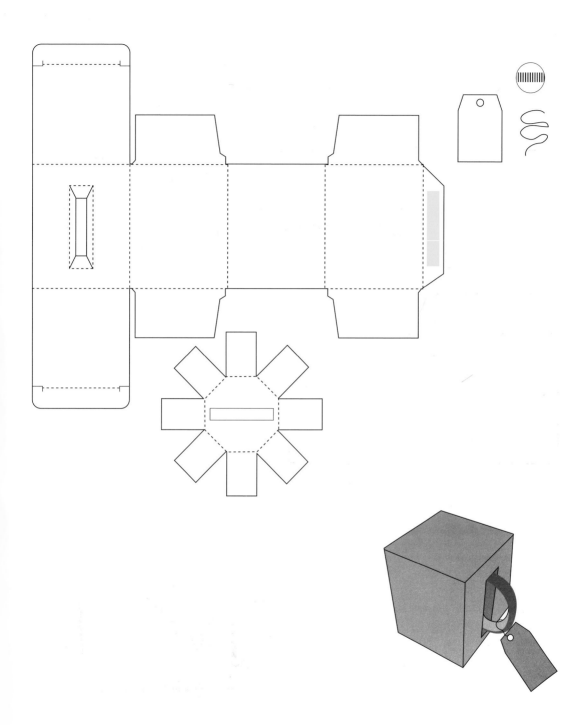

Kit consisting of die cut card for a mug, interior holder and perforated card

Kit composé d'une boîte ajourée pour *mug*, d'un support intérieur et d'une carte perforée

Kit compuesto por caja troquelada para *mug*, soporte interior y tarjeta perforada

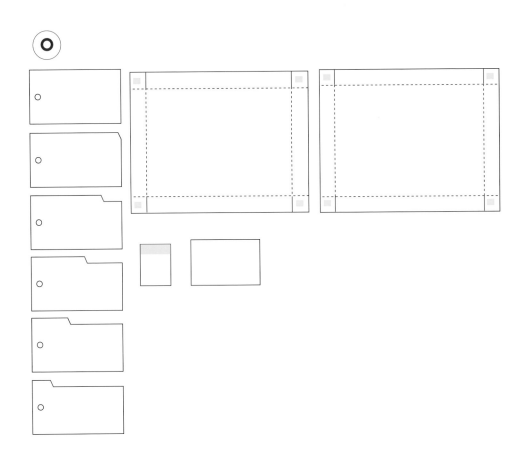

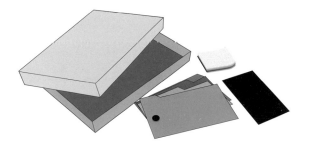

Kit consisting of various formats of sample cards, stickers, card and box
Kit composé d'un échantillonnage de fiches de différents formats, d'adhésifs, d'une carte et d'une boîte
Kit compuesto por muestrario de fichas de diversos formatos, adhesivos, tarjeta y caja

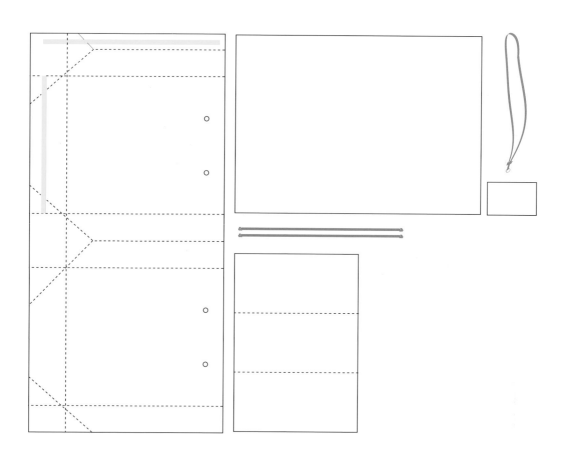

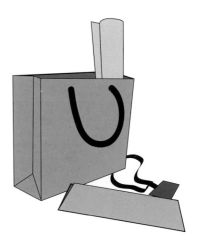

Kit consisting of bag with handles, poster, three-page leaflet, lanyard and card

Kit composé d'un sac avec anses, d'un poster, d'un dépliant à trois volets, d'un *lanyard* et d'une carte

Kit compuesto por bolsa con asas, póster, tríptico, *lanyard* y tarjeta

Photo credits
Crédits photographiques
Créditos fotográficos

Anders Gramers, Liberty Fabric Design Department (66-69)
Jimmy Vandenheuvel (74-75)
Bissinger, David, Slowik (154-157)
Franck & Ines Dieleman (184-187)
Pepe Ruz (202-205, 232-247, 270-273, 280-301, 306-331, 314-317)
Patricia Schwoerer (258-259)